FORGING THE FRANCHISE

FORGING THE FRANCHISE

The Political Origins of the Women's Vote

DAWN LANGAN TEELE

PRINCETON UNIVERSITY PRESS
Princeton and Oxford

Published by Princeton University Press,
41 William Street, Princeton, New Jersey 08540

In the United Kingdom: Princeton University Press,
6 Oxford Street, Woodstock, Oxfordshire, OX20 1TR

press.princeton.edu

Library of Congress Control Number: 2018931016

ISBN: 978-0-691-18026-7

British Library Cataloging-in-Publication Data is available

Editorial: Eric Crahan and Pamela Weidman
Production Editorial: Ellen Foos
Jacket illustration: detail from the April 1928 cover of *The Labour Woman*
Production: Jacqueline Poirier
Copyeditor: Wendy Washburn

This book has been composed in Palatino LT Std and Optima LT Std

Printed on acid-free paper. ∞

Typeset by Nova Techset Pvt Ltd, Bangalore, India
Printed in the United States of America

10 9 8 7 6 5 4 3 2 1

FOR SYLVIA AND MADELEINE,

AND YOUR INDOMITABLE NAMESAKES

Contents

List of Figures and Tables

FIGURES

TABLES

Preface

You cannot lift the world at all,
While half of it is left so small.[1]

In setting out to write about women and democratization, I have at several points wondered if it was enough to write about "just" women. The historical, philosophical, and perhaps even the material baggage of democracy is so weighty that it can be quite tempting to write about all of that as well. But time and again when one reads the great tracts on democracy's founding, there is scarcely a mention of the fairer sex. A sophisticated reader could be forgiven for thinking that the story of women's political emancipation has been quite separate from the progression of democracy itself.

With this book I hope, above all, to convince even those readers not particularly interested in feminism that women were not outside of history when democratic governments were born and solidified. In fact, in these new systems women's struggle against the remnants of authoritarianism bears many resemblances to the struggles of other groups, including the non-landed elites, industrial workers, indigenous peoples, and immigrants. For each of these groups, history has produced moments in which members perceived a deep contradiction in their continued exclusion from a purportedly inclusive governmental system. At times, leaders of these groups contrived methods to change the rules in ways both more congruent with democratic ideals and in line with their own economic and political interests.

There are three big lessons that have emerged while writing this book. The first is that women's inclusion was not an apolitical gift from elected leaders who knew its time had come. Many politicians and anti-suffragists of all genders were wary of the consequences of expanding voting rights, and only capitulated when they saw no other option for their own electoral survival, or when another party with entrepreneurial hopes could push it through. Second, although this book studies women's

---

[1] "The Socialist and the Suffragist," Gilman, 1911.

suffrage more or less separately from other reforms, in the future we should think of innovations, such as the adoption of proportional electoral rules, the move toward the secret ballot, and the enfranchisement of women and men, as substitute strategies for stacking a state. Finally, as we move toward a greater understanding of the impact of suffrage, we have to ask whether and how the coalitions that were formed in the course of the movements, and the victories suffragists won along the way, impacted different groups of women systematically. The cleavages that divided suffragists from one another likely influenced the efficacy of the coalition in the years after the vote was won.

In the eight years of this book's making, I have benefited from the encouragement, critique, and camaraderie of so many people. Frances Rosenbluth and Susan Stokes, my guiding lights at Yale, always reminded me that good work requires writing what one loves. Alexandre Debs and Thad Dunning were both supportive and exacting throughout this process. Along with official graduate advisors, I am grateful to Elisabeth Wood, Naomi Lamoreaux, David Mayhew, and Rogers Smith, who each provided early guidance on the project, and to my first mentors at Reed, Kimberly Clausing and Casiano Hacker-Cordón, who sparked my love of research.

This book has been scrutinized by nearly every new friend I have made. A book conference in the spring of 2016, in which Lisa Baldez, Gary Cox, and Carles Boix commented on the entire manuscript was both humbling and inspiring. Additionally, I would like to thank Kimberly Morgan (my guardian scholar), Kathleen Thelen, and Peter Hall for their guidance and support. Thanks, too, to Daniel Ziblatt, Isabella Mares, Steven Wilkinson, Dan Kelemen, Mark Pollock, Phillip Ayoub, Marcus Kreuzer, Tom Pepinsky, Jim Mahoney, and Mala Htun. My friends and colleagues have allowed this project to be infinitely more fun and undoubtedly more rigorous. Michael Weaver, Rory Truex, Kristin Plys, Erin Pineda, Mona Morgan-Collins, Dorothy Kronick, Anna Jurkeviks, Yue Hou, Alexandra Hartman, Allison Sovey Carnegie, David Bateman, and Jessica Stanton are all on this list. Huge shout-outs, too, to Tulia Falleti, for generously reading everything, including the footnotes, multiple times, and the singular Julie Lynch, for her multifaceted support.

On the United States chapter I would like to thank Stephen Skrowneck, Des King, Corinne McConnaughy, and Andy Eggers, who each made suggestions that are reflected herein. Part of this chapter has appeared in *The Journal of Politics* thanks to the support of Jeff Jenkins, Christina Wolbrecht, and anonymous reviewers. The work on Great Britain was the first and benefited tremendously from the input of others. Initial conversations with Adam Tooze, Jay Winter, Iain MacLean, and David Soskice were especially helpful. Thanks, too, to the editors of *Politics & Society*, especially Mary Ann Twist and Molly Nolan, for their enthusiasm and thoughtful feedback on a segment published in their journal. Special thanks to Brendan O'Leary, whose detailed comments taught me a good deal about Ireland as well. On the study of France I am indebted to John Merriman, Steven Hause, Timothy Tackett, and Paul Smith. Grey Anderson and Alexandra Cirone also deserve recognition as reliable first stops before the reference section for all matters related to French politics in the Third Republic.

It heartens me to acknowledge the many sources of funding and the many contributions of friends, family, and colleagues to this process. Yale, the LSE, and Penn have all been generous institutions, and I am so grateful for their progressive parental leave policies. A prize from the Carrie Chapman Catt Foundation and the National Science Foundation's doctoral dissertation research improvement grant gave much needed provisions during graduate school. These grants allowed me to do research abroad for long stretches of time, and to employ a few excellent people to help with my data collection efforts, including Katie Rader, Shira Pindyk, Joshua Kalla, Michelle Fogarty, Stephanie Gustafson, Mohamed Gamal, Casey Libonate, Daniel Almedia, Julia Hug, Samira Noronha, and Èvelyne Brie. Thanks are due, too, to Marie Cornwall, Erik Engstrom, Lee Ann Banaszak, and Alexandra Cirone for generously sharing with me datasets which they labored to build.

At several points I relied on advice from archivists at the New York Public Library and Yale's own collections. I also spent many months in England at the Women's Library, the People's Library, Manchester Local Studies, the Cumbria Archive Center, the British Parliamentary Archives, and Oxford's Bodleian Library. In France I had help at the Bibliothèque nationale and from Jean-Antonin Caheric at the archives of the Assemblée nationale. In addition, the editorial team at Princeton University Press has been fantastic. Thanks to Eric Crahan, for pursuing this project, and to Wendy Washburn, Ellen Foos, and Pamela Weidman for help pushing it to the finish.

The support of my family has been no less important for this project even though most of its members thought they were cheering me on for a career in politics. The fieldwork, conferences, and two transatlantic moves would not have been possible without Emmy, Aunt E, Amy, LaLa, Maw and Poppy, Dad and Suzy, and Pops, who have each stepped in as child minders during crucial career moments. And to 'Ria, who keeps everyone afloat.

At last I must shower praise on my husband Josh Simon, who has scrutinized my writing and thoughts since our early days at Reed. This book is a product of years of arguments during walks around the well-trod paths of West Rock, the Heath, the Woodlands, and Oswald West. A constant companion in this life of scholarship makes it harder, but also better.

FORGING THE FRANCHISE

1

Introduction

The masculine nouns that describe belonging to a nation, such as citizen, citoyen, ciudadano, and Bürger, are often vested with universal meaning: in constitutions and jurisprudence, many of the duties of a citizen apply equally to both sexes. But once upon a time, albeit not very long ago, the rights and privileges associated with political membership applied only to men. This was the case even in the world's first democracies, and it was true in spite of the fact that as organizers of tea boycotts, white-clad rabble-rousers marching on the Bastille, and invaluable supporters in the supply chains of revolution, women played significant roles in democracy's origins.[1] One hundred years passed before the first declaration of universal manhood suffrage in France gave way to a truly universal suffrage in New Zealand in 1893.[2] Since then, though, voting rules across the world have shifted dramatically toward political equality of the sexes. Almost without exception, the very first petition for reform in any given national legislature was rejected. Yet without exception, democratic countries eventually gave women voting rights. What caused this shift? That is to say, why did male politicians agree to extend the vote to women?

---

[1] Women have played important roles in democratization and revolution. See Baldez 2002; Friedman 2000; Flexner 1995: ch1; Jayawardena 1986; Macías 1982; Montes-de-Oca-O'Reilley 2005.

[2] The Isle of Man, in the British Isles, extended voting rights to women via its independent legislature, the Tynwald, as early as 1881. New Zealand was the first of today's advanced industrial economies to extend the franchise in 1893. Unlike Australia, which formed a federal commonwealth in 1901 and excluded aboriginals in its initial constitution, New Zealand's colonists included Maori voters among their electorate. Norway was the first independent country to enfranchise women in its founding constitution in 1906. But the first place where women were given the vote was the Pitcairn Islands in 1838. Markoff (2003: 102–103) recounts the tale of the British Captain Elliott, who, passing through the Tahitian archipelago, took a moment to provide a few regulations for the island which included a provision for equal suffrage. The Pitcairn settlers were the survivors of the HMS *Bounty* mutiny. Numbering 194 in 1856, they maintained the female franchise upon their relocation to Norfolk Island.

   The emergence of democratic governments and industrialization are background features in the story of women's political inclusion. As figure 1.1 shows, the pattern of women's enfranchisement mimics the pattern of democratization more generally, with distinctive spells surrounding the 1920s, 1940s, and 1960s.[3] In the early period, women's changing social and economic roles may have opened up a space in which their public presence was up for debate. In the later period, women's enfranchisement peaked in the 1950s, a decade in which many colonial territories won independence for the first time. Over the course of this history, there were four primary settings in which women gained national voting rights: as part of a universal franchise bill (14 percent of today's countries), as a result of external imposition (30 percent), gradually, after some men had already gained political voice (42 percent), and a hybrid category where combinations of the other three appeared, often due to multiple transitions between political regimes (14 percent).[4]

   In the *universalist path*, all adults won the right to vote at the same time. This generally occurred during a "founding" moment when a new constitution sought to establish representative institutions for all citizens. For example, following the elimination of an absolute monarchy, the Thai Constitution of 1932 established a constitutional monarchy and enfranchised all Thai people regardless of sex.[5] Countries like Finland

---

   [3] The figure depicts the decade of the first major legislative reform that allowed most women to vote. In all, I was able to find and cross-check this information for 172 of today's countries. Existing literature on the granting of women's suffrage (Paxton and Hughes 2016; Przeworski 2009), almanacs (Martin 2000), and data handbooks (Nohlen 2005; Nohlen et al. 1991, 2001), provide conflicting dates of the female franchise. At times these inconsistencies are due to simple error (particularly in Przeworski 2009), or different coding rules, which, for example, might record suffrage as occurring in the year it passed the legislature, or was finally signed into law by executive or monarch, or the first election in which women voted, or the date can refer to the year in which universal suffrage—the right to vote regardless of race, social status, belief, or gender—was granted. A potentially bigger problem, though, stems from different interpretations of what it means for "women" to gain voting rights, for example, when women gain the right to vote with certain restrictions, such as those regarding literacy, age, or, as in the case of Bulgaria, marital status (Hannam et al. 2000: 45). My coding tries to reflect 1.) the first major reform that would have included most women and 2.) the year the relevant enfranchising bill passed in the national legislature. See appendix I for further details. Pitcairn Islands are not pictured here.

   [4] Classification of countries into paths was done based on the dataset described in the previous footnote, cross-referenced with information on universal and manhood suffrage extension from Boix et al. (2013), Caramani (2004), Mackie and Rose (1991), and Colomer (2016). Dates of independence and colonial relations are from the CIA Factbook.

   [5] Loos 2004.

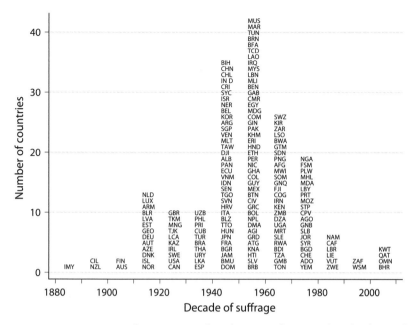

FIGURE 1.1. "Listogram" of Women's Enfranchisement by Decade. The figure displays a three-letter code for each country and the decade in which women were enfranchised. The y-axis counts the number of such extensions per decade. The countries lower down in each column extended the vote earlier in the decade than those higher up.

in 1906, or several states in the Caucasus from 1917 to 1919, just prior to the emergence of the Soviet Union, also followed the universalist path.[6] The *imposed route* to suffrage arose when an occupying power or a colonial metropole required entities under its influence to extend the franchise. Examples of this path include many of the French colonies, such as Cameroon, Madagascar, and Malta, where the *Loi Cadre* promulgated in 1956 extended voting rights to women in the colonies. Typically,

[6] For a variety of reasons, founding moments that occurred after 1945 typically produced constitutions that included universal franchise rights for men and women. After 1950, every newly independent state included women in the franchise. Ramirez et al. 1997. Today, in the words of Schedler (2002), formal disfranchisement is uncommon "even in the most hard-boiled electoral autocracies." And international influences have been a large factor in more recent democratizations. Geddes, 2007; 330. See Towns (2010a and 2010b) on the importance of global norms and international organizations, in particular the Inter-American Council of Women, for transforming suffrage into a reality in Latin America. Finally, see Marino (2018) on the Latin American origins of Pan-American feminism.

a country that had the vote imposed by an external power would keep equal franchise laws after independence. Third comes the *gradualist path*, wherein many, though not necessarily all, men enjoyed voting rights before women won the vote.[7] Examples of the gradualist path include Sweden, Mexico, and the United States.[8] Finally, in the remaining countries, a hybrid path to women's suffrage arose, often because of new rules following regime transitions. Examples include France, which, after several bouts of manhood suffrage in the mid nineteenth century, successfully maintained it beginning in the 1870s but denied women the vote until the Fourth Republic was established, and Japan, which allowed men to vote in the early twentieth century, but where the United States, as an occupying power after the Second World War, pushed for the reform in its postwar constitution.

The path that a country took toward women's enfranchisement depended, in an important sense, on the institutional arrangements in place during the past 130 years.[9] The universalist path is most often associated with having transitioned from authoritarian or monarchial institutions in the twentieth century; the imposed path with colonial subordination or, less commonly, defeat in war; the gradualist path with having established minimally representative electoral institutions in the

[7] The complexity does not end here. Many countries that gradually extended the vote initially used restrictions that were different than men's, such as age differences (e.g., the UK 1918–1928, Chile 1934–1949), specific income requirements (e.g., Bolivia 1938–1952), educational requirements (e.g., Kenya 1956–1963), racial distinctions (e.g., Australia 1902–1962, South Africa 1930–1994), differences within federal entities (e.g., Canada 1916–1920, US 1893–1920, Switzerland 1959–1971), and even based on distinctions related to husbands, such as whether he had served in the military (Canada 1917–1920, Romania 1929–1946) or if they were widows (e.g., Bulgaria 1937–1944).

[8] In several countries, such as Venezuela in 1947 and Guatemala in 1945, men could vote in earlier periods, but constitutions that followed episodes of autocratic rule ultimately included women as voters. Towns 2010b: 785 and footnote 19.

[9] There are some documented reversals in women's right to participate. In the medieval period, societies in which communal right rested on a material basis (such as property ownership) sometimes included propertied women in communal suffrage, so the transition to absolutism and then later to representative institutions may have taken rights away from women with material resources. Ostrogorski 1891: 679–680, 684. After 1868 in post-Meiji Japan, women exercised the vote in some local elections until legal loopholes were closed in 1888. Hannam et al. 2000: 156; Molony 2004. The Clergy Endowments Act in "Lower Canada" (present-day Québec) allowed all landlords, regardless of sex, the right to vote. Although only 2 percent of eligible women used this right, it was taken away by the Parliament of the Province of Canada in the mid-nineteenth century. Darsigny 1990: 2. Many feminist scholars argue that the transition to industrialization actually brought diminished rights for women that had to be wrested back through social movements. See footnote 9, chapter 2.

nineteenth century; and the hybrid path with multiple regime transitions in the twentieth century. Given the diverse institutional and historical conditions that gave rise to women's voting rights, it is unlikely that a single set of actors and interests can help to explain why women won the vote when they did. But within each path, the distinctive political features that sparked debates about suffrage may share commonalities with other cases in the same group.

This book is about the politics of women's enfranchisement in countries that extended voting rights gradually, under institutional arrangements that I term "limited" democracy. A limited democracy is a regime that uses elections as a decision rule for appointing rulers and where turnover of leaders is possible, but which may lack many features that are considered essential to full democracy today including, but not limited to, freedom of the press, secret voting, direct-election of all legislative houses, and voting rights for all citizens.[10] In contrast to non-democratic systems, in limited democracies a reorganization of the laws that govern political participation can have quite substantial effects on electoral politics and programmatic policies. These potential effects shape the incentives politicians face and their ultimate decisions over whether to reform the law. They also constrain the set of options available to identity groups that are mobilized for reform.

In the cross-national context there are several issues that must be attended to for a clear picture of women's enfranchisement in limited democracies to materialize. One is the fact that suffrage movements did not emerge in every country, nor did suffragists always seek a mass basis. Why did women who wanted to vote strive for a large movement in some countries but remain satisfied with a small movement in others? This is a particularly intriguing question in places where suffrage reform was debated but failed to produce reform, in spite of a strong women's

---

[10] Building on Dahl's concepts of "competitive oligarchy" and "inclusive hegemony," and O'Donnell and Schmitter's concept "democradura," a political community can be described as a limited democracy if an elected body has the power to legislate, if elections are held regularly, and if there is some potential for turnover of office. Dahl 1971; O'Donnell and Schmitter 1986. Note that the concept of limited democracy is somewhere between Przeworski's 1999 "minimalist" binary and Dahl's richer definition of polyarchy, which requires regimes to be highly liberal—in that they accept public contestation as a core principle—and highly inclusive—in that they put few restrictions on political participation. Writing about the pre-WWII democracies, Geddes states the idea of a limited democracy succinctly: "legislatures existed, elite parties or proto-parties competed for office, and struggles by legislatures to limit the power of monarchs or executives had played an important role in determining the shape of political institutions." Geddes 2007: 331. She calls them non-democracies.

movement. Second is a puzzle of why leftist parties supported reform in some countries while conservative parties were the first to propose the change in others, and why in many countries the longest standing resistance to women's inclusion came from centrists. Last is the issue of timing—why did some legislatures enfranchise women shortly after the first demand for reform while others clung to the status quo for decades? Why were some legislatures the site of short-term reversals, passing reform just a year or two after refusing to do so?

THE ARGUMENT, IN BRIEF

The answer I provide for all of these questions is a strategic one: winning the vote depends on the alignment of interests between elected politicians and suffragists. The institutional legacies that followed the transition to representative institutions and the nature of political cleavages in a given country determined which forms of women's enfranchisement would have been considered legally and normatively feasible, and influenced the ideas that both suffragists and politicians had about the political ramifications of women's enfranchisement. Both suffragists and politicians were concerned with the impact of women's votes—suffragists because their interests along dimensions other than gender may have been better served by keeping other women from voting, and politicians because their very seats were at stake if the new voters were not natural allies. The uncertainty surrounding women's future loyalties drove a bias toward the status quo electoral rules that could only be overcome when competition was high or during a moment of political realignment. Competition and the threat of losing power inspired entrepreneurial thinking among elected leaders, as it put them in a situation where they needed more votes in order to win. But it was only if at least one political group thought it would have a mobilizational advantage among the new electorate that electoral reform became a political possibility.

The information that politicians had about women's future political loyalties depended in large part on the activities of the suffragists themselves. Suffragists were concerned with the impact of women's enfranchisement, and could deliberately choose to keep the movement small or to grow it, depending on their expectations about what women's votes would do for their broader programmatic agendas. Because gender is, arguably, the ultimate crosscutting cleavage, even women who wanted rights in theory may have been willing, in highly stratified societies, to set this desire aside so as not to undermine other political priorities. But, in contexts where suffragists decided to pursue a broad movement and mobilize across political cleavages, this was a signal that elite women's preferences were not so far removed from the preferences of other groups, and gives a clue that the votes of women in the middle of the distribution may actually have been up for grabs. In this sense, suffrage mobilization was a demonstration of the potential voting power of the group, and when there was some degree of ambiguity about women's preferences, parties subject to high levels of political competition become open to the challenge of fighting over the women in the middle.

On the electoral side, politicians used information generated by observing and interacting with the suffrage movement to inform their understanding of which women were likely to be politically active in the event of reform. In general, the conditions under which reform was likeliest was when politics was highly competitive and when a political group with enough power to change the laws believed it could capture the majority of women's votes. A key finding of this work is that parties rejected bills related to voting rights reform either because they did not think the disfranchised groups would support them, or because they did not need the extra votes in order to win.

These general arguments can help to shed light on the pattern of political inclusion for many groups both within and between countries. The argument applies best, I believe, to the set of cases where women sought the right to vote in limited democratic systems.[11] The strategic account might not explain universalist reforms in places such as Finland, which gave both men and women voting rights in its founding constitution in 1906. Although there was substantial mobilization by Finnish women for the vote, the immediate concerns of electoral politics may not have driven their enfranchisement.[12] Instead, women were included

---

[11] As Krook (2010: 208ff) suggests for the adoption of electoral gender quotas, there are arguably multiple causal pathways to women's suffrage.

[12] Prior to 1906 Finland had been a "Grand Duchy" of Russia. Between 1886 and 1899 the Finnish Diet had some independent legislative authority, but a maximum of 8 percent of the male population would have been allowed to participate in elections. Taxpaying women were given a municipal franchise in the countryside in 1863 and in the towns in 1872. In 1897 the Finnish "Women's Association" brought a petition for full suffrage to Diet, which did not reach a second reading. In 1904 a suffrage rally in Helsinki drew 1,000 protestors, which was followed by another mass meeting of suffragists in December 1905. On the tails of a general strike in 1905 (which included male and female leaders), the radical Social Democratic Party came into power. The party overhauled the structure of the legislature and the electoral laws, extending universal suffrage to men and women in 1906. In 1907 the first election took place

because of their ties to the anti-imperial movement before the constitution was established. Nor will it provide a complete story for many moments of reform after WWII, for thereafter suffrage appears to have become a global norm, enshrined in international organizations and peace negotiations thanks in part to the advocacy of transnational women's movements.[13]

But the strategic account of enfranchisement can help us make sense of the long road to suffrage in places like Switzerland and Québec. Switzerland adopted a limited set of democratic principles in 1848 but kept women from the polls until the 1970s. Although one might surmise that the late extension in both had to do with Catholicism, it is important to stress that there were several Catholic countries—Austria, Ireland, Poland, and Belgium (to a lesser extent)—which were first-wave adopters of the franchise.[14] Moreover, Catholic women in Switzerland tended to be the leaders of the movement for the vote, while socialist women were more or less uninvolved in the issue until 1957. This, despite the fact that the Social Democrats were in power long before that late date. With very little turnover in national elections, the Swiss parties did not need women's votes to maintain political power, and thus had little incentive to pursue reform. Divided by the cultural and political cleavages across cantons, Swiss suffragists were initially more concerned with the implications of organizing across cantons than with challenging the status quo legal framework. After a resurgence of political competition and a re-grouping of the suffrage movement in the 1960s, an innovative

---

under the new laws and brought 19 women into national office. These women constituted the world's first female legislators. The universal franchise law was reaffirmed in 1919, after the fall of the Russian Empire. See Anthony et al. 1969 volume VI: ch. LIII; Collier 1999: 35; Ray 1918.

[13] See Towns 2010a and 2010b. This is not to say that norms were irrelevant in the earlier period. In 1931 Sri Lankan women were enfranchised on the same terms as men, meaning that whatever educational and property requirements applied to men would also apply to women. The documentation on this extension points not to the electoral advantage for certain political parties of including women, but rather to the desire of local parliamentarians, both indigenous Sri Lankans and creole colonists, to modernize in line with the British metropole. Female enfranchisement in Sri Lanka came after a report called the "Donoughmore Commission" mentioned it favorably, though Jayawardena (1986: 122ff) does mention limited calls for the measure by bourgeois Sri Lankan women, both national and creole.

[14] Belgium, another Catholic country, extended some national level voting rights in the first wave. The law of 1919 gave the right to vote in national elections to the widows and mothers of servicemen killed in WWI, to the widows and mothers of citizens shot or killed by the enemy, and to female political prisoners who had been held by the enemy. The majority were enfranchised in 1948. Martin 2000: 34; Cook 2002: 88.

cross-cantonal strategy with large-scale mobilization and direct action tactics helped most Swiss women gain political rights.[15]

A similar argument might also apply to Québec, where the Liberal Party, which held power for four decades after the 1920s, had little need for more votes and, what is more, operated with the assumption that women would vote for the Conservative Party.[16] After the party was ousted from power by the conservative National Union Party in 1936, the Liberals put suffrage on their platform, formed a coalition with suffrage organizations, and were re-elected. Both a federal MP and a well-known Québécois suffragist convinced the ousted Liberal leaders that women's suffrage, and the votes of women, would benefit their party in the coming elections.[17] Thus, after two decades of voting in federal elections, in 1940 Québécois women could finally vote at the province level. In both Switzerland and Québec, the incentives of political leaders stalled reform, but when the political tides shifted, suffragists were able to exploit the opening to win the vote.

SUFFRAGE POLITICS IN THE UNITED KINGDOM, THE UNITED STATES, AND FRANCE

Although I will present evidence from many countries along the way, the present text is primarily concerned with showing how political competition and the alignment of interests between suffragists and politicians helps explain women's enfranchisement in the United States, France, and the United Kingdom. These three countries are apt for comparison: they were among the first to experiment on a large scale with representative institutions, and they produced some of the earliest and most vociferous feminist political thought.[18] In 1900, all three countries

[15] I am interpreting evidence on the Swiss suffrage movement by Banaszak 1996b: 218.
[16] Dupont 1972: 415. Dumas 2016.
[17] Genest 1996: 112. The suffragists may have been mistaken, as that was the last election the Liberals would win until 1960.
[18] Offen 2000 is the major text on feminist political thought in Europe. In 1791, during the French Revolution, Olympe de Gouges authored a *Declaration of the Rights of Women*, proclaiming that "Woman has the right to mount the scaffold; she must have the right to mount the rostrum" (Hause and Kenney 1984: 5; Offen 1994: 152). Her calls were not heeded. Instead, de Gouge was guillotined. In Britain, Mary Wollstonecraft's *A Vindication of the Rights of Woman* reverberated through British "salons" after 1792, followed, in 1869, by J. S. Mill's *The Subjection of Women* (1989, original 1869), long thought to have been influenced through his relationship with the able Harriet Taylor (see Holton 1986: ch 1). Finally, the

had well-established and growing suffrage movements, and all were on the winning side of the First World War. Shortly after the war, all three had high levels of electoral contestation, and at least one chamber in each country's national legislature passed a woman's suffrage bill. Although they are by no means identical, the similarities across these three countries make the difference in suffrage expansion curious: by 1920 both the United States and the United Kingdom had agreed to let women into polling stations; but France, which was always the boldest in its institutional reforms, had many opportunities to extend the franchise in the 1920s, but refused women until the late date of 1944.[19] A central project of this book is explaining these divergent outcomes.

Any expert on the US, France, or the UK might aver that these distinctive outcomes are due to each country's singular politics—a fact that might render any comparison fraught. And indeed, the sectional conflict in the United States, which divided North from South, slave state from "free" state, and primary product markets from finished goods markets, make the racial and regional divides seem particularly fractious. But of course the Irish question—that is, what should be done about the Catholic Irish that were eager for and rebelling in the name of self-government—set British Liberals and Conservatives, not to mention the Irish themselves, in an existential conflict that threatened the stability of the state. So too did the French republicans' concerns about church involvement in national affairs, which, far from having been superseded in the Third Republic, set the lines of contestation throughout the period, giving way to the Vichy regime during World War II. The legacies of institutions such as the Church in France, slavery in the United States, and empire in the UK informed suffrage politics insofar as they created the political cleavages that influenced incentives, beliefs, and therefore the strategic interactions between suffrage movements and elected politicians.

What each of these different but nevertheless major conflicts did was to draw the battle lines in clear ways. That France fell behind might be attributed to Catholic ideology and the relegation of women to the

---

famous 1848 Women's Rights Convention, which took place at Seneca Falls, New York, produced a second *Declaration of the Rights of Woman*, spurring the formation of the world's first organized movement for women's suffrage (see Flexner 1995: ch. X).

[19] Sociologists of the US suffrage movement often stress that the ease of amendment influenced whether suffrage laws passed. France would have been the easiest on this front— all that was required was "a change of wording in a regime of textual law." Offen 1994: 156.

"private" sphere. And indeed, at the dawn of the twentieth century, given the legacy of the Catholic Church and Napoléon Bonaparte's civil code, French women may have had fewer civil rights than their counterparts across the English Channel and the Atlantic Ocean. But other stubborn facts complicate this argument: married French women had easier access to divorce by consent than women in the US and the UK, and unlike women in the US, married or pregnant French women were not easy to force out of their jobs.[20] Moreover, women's overall level of economic participation in France was quite high, including by married French women, who were two times more likely to work outside the home than married women in the other two countries.[21] Instead of Catholicism per se, the religious cleavage impacted suffrage in France because French women's education remained under the Church's auspices long after republican men were educated in public schools.[22] This led to a popular perception that French women would side with the Church on political matters—a belief that influenced both political parties' decisions and suffragists' strategies. In other Catholic countries such as Austria, where the church and state were initially aligned, women won national level voting rights in 1918.[23] In other words, political cleavages influenced popular perceptions of women's future political loyalties, and these expectations influenced the groups that believed they would win or lose from franchise reform.

Beliefs about women's political preferences became politically salient during moments of heightened competition. The postwar realignment of power in the UK, and the threat of realignment in the US, brought several parties that hoped to benefit from women's votes into a position to fight for reform. Although the French political system was similarly in flux, prominent members of the Radical Party expressed fears that women would not support their republican agenda. Since the Radicals had veto

[20] See Morgan 2006: 43. See Goldin (1994: 160ff) on "marriage bars," policies that effectively kicked women out of companies when they married. These practices did not decline in the US until the 1950s, and eventually became illegal.

[21] Moreover, we should not overstate women's civil rights in the United States or the UK. In 1907, the US Congress passed the Expatriation Act, which denaturalized—i.e., stripped citizenship from—any American woman who married a foreign man. See Gunter 2017: 6.

[22] See Pedersen 2014: 38 and Clark 1984: table 1.

[23] Many scholars of gender complicate the relationship between religious institutions and ideology on the formation of progressive gender policies, arguing that it is the relationship between the church and the state, not just the existence of a strong state, that is important. Morgan (2006) makes this point with regard to maternalist welfare state policies in Europe, as does Htun (2003) for understanding the complex politics of divorce, abortion, and women's civil rights in Latin America.

power in the upper chamber of the legislature throughout the 1920s and 1930s, they were able to block women's suffrage for two decades. Leading French suffragists also expressed similar reservations—that the majority of French women would vote as the clerics told them—and so they did not build a coalition across the dominant cleavage, of the sort that proved crucial in the US and the UK, to fight for reform. In each country, an analysis of periods in which successive legislative debates failed, and ultimately were successful, reveals the conditions under which an alignment of interests between elected politicians and the organized women's movement promoted women's suffrage. Together, these within-case analyses illuminate the broader cross-country questions.

READING THIS BOOK

This book can be read in several ways. For those primarily interested in understanding the actual dynamics of suffrage politics, any of the case studies should be fine to read on their own. Chapter 2 provides a longer discussion of different social scientific arguments about women's enfranchisement, and describes the theoretical claims forwarded in the text in detail. It evaluates several alternative explanations of women's enfranchisement, such as economic modernization, growth in women's labor force participation, sex ratios, and warfare, that have been generated from scholarship on male democratization. It lays out an alternative argument that links political cleavages and electoral competition to politicians' and suffragists' strategies surrounding suffrage. Drawing on the massive literature on suffrage movements, which has historical and social scientific branches, the theory forms insights into the tensions among suffragists and between suffrage organizations, and outlines the political hurdles that suffragists must overcome to make suffrage bills become law.[24] I rely, finally, on several rich texts on women and politics that have theorized the conditions under which women's movements can best

---

[24] These insights come from three waves of historical scholarship on women's suffrage. The first wave began with histories of bourgeois movement leaders; the second moved toward revisionist accounts of suffrage movements which stressed the importance of "militant" activism; and the final wave settled into new political histories and social scientific accounts of the women's movements. Writings from all three of these schools appear in the footnotes of this text, but the recent political accounts are given more weight in the book as a whole. The work by political historians such as Holton (1986, 1996), Pugh (1974, 1985, 2000), Hause and Kenney (1981, 1984), Morgan (1972, 1975), and Smith (1996) and that of social scientists, such as Banaszak (1996a,b, 1998), McConnaughy (2013), McDonagh and

contest exclusion to describe the way in which political competition and women's mobilization together form a logic of suffrage reform.[25]

Chapters 3, 4, and 5 substantiate these arguments through case studies of the UK, the US, and France. They attend specifically to three puzzles: why the Liberal government in the United Kingdom refused to support a women's franchise bill from 1906 to 1914, but ultimately included women on the Reform Act of 1918; why the western United States were early adopters of women's suffrage when, by conventional accounts, the movement was stronger in the East; and, finally, why a successful suffrage measure that was passed by the French Chamber of Deputies in 1919 received no hearing in the Senate throughout the 1920s. These chapters suggest that the confluence of a targeted movement strategy and shifts in political power allowed American and British women to vote much earlier than their French counterparts, as in France the party with veto power expected to lose women's votes.

Some readers may be curious about the bigger picture—what these three countries reveal, theoretically and empirically about women's suffrage in a larger set of countries. For this, turn to the conclusion, which delves into a discussion of what thinking about women's suffrage can teach us about the comparative politics of democratization, and about the study of gender and political development more generally.

Price 1985, McDonagh (1989, 2002), McCammon and Campbell (2001), and McCammon et al. (2001), are explicitly concerned with understanding relationships between suffrage activists and legislative politics. In other words, they provide insight into the strategic interactions that, I argue, are key to understanding the political origins of the female franchise.

[25] E.g., Baldez 2002, Htun 2003, Beckwith 2014, and Friedman 2000.

2

Democratization and the Case of Women

In most of the world's first democracies, the lag between the initial extension of voting rights to men and later laws that brought women to the polls was quite long. Nearly 144 years passed from America's democratic founding until 1920, when the Nineteenth Amendment enfranchised women nationally. In the Southern Hemisphere, women in Argentina, Uruguay, and Chile waited, respectively, 94, 102, and 119 years between the time that men could vote and women's political inclusion. Similar gulfs materialized all over Europe, where, in the most extreme case, many Swiss women were prevented from voting until 1971.[1] The majority of these countries gave women the vote after they had already begun to experiment with elections as a way of choosing leaders.

The story of women's enfranchisement in limited democracies is fundamentally one of democratization. It is about changing electoral institutions to increase the political voice of an historically marginalized group, and about enhancing contestation for political power based on the new issues and ideas favored by female voters. These themes are all in the purview of comparative politics, but for the most part the field has considered women to be "outside history" during the first key era of democratic transitions.[2] In seminal works on democratization, women, either as political actors who have taken part in the process or as beneficiaries of the fruits of democracy, have rarely been given center stage.[3] This is true even

---

[1] Even the Swiss federal reform in 1971 did not guarantee women the vote in all elections: in some cantons they had to wait until the 1980s.

[2] The work of Göran Therborn is perhaps an exception that proves the rule. Therborn (1977) conceded that many of the world's democracies in earlier periods would be more accurately labeled "male democracies." The phrase "outside history" comes from Eric Hobsbawm, an august Marxist historian who has written important economic and political histories of the nineteenth and twentieth centuries. He is quite candid: women did not make the politics, wars, or revolutions that defined the Age of Empires, and so are irrelevant to its telling. Hobsbawm 2010: 196.

[3] In the classic texts written, for example, by Barrington Moore, Samuel Huntington, and Seymour Lipset, there is scarcely a mention of women, let alone as actors relevant to the

though mass mobilization by women was a striking feature of the early twentieth century in several countries—prior to 1950 women in more than 29 countries mobilized for the vote—and the omission exists even when scholars have focused on episodes of reform where women won the vote at the same time as men.[4]

To be sure, there is a rich literature on gender and politics that theorizes the conditions under which women protest against political regimes, the efficacy of women's movements when they align with different types of political party, and the way that moments of rupture and state reconfiguration influence women's access to institutions and political power.[5] Nevertheless, as several feminist scholars have pointed out, in game-theoretic accounts of regime transition and in almost all quantitative studies of democratization, women are missing. In statistical studies, it is common for scholars to label a country democratic if 50 percent of its male citizens have the right to vote, implying that countries can completely exclude women but nevertheless be considered fully democratic.[6] The study of democratization is therefore most accurately described as the study of democracy for men.

To justify the focus on male democratization, many scholars simply assume, with Daron Acemoglu and James Robinson, that there is nothing

---

process of democratization. Moore (1966) mentions women nine times in the tome. Almost all of these references are to a feudal lord's rights over women in his demesne. Huntington (1993) does not mention the big surge of women's enfranchisement in the "second" wave; nor does he consider women's role in the decolonization struggles that demarcate democracy's "third" wave after 1974. For an account of women's role in decolonization struggles, see Jayawardena (1986). Note, though, that the phenomenon of women's suffrage did not pass unnoticed by contemporary political scientists. See Ray 1918, Stuart 1920, Turner 1913.

[4] E.g., Collier 1999. Women got the vote during several of the "joint project" episodes she studies in depth, including Finland (1906), Germany (1918), and the UK (1918). The omission of women from her text is especially curious in the UK because it was women, rather than men, who had mobilized extensively for the 1918 reform. On women's activism for suffrage worldwide, see Chafetz et al. 1990.

[5] E.g., Baldez 2002; Beckwith 2000; Banaszak 1996b; Alvarez 1990; Chowdhury et al. 1994; Friedman 2000; Rucht 2003.

[6] Caraway 2004; Ferree and Mueller 2004: 577; Crasnow 2015: 152–154. Paxton's (2000) article on measurement validity in democratization studies brilliantly shows how, despite having a conception of democracy that features universal inclusion, most studies in practice utilize a "50 percent male" benchmark as an operational measure. In spite of these criticisms, more recent operationalizations continue to use 50 percent male enfranchisement as the benchmark for democracy, e.g., Boix et al. (2013), Ansell and Samuels (2014). Cf. Therborn (1977), who adopts rigorous standards of full inclusion for countries to be labeled democratic. See too the new initiatives toward a feminist institutionalism in Krook and Mackay (2010).

mysterious about the politics of women's inclusion, so that "when the roles began to change as women entered the workforce, women also obtained voting rights."[7] Or they agree with Dietrich Rueschemeyer, Evelyne Huber Stephens, and John Stephens that the "dynamics of [women's] struggle follow quite different principles from the inclusion of subordinate classes or ethnic groups and would require a whole separate analysis."[8] Statements like these, which are used to define the theoretical scope of a particular study, convey the impression that there is either no puzzle surrounding why women gained entry into the body politic, or, if there is one, its solution is distinct from most other instances of political inclusion. Let us reserve for the book's conclusion the question of whether the politics of women's enfranchisement does require a completely separate analysis from the inclusion of other groups, and begin instead by exploring the relevance of several general hypotheses about democratization for the case of women.

THEORIES OF FRANCHISE REFORM

There are three general forms of explanation of women's enfranchisement: those that focus on macro-historical processes like economic modernization, warfare, and the distribution of men and women in the population; those that have micro-behavioral roots where suffrage is seen as the outcome of bargaining or elite incentives; and arguments that focus on the role of suffragists and women's movements in forging reform. I examine whether these ideas are consistent, more or less, with the pattern of enfranchisement around the world. Presenting comparative historical data over the last century, I find that countries that enfranchised women earlier tended to be among the first to industrialize, but there is no convincing evidence that women's labor force participation grew dramatically prior to reform. Nor do sex ratios or warfare evince strong connections to enfranchisement. Instead, I argue that more direct political factors are likely to account for suffrage, such as the level of political competition, politicians' beliefs about the women's vote, and the degree of mobilization by women.

---

[7] Acemoglu and Robinson 2006: 8.
[8] Rueschemeyer et al. 1992: 301.

Macro-Historical Processes and Women's Suffrage

The Modernization Thesis. The first potential explanation for the global pattern of women's enfranchisement is a form of "modernization" thesis, the notion that economic development drives democratization and, by extension, women's enfranchisement. Since industrializing countries were among the first to experiment with representative institutions, the emergence of industrialization is undoubtedly a background feature in the story of women's political inclusion.[9] With technological innovation, mass migration, and falling birthrates, the industrial revolution produced new orderings of society and the economy. In the nineteenth century, many of the traditional rules of "coverture"—in which fathers and husbands were the public representatives of women—were upended as women became better educated, and delayed marriage in order to work. These changes set the stage for transformations in the legal environment, so that women eventually gained enhanced rights to property, inheritance, earnings, and custody in the case of divorce.[10]

Figure 2.1 presents a snapshot of the sectoral composition of economies around the time of suffrage in sixty-four countries for which data are available.[11] The top panel shows the percentage of the workforce

---

[9] It should be noted, though, that many Marxist political economists and sociologists suggest that the division of labor in capitalism gave rise to *greater* gender inequality than existed in agricultural societies. See Hartmann 1976, Folbre 1982, Federici 2004, Mies 1980: ch 3, and Engels 2010. Further, in a macro-anthropological study, Sanday 1981 finds that gender equality varied widely among pre-industrial tribes depending on the mode of production and cultural narratives. This implies that women's subordination is not a universal phenomenon.

[10] The question of whether women were citizens, and whether, by virtue of being citizens, they had the right to vote, was adjudicated in several countries. In *Minor v. Happersett* (1874) the US Supreme Court held that the Constitution did not confer voting rights on citizens, that suffrage was not a right of citizenship, and that the states had the right to withhold voting rights from certain groups of citizens (see Flexner 1995: 161ff.). In the 1880s, French feminists appealed to various ministries and the courts for a decision as to whether the words *citoyen* and *Français*, used in constitutions to confer political and civil liberties, applied to women. Several rulings implied that these words had different meanings in different contexts: that women did not fulfill all the legal conditions to make them French citizens, but that tax law could apply to women so long as a qualification for taxpaying did not require enjoying full civil rights (Hause and Kenney 1984: 11–12; Offen 1994: 156).

[11] The country-level data on economic sectors, women's labor force participation, and population that appear herein have been digitized from Mitchell 2003, 2007a, 2007b. Mitchell used national level censuses, which are admittedly more complete for the advanced industrial economies and as we get into the late twentieth century. I used his categories of manufacturing and service employment, which he intended to be comparable, but there are undoubtedly mistakes and inconsistencies in definitions across countries and even across censuses within countries. Since census data are typically recorded every ten years, I linearly interpolate values in the intercensal years using Stata's "ipolate" command.

(a) Industrial workforce in year of women's suffrage

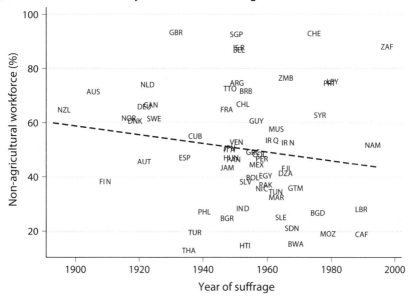

(b) Changes in industrial workforce surrounding women's suffrage

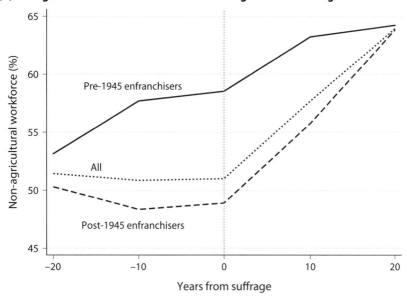

FIGURE 2.1. Economic Development and Women's Suffrage. Panel (a) presents a cross-section of the year of enfranchisement and the non-agricultural workforce as a fraction of all laborers, marked with a country code ($n = 64$). Panel (b) presents the average of the non-agricultural workforce before and after suffrage was extended, centered around the year of suffrage, for countries that enfranchised women before and after 1945 ($n = 64$).

engaged in non-agricultural activity in the year that women's suffrage was extended. Overall, as with democratization more generally, the economies where a greater proportion of workers was involved in non-agricultural work were earlier on the road to women's political inclusion.[12] This does not imply, however, that rapid changes in the composition of the economy precipitated women's suffrage. Panel (b) looks at changes in the economy surrounding suffrage in sixty-four countries after separating countries by whether they enfranchised women before or after 1945.[13] Data are available for fourteen countries that enfranchised women before 1945 and fifty countries that did so after the Second World War. Each line is constructed by taking the average level of non-agricultural employment for all countries in a given group after centering the data around time "zero"—the year of women's enfranchisement in each country. The lines of averages show that countries in the group that enfranchised women before 1945 had higher levels of non-agricultural participation prior to the extension of the franchise to women than countries that enfranchised women after 1945. But note that within the early enfranchising group, the average increase in non-agricultural labor in the ten years prior to suffrage was small, around three percentage points. Countries in the later group for which data were available had lower levels of economic development prior to enfranchisement, with little change in the ten years prior to reform. At the same time that early enfranchisers tended to have higher levels of industrial workers, these figures do not show rapid growth in the industrial workforce prior to suffrage in either the early or later group.

Women in the Workforce. A second variant of the modernization thesis suggests that women's rights emerged after women entered the workforce in larger numbers.[14] Is women's economic participation, or growth therein, directly correlated with women's enfranchisement? Using data compiled from historical censuses, I was able to locate information on the share of adult women engaged in economic activity for forty-seven countries in the years surrounding suffrage.[15] The top panel of

---

[12] See, e.g., Boix et al. 2013.

[13] I chose these groupings because many scholars think that suffrage became a global norm after 1945, and so suffrage and the economy may have had different relationships over time. Ramirez et al. 1997. Towns 2010a, b.

[14] Acemoglu and Robinson 2006: 8. Doepke and Tertilt 2009. Bertocchi 2010.

[15] Labor force participation includes economic activity in manufacturing, agriculture, and the service sector. The figures have been coded from Mitchell (2003, 2007a, 2007b: various pages).

(a) Women's labor force participation in year of suffrage

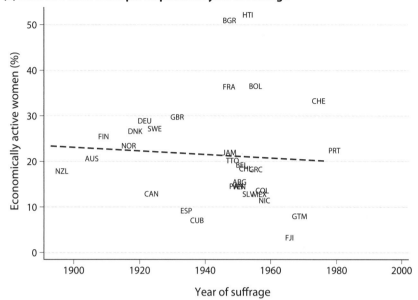

(b) Changes in participation surrounding suffrage

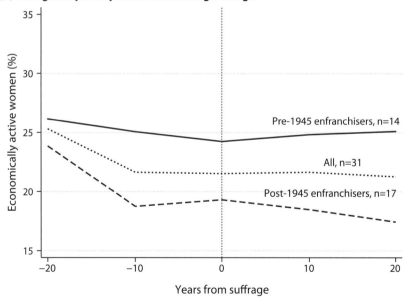

FIGURE 2.2. Women's Labor Force Participation in the Year of Suffrage. In panel (a) the three-letter country code marker appears in the year suffrage was extended ($n = 47$). Panel (b) plots the average percent of women who were economically active over time for countries that enfranchised before and after the Second World War ($n = 31$). The graph is centered on the year of suffrage.

figure 2.2 plots the year of enfranchisement along the x-axis against the share of women that were economically active in the year the vote was extended on the y-axis. Surprisingly, the bivariate relationship between suffrage and women's labor force participation shows that several of the first countries to extend the electoral franchise to women, such as New Zealand and Australia, had quite low female labor force participation when women won the vote, while several of the later cases—like France—had much higher labor force participation overall.

The bottom panel of figure 2.2 can shed light on whether there were major changes in women's labor force participation prior to electoral reform. It groups thirty-one countries for which a longer series of data is available surrounding enfranchisement by whether they enfranchised women before 1945 (fourteen countries) or after (seventeen countries). The graph, which is centered on the year of suffrage, takes the average of women's labor force participation in each group for twenty years before and after suffrage. Although the earlier enfranchisers did have higher labor force participation surrounding suffrage on average—24 percent instead of 19 percent of women were economically active in the earlier cases around the time of suffrage—there is no obvious increase in women's labor force participation surrounding the reform. Some countries saw growth in women's economic activity while others saw declines, but mainly the lines appear to be flat. Together, these figures cast doubt on the existence of a simple association between changes in women's economic activity and suffrage reform.[16]

Wars Bring Enfranchisement. A third potential explanation for women's suffrage is that war set the stage for women's political inclusion as it did for democratization more generally.[17] Two different camps link warfare to democratization—the pessimists argue that war reduced the political costs of enfranchisement because it elevated a global elite above the threat of expropriation by the masses—while the optimists argue that because mass warfare requires society-wide

---

[16] Note, too, that in the US, at least, suffrage was granted in an era of women's declining economic activity: Goldin and Sokoloff (1982: 748) find that women's economic participation actually fell during the nineteenth century, with peak activity in the 1840s.

[17] See Bermeo (2003) on war and democratization. On suffrage and war see Adams 2014, Therborn 1977, and Dangerfield 2011.

cooperation, it allows ordinary people to extract concessions from leaders.[18]

Warfare enters the politics of women's suffrage in some interesting ways. Elite women often pointed to a seeming contradiction when the "masses" of men were allowed to vote while they could not, while politicians confronting this logic often justified women's continued exclusion from political participation on the grounds that men were called to make greater bodily sacrifices for the state in times of war. Suffragists learned to counter this argument, especially during and after wars, by pointing to the very real contributions they made to their countries in the course of conflict.[19] War could exact a high toll from women insofar as they would be left childless or widowed or if the necessary economic preparations brought them into new daily roles. And indeed, women often entered the workforce in large numbers when men were at the front. Because of their wartime sacrifices, war may have given women leverage over leaders to secure the vote.

There are ninety countries for which I was able to gather information on warfare (interstate, civil, or extrastate war) prior to suffrage.[20] In the

---

[18] The pessimists include Therborn (1977) and Boix (2003). The optimists include Scheve and Stasavage (2011), who find that mobilization for war is associated with higher pressure on governments for progressive taxation, and Adams (2014), who attributes the first wave of suffrage to the First World War.

[19] While admitting that suffragists saw war as opening up new possibilities for change, I want to stress that this hope was not confined to World War I. In an address to Congress in 1866, just after the Civil War, Susan B. Anthony used the war to argue persuasively that women were deserving of equality:

> With you we have just passed through the agony of death, the resurrection and triumph of another revolution, doing all in our power to mitigate its horrors and gild its glories. And now think you, we have no souls to fire, no brains to weigh your arguments; that after education such as this, we can stand silent witnesses while you sell our birthright of liberty? ... Our demand must ever be: "No compromise of human rights. No admission in the constitution of inequality of rights, or disfranchisement on account of color or sex." [Quoted in Catt and Shuler (1923: 39).]

Shortly after Anthony's plea, the Republican Party decided to support a variation of the Fourteenth Amendment which stated that voting rights could not be abridged on the basis of race, but which did not include sex as a protected category. This, in spite of the fact that earlier drafts of the amendment had included women. When questioned by Elizabeth Cady Stanton as to why the same arguments made on behalf of black men would not also apply to women's enfranchisement, Congressman John Bingham, a principal architect of the Fourteenth Amendment, quipped that "he was not the puppet of logic but the slave of practical politics." Catt and Shuler (1923) see this move in entirely strategic terms. See chs. III and IV.

[20] The warfare data are modified from the Correlates of War database (Sarkees and Wayman 2010) thanks to my colleague Alex Weisigar.

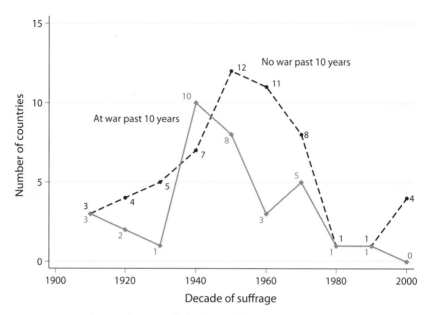

FIGURE 2.3. Warfare in the Decade before Suffrage. The figure presents the number of countries that extended the vote in a given decade based on whether or not they had been at war in the prior 10 years. The marker labels are the number in each group.

sample as a whole, twenty out of ninety countries (22 percent) were involved in some form of war in the year that the majority of women gained the right to vote, and thirty-four out of ninety (37 percent) were involved in some form of warfare in the ten years prior to women's suffrage. Figure 2.3 presents aggregate information on countries' involvement in war in the ten years prior to the extension of the franchise to women. The x-axis represents the decade of suffrage, and the y-axis represents the number of countries that extended the vote in that decade by whether or not they were involved in a war. As the figure shows, nearly 60 percent of countries that extended suffrage in the 1940s had been involved in a war in the ten years prior to reform. But generally speaking, from 1900 to 2000 the majority of countries that gave women voting rights had not been at war in the previous decade.

Looking within the first wave of women's enfranchisement, there is not a clear connection between wartime mobilization in World War I and franchise extension. Germany and Austria, two mobilized, belligerent states, extended voting rights right before the war ended. But some of the earliest countries to enfranchise women in the period remained neutral throughout the conflict, including the Netherlands and several countries in Scandinavia.[21] Levels of wartime mobilization also do not present an obvious pattern for the allies. The UK, France, and Italy were highly mobilized for the war, yet only the UK extended the vote at its close. Across the Atlantic, Canada and the United States each extended suffrage in some form around this time, yet neither was highly mobilized in the war effort. These diverse outcomes do not provide support for a deterministic model of warfare and women's enfranchisement.

What I want to suggest, instead, is that to the extent that war and electoral reform are related, it is because war sets the stage for major contests in the domestic political arena. New issues emerge as salient in the public sphere, and, because even a war won will have many detractors, it heightens the level of competition at home. War can even affect politics in neutral countries if some citizens question the decision to stay neutral and if others see the need to protect interests in a new world-wide realignment. As we will see in later chapters, the suffrage legislation that was adopted after the war in the US and the UK was on the docket well before conflict broke out, but the unfreezing of old political alliances and the desire to forge new ones once the war ended opened up avenues for entrepreneurial activity along the lines of electoral reform.

Women's Scarcity. A fourth idea that has been invoked to explain women's enfranchisement theorizes that women are more likely to gain voting rights when there are fewer of them. Scarcity increases bargaining power, allowing women to ask for more and better rights, and it might also make female voters less of a threat to men because their smaller numbers reduce the risks associated with reform.[22] This argument has been used to explain the pattern of adoption in the United States, where the male-packed western states gave women voting rights before states in the East.[23] But, as figure 2.4 shows, the negative correlation between sex ratios and enfranchisement is rather weak: within the set of countries that

[21] Hause and Kenney 1984: 202.

[22] Braun and Kvasnicka 2013. Although there is a stronger negative correlation between sex ratios and the date of suffrage in the US than globally, early-adopting Utah (1869 and 1870) had nearly equal numbers. Alexander 1970, 21. In some sense the scarcity argument and the war thesis are mutually exclusive, as wartime mobilization which reduced the male population actually made women more numerous.

[23] Although see chapter 4 on the United States, which shows that western states did not offer women a better package of rights prior to enfranchisement than states in the East.

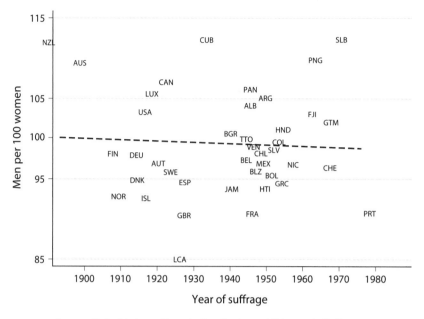

FIGURE 2.4. Male-to-Female Sex Ratio and Women's Suffrage.

gave women the vote prior to 1920, there were as many with a low ratio of men to women as with a high sex ratio. As with women's economic activity, the pattern of sex ratios was relatively stable before and after enfranchisement.

Micro-Behavioral Accounts of Enfranchisement

Men's Preferences. Moving from sweeping theories of suffrage to arguments that focus on individual level incentives is an idea that women won the vote when it was politically expedient for men. There are several variations on this theme. Political economists have used models of household production to argue that men will begin to advocate for women's rights because their shared preferences will be amplified in government if both partners can vote.[24] Alternatively, as the fertility transition in the nineteenth century reduced the average number of children born into households, fathers may have desired more rights (to inherit, to go to school, to vote) for their daughters and hence advocated for women's inclusion.[25] Both the bargaining models and the models of

[24] Bertocchi 2010.
[25] Doepke and Tertilt 2009.

household production usefully point to the incentives that men may face when confronted with demands for women's voting rights, but the reality that the vast majority of suffrage organization members were women does not suggest that *mass* male advocacy was key to reform. Moreover, these models do not consider the crucial political actors—elected politicians—who have both the actual power to change the laws and stand to become the immediate winners or losers after women start to vote. In this sense, the bargaining models neglect the importance of elite incentives.

Elite Incentives. The incentives that underlie politicians' choices about whether to extend the franchise are the subject of a great body of work on male democratization. There are three prominent arguments about elite incentives: politicians may support reform when elites are split and driven into party competition based on divergent sectoral interests or programmatic preferences;[26] elites may concede the vote when they are already powerful or have such well-insulated economic interests that they do not fear popular participation in politics;[27] lastly, many scholars are drawn to the idea that "revolutionary mobilization"—public displays of discontent against the regime that signal a willingness to use violence to achieve political ends—plays a key role in democratic reforms.[28] Models of the first sort conceive of different partisan agendas as fundamentally linked to economic interests—such as urban versus rural political conflicts—and they generally presume that politicians know ex ante which parties will win the votes of the poor. Because women are situated among all classes and have incomes that draw from all sectors, these models would not produce an obvious political winner based on gender. Models of the second sort assume that the vote comes when electoral politics have become irrelevant to power. But of course, there are many instances where the laws were carved with obvious partisan and strategic interests in mind, such as when the UK Conservatives conceded the vote to wealthy older women at the same time that the other parties won manhood suffrage; or when Canadian women were not allowed to vote in province-level elections in Québec at the same time that they won the federal vote. If elections did not matter, then it makes little sense for countries to allow men of the working classes to vote but not allow

[26] Ansell and Samuels 2014; Collier 1999; Lizzeri and Persico 2004; Llavador and Oxoby 2005.
[27] Boix 2003; Therborn 1977.
[28] For a longer discussion of revolutionary unrest in models of democratization, see the conclusion.

women the same rights, especially in places where women were actually demanding the vote.

Finally there is the prominent argument that revolutionary unrest leads to enfranchisement.[29] Because many of the world's revolutions have led to major changes in the electoral franchise, scholars have been right to focus on the importance of revolutionary unrest as one key driver of democratization.[30] But revolutionary unrest was not, strictly speaking, the major force behind women's enfranchisement. To begin with, "militancy" as such did not exist at all in most countries in the world, including the early enfranchisers like New Zealand and Australia, any countries in Latin America, or the late enfranchisers like Portugal (1974) and Switzerland (1971).[31] In France, too, there was virtually no militant movement.[32] More importantly, even in suffrage movements with militant flanks, the actions

[29] E.g., Acemoglu and Robinson 2006, Aidt and Jensen 2011, Przeworski 2009.

[30] The usage of "revolutionary unrest" in the democratization literature definitely signals violent contestation. But there is an alternative account of what revolution means. Following McAdam et al., revolution is "a rapid, forcible, durable shift in collective control over a state that includes a passage through openly contested sovereignty" (1996: 24). Note that violence is neither necessary nor sufficient for revolution. Revolution, rather, is a re-ordering of the way that decisions are taken for the body politic. Pincus 2007: 398. In this sense, suffrage historians' treatment of militancy can fit a conception of revolutionary behavior, but it would not match the intonation of most of the democratization literature. For a treatment of non-violent revolutions in the late twentieth century, see Nepstad (2011).

[31] The "militant" wing of the suffrage movement—led by the famous Pankhurst family and the Women's Social and Political Union in the United Kingdom and by Alice Paul and the National Woman's Party in the United States—have been celebrated in books (e.g., Ford 1991 and Lunardini 1986) and recent popular movies about the suffrage movement. Thus it may come as a surprise to some readers that militancy, as a form of revolutionary unrest, does not get credit for winning women the vote. For example, *Iron Jawed Angels* (2004), about the United States, and *Suffragette* (2015), about the militant movement in the United Kingdom.

[32] The few militants in France include Hubertine Auclert and Madeleine Pelletier. In 1876 Auclert formed the first sustaining French suffrage league, *Suffrage des femmes*, which was militant (in the sense of uncompromising) from the first. She encouraged women to stop paying taxes and organized public marches—which were uncommon in the French suffrage movement—and publicly burned pages of the *Code Napoléon*. Auclert's violent actions began in 1908 with an attempt to knock down urns containing ballots filled out by men, but her organization had no more than twenty active followers, reaching fifty at most. Hause and Kenney 1984: 9, 47, 76, 102. Also see Gordon 1990. In the United States, militancy emerged after 1913 when Alice Paul returned from a study trip with the British militants and formed the Congressional Union, which later became the National Woman's Party (Flexner 1995: 276ff.). But the majority of states in the US gave women the vote prior to the founding of the NWP. In the United Kingdom, where the militant Women's Social and Political Union gained 4,000 adherents by 1913, it is perhaps more difficult to discount the importance of militancy in driving suffrage reform. We can get part of the way by pointing out that in the same year the mainstream movement, led by Millicent Garrett Fawcett and the National Union of Women's Suffrage Societies, was, with 53,000 members and over 380 branches, vastly larger than the militant wing. Pugh 2000: table 8.4.

of suffragettes were not revolutionary in the sense used by the literature on male enfranchisement. Instead, the militant suffragettes selectively used violence to gain inclusion in an established regime, albeit with substantive changes in political culture and the rules of the game. I return to the issue of revolutionary unrest in more depth in the book's conclusion. For now, I submit that to theorize elite incentives and the ultimate outcome of debates about women's enfranchisement requires thinking about how ordinary, non-violent mechanisms of contestation can play a role in democratizing reforms.[33] The theory outlined in the rest of this chapter is motivated by two questions: first, how do politicians make predictions about how a group as diverse and diffuse as women will behave politically? Second, under what conditions do the choices made by organized women influence the ultimate outcome of suffrage reform?

The basic outcome that I seek to explain is the extension, or the rejection, of voting rights to women in any given context. Countries that elect leaders tend to have many levels of franchise, and often women have been given local level participatory rights, such as in school board elections or at the municipal level, prior to national rights. But even at the national level, there are many examples of partial enfranchisement in limited democracies, such as in Norway in 1906, when only wealthy women were given the vote, or Chile in 1934, when the franchise was extended to literate women. In this sense, the explanandum is not only whether the vote was extended, but along what lines. To understand women's suffrage, we must consider which women are included and the basis of the law.

THE LOGIC OF WOMEN'S SUFFRAGE

Electoral reforms can have many possible consequences. Adopting the secret ballot may embolden peasants to vote against their lord's favored parties; adopting majoritarian electoral rules can drive people to vote strategically for larger parties that have a greater likelihood of winning; and allowing citizens to vote by mail can increase voter turnout in places where participation was previously low. The extension of the franchise is similar to these other electoral reforms insofar as it marks a change in the rules of the game, which has the potential to upset the bases of political power in approaching elections. There is also a chance that longer-term changes will be set into motion, some of which may be unpredictable

[33] See Teele 2014.

ex ante.[34] The uncertainty that surrounds expansions of voting rights matters to both politicians and suffragists. Members of these groups voice explicit and implicit opinions and fears about the potential consequences of women's enfranchisement, and I contend that both groups' actions are consistent with trying to minimize their own uncertainty about politics after the vote is won. The conditions that ultimately produce or hinder reform stem from an *alignment of interests* between elected leaders and organized suffragists.

Figure 2.5 presents a schematic of the logic of women's suffrage. The first thing to note is that political cleavages and party competition appear as two important background features in the politics of suffrage. Cleavages are deep-seated political conflicts that shape the lines of competition and ideational discourse about reform, and competition describes the level of uncertainty in the electoral arena. In the long term, both cleavages and competition can be influenced by suffrage politics, but in any given year (or when studying any given suffrage bill) it is useful to think of the structure of political cleavages and the levels of competition as being determined "outside" the system. In this sense, cleavages and competition are the crucial inputs that set the terms of debate and that influence the incentives of elected leaders and suffragists at any moment in time.

In what follows I describe the logic of the argument working from the bottom of the schematic in figure 2.5 to the top. Beginning with the preferences of parties and politicians, I theorize that electoral competition and expectations about how women will vote are the primary criteria that condition choices on reform bills. Expectations about how women will vote are themselves related to political cleavages, but they are also formed with reference to the strategies of mobilization employed by suffragists. To the extent that women's preferences replicate men's, knowledge of the big political cleavages—the issue areas, the partisan groupings that emerge around these issues, and the geographic distribution of partisan support—will give politicians a sense of how many new voters will be associated with each existing group. If, on the other hand, women have distinctive preferences, then politicians will have less certainty about women's future loyalties. The strategy of the suffragists can serve to reveal this information; the women that mobilize and the issues they fight for can inform expectations about the preferences of women that are the most

---

[34] Acemoglu and Robinson (2006) describe this as giving the people de jure and de facto power into the future.

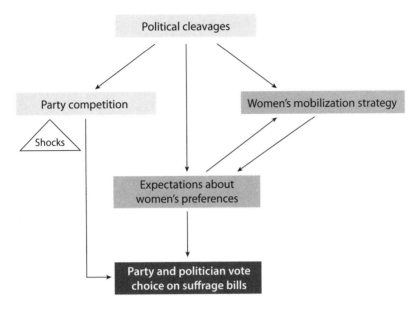

FIGURE 2.5. The Logic of Suffrage.

likely to be politically active once suffrage is extended. Mobilization can also establish gendered policy priorities that are not defined solely with reference to the old cleavage, allowing new coalitions to emerge between women across different groupings. The strategy of suffragists is, finally, related to female leaders' own concerns about the implications of voting rights for all women.

Politician and Party Vote Choice on Suffrage

In limited democracies—countries that have representative institutions but are far from mature electoral democracies—reform of electoral laws will sometimes require an amendment to the constitution, and will almost always require a bill to pass in the legislature, often in two chambers. Legislatures are composed of elected leaders and, generally speaking, elected leaders will affiliate with specific political parties. All members of a given party may vote together on suffrage, or individual leaders may vote independently depending on the strength and cohesion of parties within the system.[35] To understand suffrage expansion, both the overall

[35] I am not assuming that parties are mere aggregators of preferences, as the responsible party government model of E. E. Schattschneider (1942) would hold, nor do I agree fully with Joseph Schumpeter (1950: 263), who claimed that "the will of the people is the product and

position taken by political parties on the issue, as well as the choices made by individual members, are potentially of interest.

Strategic enfranchisement by elected leaders has two components: the electoral landscape in a given polity and politicians' beliefs about the preferences of the new group of voters. In general, most scholarship on enfranchisement assumes that politicians will reform the law so long as they will win more votes under the new rules than they won under the old.[36] But I propose that incumbents will be reluctant to enlarge the set of electors if they already have enough support to maintain power and to push their preferred policies through. As suggested by Carles Boix's discussion of the adoption of proportional representation in today's advanced democracies, parties can reform the nature of electoral institutions to insulate themselves from losses.[37] And, as Kathleen Bawn has argued, institutions tend to be stable insofar as elites have a common interest in maintaining them. This is especially true because electoral reform has high costs: it can take precious legislative time away from other political priorities, and, because even sophisticated polling does not predict elections very well, reform is shrouded in a good deal of uncertainty. Thus politicians must face a real threat of losing power (or, if out of power, must have a chance to win it) to produce enough momentum for reform. In this sense, it is only when politicians are, or become, vulnerable to challengers that they might be willing to take a chance on enlarging the electorate. Politicians will only support reform, then, when they need new voters in order to win. In addition, they will not support reform if they think the new group of voters will vote against their party.[38]

The schematic in table 2.1 helps to clarify the argument by specifying when individual legislators will support suffrage. The horizontal axis of table 2.1 displays the level of competition. When competition is high, incumbent leaders are insecure in their power, likely facing a real threat in the next election. Conversely, when competition is low, leaders may believe their position to be secure now and into the future. Arrayed

---

not the motive of power in the political process," but instead I lean toward the perspective that in the course of politics and over time, both party platforms and voters' preferences are subject to change, often based on how elites and identity groups interact with one another.

[36] An early defender of this idea is Schattschneider (1960, 100), who argues that the rise of party competition led to competitive enfranchisement as parties sought bigger constituencies to help them win electoral fights.

[37] Boix 1999, 2010; Bawn 1993: 987.

[38] More specifically, they must perceive a net gain of votes, so that whatever new voters come to their party will not be washed out by the departure of current constituents.

TABLE 2.1. Electoral Incentives and Enfranchisement.

Leader/Party thinks it can mobilize women		Political Competition	
		Low	High
	Yes	do nothing	**support**
	No	resist	resist

Note: Cells describe the action of any given legislator, which, when aggregated, will produce the average position on suffrage by a given party.

on the vertical axis of table 2.1 are leaders' expectations about whether they will be able to mobilize women in coming elections. Inside the cells are predictions about a legislator's actions when the issue of franchise extension is brought to a debate.

Basic rationality suggests that a legislator will always "resist" enfranchisement when he thinks he cannot win women's votes. This is the bottom row of the matrix. On the other hand, garnering support from female voters alone is not enough to prompt him to support enfranchisement. In the top left cell, when political competition is low, a leader will "do nothing" to change franchise rights because he is already secure in his position and perceives he will continue to hold power in the future. Because the leader is already winning, he has no reason to change the rules of the game; he will not play a card before he needs to. The only time a leader supports enfranchisement is when the top right cell is reached— that is, when he faces a high degree of competition and thinks he can court the new group of voters.

Because the electoral logic applies to individual legislators, and legislators tend to be members of parties, an aggregation of choices by individual members of parties can be interpreted as a given party's overall choice. Party leaders will provide their members with a framework for thinking about the impact of suffrage reform, and when parties are strong and cohesive most members will vote the party line.[39] But even if party leaders believe that the party will, in general, benefit from reform, some individual legislators may not see it that way. In an environment where deviations from the party are common, that is, when parties are weaker and less cohesive, individual legislators may deviate from the party position based on values, or based on the distinctive electoral incentives they

---

[39] There is a healthy debate about the influence of strong versus weak party systems on the quality of democracy. See Stokes (2001, ch. 4) for a review. In an analysis of policy switching, Stokes finds longevity, a proxy for strength, to be negatively related to reneging on campaign promises once elected. In this sense, strong parties may be good for democracy.

face in their own districts.[40] Although there are examples of legislators refusing suffrage on moral grounds, and examples of politicians that supported suffrage because they believed in the justice no matter the effect, I contend, and hope to convince in the empirical chapters, that the majority of legislators with less extreme normative commitments voted based on partisan and individual-level incentives. In this sense, both party-level choices as well as individual politicians' decisions about suffrage should be conceived of as reflecting strategic calculations.[41]

The proposition that emerges from this discussion is that *political change should be unlikely when competition is low, but it becomes likelier when competition is high. In high-competition environments, the legislators and parties that think they can mobilize women will be more supportive of reform.*

Expectations about Women's Votes

The preceding discussion suggests that in contexts where political competition is robust, politicians will be more likely to extend the franchise to women when they believe women can be mobilized for their group. Scholars have long debated the optimal strategy for mobilizing voters: whether parties should target voters that form their "core" constituencies, or "swing" voters that can be swayed to vote for them, and whether they should do this in safe districts or in swing districts.[42] Underlying these theories is a crucial assumption that parties already have a good deal of information about who their supporters are and where these supporters

[40] Politicians' preferences do no perfectly overlap with the general position of the party, but party can trump preferences in key decisions (Ansolabehere et al. 2001). Deviation from the average party position may be more common in some legislative arenas, such as social policies, than in other arenas, like economic policy (Washington 2008).

[41] The logic can be as easily applied in cases when there are two parties as when there are three or more. Finally, legislative rules, which may make electoral reform more difficult if, for example, reform requires support by a "super-majority." In this case, support for reform may be very high, and located in the expected places, but there may not be enough votes to see the bill passed. For example, amendments to New Mexico's state constitution were nearly impossible, as they required three-fourths of the vote in both state legislative houses, three-fourths of the vote in a public referendum, and a two-thirds majority in each county, McConnaughy (2013, 196), McCammon and Campbell (2001) measure the ease of the amendment process in the United States but did not share their data with me.

[42] In Gary Cox's (2009) language, entrepreneurial politicians can "mobilize" supporters by increasing the turnout of those who are entitled to the vote but do not generally participate in politics, or they can try to "persuade" voters with weak political loyalties to join their cause. When none of these possibilities seem strategically appealing, politicians can also reform the rules governing who has the right to vote. In some situations, as Trounstein (2009) has shown for municipal reform movements in America after 1950, this means selectively *disenfranchising* certain groups.

reside. Most likely, politicians gain this information by observing previous elections. In the case of enfranchising a new group, though, this type of information may not be available.[43] In this context, people will have to form guesses about women's future political loyalties using whatever information they have at hand.

Suffragists and politicians could make three distinct predictions about women's future loyalties: that women's voting behavior would mimic men's; that women would be more conservative than men; or that women would be more liberal. Each of these predictions can be backed up by a compelling theoretical argument. Women's votes might mirror men's because women and men are found in similar proportions in all of society's groups, and male and female relatives and spouses may have the same political interests and views. Women's votes might be more conservative than men's because they have been the bearers of tradition and religion within families. And women's votes might be more liberal than men's because women are more economically vulnerable and may desire a larger safety net in the event that their marriages dissolve or they become widowed.[44] In addition to being theoretically plausible, each of these lines of reasoning can be supported qualitatively as they all surfaced in discussions of women's suffrage in the press, within suffrage organizations, and among politicians.

Depending on contemporaries' views about women's political preferences, that is, which view was the most prominent, a logic of strategic enfranchisement will produce different predictions about the parties that should support reform. I do not claim to provide a theory of which perspective was the most common across time and space. Indeed, context-specific factors related to women's work, education, religiosity, and political mobilization, as well as demographic patterns, age distributions, and marital rates, can each influence the relative preference that women

---

[43] The democratization literature has tended to assume an economic model of voting whereby those with high incomes will prefer a lower level of taxation and less redistribution, while those with lower incomes will prefer higher rates of taxation and more redistribution. When considering the enfranchisement of lower-class men in this framework, the Meltzer-Richards theory suggests that working-class voters will be more sympathetic to leftist parties. A corollary of this preference would hold that leftist parties should be more supportive of universal franchise reform. This simple but powerful idea has spurred an enormous amount of scholarship that debates whether working classes do naturally prefer parties with redistributive platforms. See, e.g., Lee and Roemer (2006) for a formal and quantitative account of why economic voting breaks down in the context of racism.

[44] This is a key claim of Folbre (1982) and other Marxist feminists. Bertocchi (2010) develops a formal model supporting this argument.

have for parties on the left or parties on the right.[45] Instead, I make a logical claim that if parties expected that women would double the vote, then we should not see enfranchisement in competitive environments. This is because there will be no clear benefit for any party from extending the vote, and a great deal of uncertainty. If, on the other hand, we observe that the vote is extended in environments of heightened competition, it is unlikely that politicians expected that women would vote exactly like men.

This argument deserves unpacking, as it provides a key theoretical tension between the strategic account here and the most recent major book in political science on women's enfranchisement. In an expansive text on state-level suffrage in the United States, Corinne McConnaughy argues, first, that many politicians expected women to replicate their husband's votes. And second, that in light of this belief, women would not have been a solid bloc of voters for any party. Under these conditions, suffrage would not have mattered for electoral politics and hence suffrage extension could not have been "strategic."[46] It is true, as McConnaughy suggests, that plenty of contemporaries espoused the double-the-vote theory. Many also, as she admits, voiced the idea that women would be distinctive voters.[47] The fact that both arguments were present suggests

[45] I agree here with Inglehart and Norris (2000) that changes in women's working patterns will lead to changes in voting behavior, but I do not think that women were inexorably conservative prior to 1950.

[46] E.g., McConnaughy (2013: 262). The argument is nuanced—while McConnaughy presents evidence that some politicians did hope to strategically enfranchise women, she finds that these arguments were not ultimately what won the day. Women's enfranchisement could be forestalled by fears about the women's vote going for the other party, but it could not be propelled by the prospect of winning women's favor alone. McConnaughy thus draws a firm line between her articulated "programmatic" explanation of women's suffrage against a more "strategic" account. But her version of a "strategic" account is unnecessarily stringent. It allows only one party, with the capacity to change the laws, to believe it can win women's votes. But in weak party systems, like the western US states that she studies, individual legislators could vote against the party position to suit their own purposes. Hence a single party need not have had all the power to change the law for reform to work. McConnaughy's theory further requires that the information parties have about women's preferences is credible, i.e., close to the truth. Finally, her argument is designed for a two-party system. Although there were two dominant parties in most of the US in that period, similarly in the UK, the challenges posed by outsider parties are key to the story in all the countries that I study, and third parties are in fact crucial to McConnaughy's argument as well as many other historians' accounts of the United States, e.g., Mead 2004, Snider 2008.

[47] In the historiography of the United States, most scholars who describe the double-the-vote argument attribute this claim to anti-suffragists, people who decried the need for women's suffrage because women would vote just like men. Schuyler 2008: 28–9. Alpern and Baum (1985: 47) suggest that prior to women's enfranchisement in the US many

that there was much more uncertainty about women's preferences than allowed for in McConnaughy's model.

But certainty is a steep requirement, especially in a setting like the early twentieth century when sophisticated polling had not been developed. If we make the more realistic assumption that that there was some degree of uncertainty about the distribution of women's preferences, a competitive environment should only produce reform if one or another party believed it had a better chance of mobilizing women. The evidence in McConnaughy's book that competition often preceded reform therefore undermines the very idea that women would double the vote: if politicians were more likely to extend the vote when politics were competitive, a logical prior belief is that they could not have expected women to vote exactly like men. Otherwise, there would have been no benefit at all and a considerable amount of risk in the action; a reform which would *probably* double the vote would have introduced too much uncertainty for the risk to be worth taking. On the other hand, if parties thought that the distribution of women's preferences did not perfectly mirror men's, then the party that believed it could capture a larger share of women's votes should, under conditions of high competition, support electoral reform.

There is ample evidence that party elites and suffragists expected the female vote to be different from the male vote, and it was precisely because suffragists felt that women had political priorities that could not be represented by men that many desired the vote in the first place.[48] Looking beyond the boundaries of the United States, one telling example comes from communication between Lord Onslow, the British Governor of New Zealand, and Minister Hall, a representative in the New Zealand legislature. Before the first election that included women, Onslow wrote, "It will of course very largely affect the attitude which we in the Conservative party [in the UK] may take in respect to women's suffrage when we learn in what matter it operates in N.Z."[49] In other words, British MPs prepared to look at women's voting behavior in New Zealand to draw inferences about how women would vote in the UK, and they planned to use this assessment to guide their own thoughts about allowing women to vote in their country.[50] In many contexts, male

---

contemporaries believed women would vote differently than men, but then afterwards this was reversed: people thought wives voted like their husbands.

[48] Gustafson 2001: 133–4; Corder and Wolbrecht 2016: 131–135.

[49] Quoted in Grimshaw 1972: 104.

[50] Of course, the comparison between New Zealand and the UK seems rather problematic given the more compressed political and class structure in New Zealand compared to the

politicians went to great lengths to pronounce upon what the votes of women would be, some seeing promise for themselves—the Liberals in New Zealand were sure women would champion liberal causes and improve charity and welfare—and others seeing doom—Radical Party members in both France and Mexico were sure that women would be swayed by the low murmurs of the confessional and give rise to a clerical constitutionalism, or worse, a return to absolutism. In the United States there were great fears that women would vote for prohibition, and politicians whose coffers were routinely filled by the liquor lobby were concerned for their own political fortunes if they supported extending the franchise.[51]

The fact that politicians often expected women to vote distinctively, but in some places thought women would be more conservative, while in others thought women would be more liberal, raises the possibility of strategic enfranchisement based on local expectations about how women would vote. This argument does not require that party actors have *correct* information to have strong beliefs. And, multiple parties can incorrectly believe that they will have an advantage in mobilizing women's votes. The important point for strategic enfranchisement is simply that party actors make the best choices they can given whatever beliefs they have.

It follows that *in places where a common view is that women are more conservative, parties on the right that are vulnerable to competition should promote women's inclusion, while in places where women are deemed more progressive should produce support for reform by groups on the left when competition is high.*

Women's Mobilization Strategy

The schematic in figure 2.5 suggests that expectations about women's votes are generated in relation to political cleavages and women's strategies of mobilization. Political cleavages inform beliefs both because actors have intuitions about how these cleavages are translated into electoral politics, and because they have some sense of the geography and density of political groups across these cleavages. Women's mobilizational efforts can help shape expectations about women's political preferences by revealing which women are likely to be politically active once the vote is extended, and by increasing awareness about the issues that pertain

---

UK, which made the Conservatives in the colony closer to the Liberals in the metropole, and the Liberals in the colony closer to the British radicals (Grimshaw 1972: 47).

[51] See chapter 4.

to women in the public sphere. These efforts influence suffrage politics through two channels: by generating information about women's future political loyalties and by creating opportunities for alliances with other political actors.

Although this book is primarily concerned with how mobilization on behalf of the right to vote influenced politicians' decisions about whether to extend the vote, the use in the schematic of "women's mobilization strategies" instead of "suffragist mobilization strategies" serves as an important reminder that not all women who organized around the issue of suffrage were suffragists. In fact, there were many women who were prominent leaders in the anti-suffrage camp, a seeming irony that has been the subject of several great books.[52] The phenomenon of female anti-suffragism, which Susan Marshall explains by reference to the "gender class position" of elite women, is actually quite useful for thinking about the tensions that emerge among women who do want to vote. Put simply, some women may want *to* vote, even if they do not want *the* vote.

For women who want to vote, their mobilization strategy will be influenced by political cleavages and by their expectations about the policy preferences of the average woman that would be included as a result of electoral reform. In countries where the male franchise was limited, elite women might prefer to argue for a narrow reform on the same terms as men.[53] But in countries where the male franchise was expansive, legal and normative barriers might have precluded an extension of the vote that was subject to restrictions along the line of class, race, literacy, and so on. In other words, in places where restrictions were infeasible, the vote would have to be extended to all women or to none. As the size of the group of women that would be enfranchised grew, the informational problem involved in understanding women's preferences would loom larger, especially if very deep group and gender cleavages separated social groups and women within them. To learn about the future female vote, political actors had to think beyond the priorities of elite women by getting a sense of what all women wanted. In manhood franchise cases, politicians would have to learn about the full distribution of women's preferences in order to be able to make well-informed decisions, a requirement, in other words, that the suffrage

[52] Camhi 1994; Marshall 1997.

[53] Kenya and South Africa are both examples where white women and, in Kenya, Asian women, were given voting privileges long before the majority African population, male or female, was enfranchised.

movement be big. But the formation of a broad movement was no easy task. First, because the cultivation of a feminist consciousness is undermined by the "crosscutting" nature of the gender cleavage. And second, because enfranchisement is not, strictly speaking, a single reform, but instead brings with it many potential changes in the nature of politics thereafter.

CROSSCUTTING CLEAVAGES AND GROUP CONSCIOUSNESS

In a seminal book on political development, Seymour Lipset and Stein Rokkan (1967) famously argued that party systems and electoral institutions are influenced by the nature of political cleavages in a given country. Partisan power and group representation emerge based on whether and how social movements can harness groups that fall within society's various cleavages. Harmonious political development can be undermined by cleavages that cut across group members, such as ethnic and linguistic heritage, nationality, and other sources of political identity. Although their focus was not on gender, we can think of the difficulty of women's collective identification and collective action as similarly related to the crosscutting nature of gender. Gender crosscuts all other cleavages because, given the nature of human reproduction hitherto, and historical patterns of household formation, women exist within all of a society's groups. As Erving Goffman writes, what is curious about women as a "sex-class" is that because of their deep ties to non-women, they are "separated from one another by the stake they acquire in the very organization which divides them."[54] Loyalty to one's menfolk may lead a woman to see herself as a person whose grievances are linked to the marginalization of her religion or to her linguistic traditions, rather than as a Dutch speaker whose gender inhibits her free movement.

It is generally thought that group consciousness—a politicized awareness of membership and commitment to collective action—requires a nontrivial number of people to identify with the group.[55] Because women do not automatically identify primarily with other women, as the vast literature on intersectionality reminds us, it takes considerable work to cultivate a form of group consciousness that can be translated into collective action.[56] As with other social cleavages, if women's social networks

[54] Goffman 1977: 308.

[55] Conover 1988: 53.

[56] Intersectionality invokes the idea that women are not a unified group, but have unique experiences of the social and institutional world depending on multiple ascriptive

are highly stratified, this might reduce any given woman's sense that she has things in common with women from other groups, and limit her ability to conceive of their shared commonalities as grievances against patriarchy, firms, or the state.[57] In this sense, the problem of organizing women is not simply one of finding selective incentives to dole out to group members, as Mancur Olson might see it, but rather that the very idea that women form a group at all is questionable. In fact, women may be fundamentally difficult to mobilize for feminist initiatives precisely because gender may well be *the* most crosscutting cleavage.[58]

WOMEN AS FUTURE VOTERS

At the same time that cleavages impinge on women's identification with other women, ideas about women's future political preferences will also influence women's mobilization strategy. In countries with an expansive male franchise, an activist's decision over whether to mobilize for voting rights reform requires that she think through the potential political consequences of including all women—many of whom will not share her same values or policy priorities—in the electorate. To choose to mobilize for a broad reform (for example, one which included all women) would require activists to prioritize contesting patriarchy over pursuing other social reforms. Activists would have to see and argue that the issues that lie along the intersecting line of "women's interests" are more important than those that lie in the other planes of identity that women occupy.

We see these tensions at play in the organization of women both against and for their own inclusion. In her book on the anti-suffrage campaign in the United States, Susan Marshall argues that the anti-suffrage ideology was driven by a desire of upper class women to preserve their positions

identities (see Hancock 2016). Women's intersectionality has implications not only for suffrage politics, but also for inquiries into institutional design, such as how to increase women's representation in politics (Htun 2004: 441).

[57] For a thoughtful discussion of marginalization, intersectionality, and women's interests, see the introduction in Weldon 2011.

[58] Olson 1971. A feminist identity emerges when people come to see their primary aim as contesting women's social and economic subordination to men. Although women's movements can take on feminist aims, and feminist movements can alter goals toward reconciling other social injustices, we can distinguish women's movements more generally from those with specifically feminist aims (Ferree and Mueller 2004: 577). This distinction recognizes that women have historically been mobilized as women in order to contest any number of social ills, such as health, child care, education, sanitation, and spiritual issues, while specifying that feminist movements are specifically concerned with contesting injustices that relate to gendered divisions of institutions, resource allocations, and status.

of privilege. "Close to the centers of power, they perceived no need of the ballot for themselves, and, like many men of their class, regarded a mass electorate as a threat to their way of life."[59] The impulse toward class preservation was so strong that by 1920 the National Association Opposed to Woman Suffrage boasted of 700,000 members countrywide. But as Marshall notes, and as we will see in the chapter on the United States, elitism and other pernicious ideologies were also keystones of the pro-suffrage campaign. Ellen Carol DuBois, one of the premier historians of the US suffrage movement, agrees: "The problem for elite suffragists was that woman suffrage meant the enfranchisement of working-class, as well as elite, women" (1987: 38). Suffrage mobilization was therefore constrained by the very factors that gave rise to anti-suffragism amongst women, namely whether the potential costs of enfranchising a diverse group of women was worth the vote.

This idea is put succinctly by a 1908 article in the *New Ireland Review*:

[T]here are first the women who want to vote at any price; there are second the women who don't want the vote at any price; and third the women who want the vote but are prepared to pay only a certain price for it.[60]

A sense of the "price" of suffrage would influence whether suffrage leaders would mobilize narrowly for their cause and risk non-reform, or mobilize broadly and risk the downstream political effects of the reform. Even women who believe that they share some common interests with women from other cleavage groups, and who want the right to vote in theory, may not want voting rights at the expense of other political priorities. That is, gendered-class positions, or gendered-racial positions, can generate strong incentives against collective action even among people who think that they should have the right to vote. Concretely, *diversity among women can influence the size of the women's movement. In political contexts with deep group cleavages, elite women may form a narrow movement and seek limited reform. In circumstances where a broad reform is the only option, a larger movement will be necessary for reform to emerge.*

Aligning Interests

To summarize the preceding discussion, expectations about women as future voters shape women's mobilization for suffrage and the incentives

[59] Marshall 1997: 5.
[60] Quoted in Kelly 1996: 34.

that politicians face when confronting a bill for women's suffrage. When a movement's demands match politicians' interests in a moment of heightened competition, an alignment of interests between these two groups can produce suffrage reform. The conditions under which interests align—when the suffrage movement has mobilized enough members to provide a good sense of women's political preferences, and when the preferences that are revealed by these efforts appeal to a party or parties that are vulnerable to electoral competition—are possibly quite rare. This, then, can help to explain the often long separation between an early demand for voting rights by a small group of women in a country with a relatively expansive male franchise, and a much later final date of reform.

Ultimately, change could only come when three things happened. First, women had to mobilize outside of parlors and exert pressure beyond sharply worded editorials and letters to political leaders. That is, they had to form a core cadre of suffragists that applied insider tactics. They did this by utilizing an elitist argument that courted privileged women from across the parties. This was crucial for convincing politicians that women actually wanted the vote, but also for communicating information about the political desires of the group. Second, they had to accrue some successes. As we will see, they had the greatest impact in places where partisan loyalties and party power itself was in greater flux. In places where power was entrenched, the risk of enfranchising women far outweighed the benefits for dominant parties. Finally, they had to coalesce around a push for a national level reform instead of settling on local-level enfranchisement. At this stage, mobilization of a mass base, that is, forming cross-cleavage coalitions, was crucial.

This account is designed to explain the actual historical unfolding of women's suffrage in limited democracies, both within countries and also across them. Importantly, though, the argument is congruent with much of what we know about democratization of lower-class men and with many accounts of how women's movements make strides within states. Within limited democracies, political parties are often seen as key barriers to the advancement of women's interests, but women's movements that take strictly "outsider" positions—that do not attempt to lobby or form alliances with political insiders—fail.[61] Parties act as gatekeepers insofar as they want all successful candidates to emerge from within their ranks, and because they want to determine and get

---

[61] Beckwith 2000: 493; Chowdhury et al. 1994: 18; Friedman 2000: 20; Rucht 2003: 29.

credit for both distributive and programmatic disbursements. To succeed in producing gender-related policy reform, then, networks of feminists have to find partisan actors with whom their priorities "fit." This is a difficult task if feminist demands run counter to the interests of major political institutions such as political parties or religious bodies.[62] In many contexts, feminists forge easier alliances with progressive opposition parties, and they tend to gain concessions from these parties in moments when the political opportunity structure shifts, such as during a political realignment.[63]

The dynamic between a competitive landscape and women's mobilization finds parallels in other major works on gender and politics. In her study of Chilean women's movements, Lisa Baldez (2002) shows that the political opportunity afforded by a period of partisan realignment allowed both conservative and progressive women's organizations to coalesce into mass mobilization. In a similar vein, Anna Harvey (1996) demonstrates that the realignment of American parties in the late 1960s provided new avenues for independent women's organizations to press for reforms, resulting in several policy concessions that the women's movement was unable to secure in the previously stable party environment. As both of these studies highlight, the competitive conditions that led to partisan realignment provided fertile ground for organized segments of women's movements to make political demands. By these lights, women's mobilization can become a more effective tool to secure voting rights reform when competition is robust. Though not revolutionary in character, the logic of women's suffrage will likely resonate with other ordinary forms of democratic transformation.

METHODOLOGICAL APPROACH

The rest of the book investigates the relationship between competition, mobilization, and suffrage by examining several logical implications of the argument. On the most basic level, concerns about women as political actors should appear in the conversations of suffragists and politicians alike. Second, enfranchisement of women should become likelier in conditions of marked political competition. Third, party-level support for suffrage should be traceable to overall perceptions about how women would vote. And finally, the actions of organized movements should reflect these strategic considerations: we should see movements

---

[62] Htun 2003.
[63] Alvarez 1990; Baldez 2002: 7; Beckwith 2003: 200; Waylen 1994.

responding to barriers in the electoral realm by working to change perceptions and beliefs and by forming alliances that can help to bolster the power of allies.

Casting the argument in this way allows for it to be corroborated (or discredited) at several levels of relief. On the micro-level, we should find evidence that suffragists and politicians were thinking about and concerned with the electoral implications of women's votes. Exploring, on the meso-level, the behavior of individual parties, we should find support for reform coming from parties that believe they will benefit from the additional voters, whereas parties that do not foresee such an advantage should resist extending the franchise. Finally, on the macro-level, that is, through large-N investigation, there should be evidence that higher competition and larger movements are correlated with suffrage reform.

The following chapters, on the United Kingdom, the United States, and France, take both a comparative historical and a statistical approach to exploring evidence for the logic of women's suffrage on both the micro- and the meso-level. The chapter on the United States also provides macro-level evidence through an analysis of the link between political competition and women's mobilization across the states over a period of forty years.[64] Each chapter considers a country on its own and dedicates substantial space to explaining the institutional context in which suffrage reform took place, and lays out the landscape of policy options being debated in each country.[65] The exploration of feminist mobilization will be discursive, drawing on the tools of process tracing to reconstruct key moments in women's mobilization utilizing primary and secondary sources on the suffrage movement. The link between mobilization and politicians' decisions on when to reform will be made with reference to actual debates, as well as using quantitative data on suffrage reform. Although some of the inferences that I draw stem from techniques of regression analysis, a thorough presentation of these results is confined to a previously published article on the United States.[66] The dynamics of suffrage are then explored during potential episodes of reform, that is, moments when a suffrage bill had the potential to become law.[67] As much

---

[64] In some sense, the macro evidence passes a "hoop" test by showing an enduring correlation between competition, mobilization, and suffrage support.

[65] Here I take up Kreuzer's (2010) call for a more thorough dialogue between qualitative and quantitative research and historical knowledge.

[66] See Teele 2018 and its online appendix: doi: 10.1086/696621.

[67] For a discussion of "episode" analysis, see Capoccia and Ziblatt (2010).

TABLE 2.2. Argument and the Cases.

	Political Competition	
	Low	*High*
Party thinks it can mobilize women	US Southern Democrats (do nothing)	**US West Parties (support)** **UK Labour 1918 (support)**
Party does not think it can mobilize women	US North (resist)	French Radicals III Republic (resist) UK Liberals 1906 (resist)

emphasis is given to episodes in which suffrage failed as to those in which suffrage passed, as each gives us insight into how mobilization strategies and expectations about women's political preferences inform politicians' decisions.[68]

Table 2.2 gives a rough guide to how the theory fits with the evidence. The chapter on the United Kingdom gives very detailed evidence about why and how a suffrage movement decides to intervene in the electoral arena, arguing that suffrage leaders that identified with multiple political parties decided that victory was worth the cost of aligning with the Labour Party to secure reform. Through a clever cross-cleavage electoral strategy, the movement expanded its base and made credible its commitment to helping Labour win. The study of the United States provides ample evidence for the importance of robust political competition in allowing for voting rights reform. Democrats in the US South were invulnerable to external challengers, and so the fact that southern white women would support their party was irrelevant. They did not promote reform but supported the status quo. In the US Northeast, political parties and machines believed women had preferences different from their base constituents, and resisted reform as well. In the western US, on the other hand, parties were much more competitive and the movement, though smaller than in the East, was able to capitalize on shifts in political power to win the vote. Finally, moving eastward across the Atlantic, an analysis of French legislative politics shows how, in a context of political weakness, an incumbent fought against reform when it believed

---

[68] The research design is different from the typical "nested" approach advocated for by Lieberman (2005), insofar as each case presents different sorts of data that can be explored. The "negative" French case does important inferential work because it highlights the importance of politicians' beliefs in preventing suffrage. Mahoney and Goertz 2004.

women were not natural political allies. Though the Radical Party was vulnerable in the Chamber of Deputies, it had enough power in the Senate to block women's enfranchisement. Together, the political circumstances of women's enfranchisement in these three countries demonstrate the importance of political cleavages, party competition, and women's mobilization in catalyzing voting rights reform.

3
Strategic Mobilization for Suffrage in Great Britain

As a constitutional monarchy with a primarily hereditary upper chamber, the United Kingdom's political system around the turn of the twentieth century had many conservative impulses. Having yet to extend voting rights to all British men, relying instead on householding and income requirements to limit participation, the two major parties vied for the votes of a group of men who were relatively more affluent than the population as a whole. On both the Tory and Liberal sides there were reservations about extending the franchise to women—for the Liberals because they believed the women to be Tories, and for the Tories because they believed they would have to make room for the masses of men should the women vote. In this relatively infelicitous political environment, where governments formed by both parties had refused to sponsor a women's suffrage bill, women in the UK won voting rights by building a more diverse coalition which allowed them to form new alliances. By itself, an electoral pact formed between the largest group of British suffragists, the *National Union of Women's Suffrage Societies*, and the Labour Party may not have produced reform, given the small presence of the Labour Party in this period.[1] But as political conditions shifted and members of the Labour Party moved into positions of power, the political opening afforded by the First World War allowed the first group

---

[1] In most of the historical period examined in this chapter, the (southern) Republic of Ireland had not yet separated from the United Kingdom of Great Britain and Ireland. Here, I use the term "British" as an adjective to describe the nationality of suffragists, which is accurate insofar as the National Union and other associations had Irish outposts, even though most of the organizations that I study, and all the archives that I visited, were based in England. It is important to note that even the use of the term "British" is not entirely accurate insofar as the Isle of Man, which is part of the British Isles, but not the UK, extended voting rights to women via its independent legislature, the Tynwald, as early as 1881.

of women on the British mainland and Ireland to exercise national level voting rights.[2]

The parliamentary system in Great Britain influenced the politics of franchise reform in three ways: it shaped the legal process by which reforms could be affected; its constellation of political power informed leaders' incentives to change voting laws; and, finally, its norms of political action molded and constrained the behavior of mobilized women in their quest for inclusion. In the first two sections of this chapter I survey this terrain, describing the political milieu in which the suffragists organized, the coalitions that ruled the House of Commons, and the preferences each party had over the suffrage issue. Using archival evidence, I document the disincentives that made suffrage reform unlikely even after the Liberal Party gained power in 1906.

Though politically weak, the Liberal Party lacked an incentive to support suffrage because both it and its coalition partners, the Irish Parliamentary Party, feared the government's demise should women be given the opportunity to vote. In spite of Liberal Prime Minister Herbert Asquith's misgivings, several bills for women's suffrage received majority support in the House of Commons. Yet without government backing these bills came to naught. Though many Liberal MPs, including future Prime Minister Lloyd George, claimed to be privately in favor of women's enfranchisement, they did everything in their power to resist reform.

In the face of these strong institutional and strategic forces militating against franchise reform, mobilized suffragists were nevertheless able to shape political outcomes. The largest group of suffragists, who mobilized under the banner of the National Union, formed an unlikely alliance with the Labour Party, exchanging access to the suffragists' vast resources for a promise by Labour not to support voting rights reform for men alone. As the Labour Party was rather small and poorly funded in this period, I argue that they stood to benefit considerably from

---

[2] In the Isle of Man, under the House of Keys Election Act of 1881, "all males, widows, and spinsters who owned, or in the case of the former, occupied property of £4 per year" were granted the right to vote (Belcham 2000: 88). In the lead-up to the discussion in the House of Keys, suffragists from Manchester gave speeches and helped local leaders to lobby for the reform (Manx Sun, 19 March 1881). The lack of a party system in the Isle of Man at the time makes analysis of the reform outside of the scope of this project, but see Butler and Templeton (2008) for a discussion of the campaign. Nevertheless, the Isle of Man Examiner (2 April 1881) reports that a Mr. Sherwood, the leader of the movement for suffrage in the House of Keys, as well as a Mr. Stephen, who was the first candidate in the Douglas district to announce his support for women's inclusion, were both returned to the House.

the influx of cash and volunteers provided to them by the flush suffrage organization.

To substantiate the claim that Labour stood to benefit from the "Election Fighting Fund" alliance, I show, first, that after the pact was implemented, the Labour Party contested a much larger proportion of seats than they had in previous by-elections. Because the geographical imprint of the Labour Party was still small, the rise in contestations marked an important first step toward becoming a national party. I further demonstrate that the EFF was accompanied by a rise in three-candidate contests. Under winner-takes-all electoral rules, if Labour chose to run against the other two parties, this could result in a Conservative victory in an otherwise safe seat for the Liberal Party. In increasing the number of these contests, Labour had a new way to exert pressure on the Liberal Party. Finally, I demonstrate that turnover of seats was more likely after the EFF was implemented than before. Taken together, these results demonstrate the potency of the EFF strategy and provide a clear justification for Labour's promise to the Liberal suffragists.[3]

Because Labour was not a pivotal group in the 1910 parliament, their commitment was not, in itself, enough to guarantee franchise reform. While a few suffragists and some subsequent scholars have claimed that women's role in preparations for the First World War paved the way for their inclusion, I argue that on its own, a shift in public opinion was not enough, nor was it strictly necessary, to guarantee women's enfranchisement. I submit, instead, that the war's greatest influence on suffrage lay in the creation of a multi-party wartime cabinet, which saw Arthur Henderson, a Labour leader and a key player in the Election Fighting Fund, appointed to the government.[4] Henderson's early and persistent lobbying prior to the 1916 "Speaker's Conference" on electoral

---

[3] While the Election Fighting Fund (EFF) has been mentioned in two works on the British suffrage campaign—Holton 1986 and Pugh 2000—it receives only one or two pages in each work. The emphasis I give it here, as well as the qualitative and quantitative analysis presented, is original.

[4] Historians of Britain are mixed as to the role of the war. Some say that women's sacrifices gave a basis to claim equal rights (Kent 1987: 220). See also the discussion in Wingerden (1999), which credits a "conversion" speech made by Asquith, and Rubenstein (1991: 242), who claims that Millicent Fawcett herself gave credit to the war. Holton (1986) does not take a stand on the role that the war played. Finally, Pugh (2000: Epilogue) claims (conveniently) that all three parties would have entered into the next election (in the absence of the war) with a commitment to votes for women. Note that Fawcett herself claims that it was the *Wartime Cabinet* under the coalition government that was responsible for the reform. The Women's Library (hereafter TWL): 7MGF/A/1/149, 9-Dec-18.

reform is, I argue, critical for understanding how women's suffrage made its way into the 1918 Representation of the People Act.

In making this argument I bring a somewhat different cast of characters to light, moving away from the fantastic careers of Emmeline, Sylvia, and the rest of the Pankhurst family and toward the leaders of the National Union, Millicent Garrett Fawcett, and its young but brilliant strategist Catherine Marshall.[5] While the militant "suffragettes" attracted considerable attention for their colorful tactics, including breaking glass, interrupting meetings, and setting empty buildings on fire, they were vehemently opposed to cooperating with political parties. National Union "suffragists" had learned from the militant movement that pledges from politicians were worth very little, but they knew that the success of suffrage depended on support from elected leaders. The National Union's chief strategists strove to understand the electoral disincentives faced by Britain's political parties and worked to create a strategy that could surmount those barriers. In the final negotiations leading to the Fourth Reform Act, too, the non-militant strategy of National Union leaders proved key.

VOTING RULES AND LEADERSHIP IN THE EDWARDIAN ERA

For most of British history those voting rights that did exist were linked to property ownership, occupation of property exceeding a specified value, or taxpaying status. Several Reform Acts in the nineteenth century—1832, 1850 (in Ireland), 1867, and 1884—relaxed these constraints, gradually enfranchising up to 60 percent of the adult male population.[6] Though sex had not previously been specified in voting laws, the delimiter "male" was inserted and thereby institutionalized in the Reform Act of 1832, a move that was justified by the British common law principle of coverture.

In the Edwardian era, the household was still the relevant unit across which votes were disbursed. Dependence upon others for their daily bread implied, at this time, that women (like domestic servants, slaves,

---

[5] The Pankhurst family, with mother Emmeline and her daughters Christabel, Sylvia, and Adela, has been a great object of study for suffrage historians. Pugh 2001 provides a comprehensive account of the formidable family, although a more sympathetic rendering of the inexorable middle sister Sylvia—the artist, socialist, suffragette, and anti-imperialist— can be found in Connelly 2013.

[6] The trend toward greater inclusiveness did not include Ireland, where an 1829 law brought the disenfranchisement of 40-shilling freeholders. The 1884 Act created a uniform franchise across the Union for the first time. Bateman 2018; Jones 1972.

and children) had no distinct *interests* of their own, and thus had no place in the political sphere. Male heads of households were considered virtual representatives of their entire family, and so women were legally "covered" in the public sphere first by their fathers and then by their husbands.[7] But as the nineteenth century progressed, the changing structure of work and family complicated the traditional application of the principle because some wage-earning women were tied neither to paternal nor to matrimonial homes. By the turn of the twentieth century, powerful arguments were made as to why women, especially those who were independent, could no longer be excluded from the electoral franchise.

In the aftermath of the Boer War (1899–1902), politics in Britain entered one of the most polarized periods in the modern era. Rising awareness of the problems initiated by an industrial economy pushed social reform into the forefront of politics. Parliamentary discussion concerned issues related to health and sanitation, the regulation and funding of schools, and Irish home rule.[8] Although suffrage activism gained a mass basis in the early 1900s,[9] with the Conservatives in power and an already large (by historical standards) male electorate, there was little movement within Parliament for voting rights reform.[10]

[7] In this framework, single women and propertied widows occupied an uncertain middle ground; while some might have been allowed to vote in school elections if they were on the tax register, single women were not enfranchised in local elections until 1869 and married women had to wait until 1894 to secure this right. Hannam et al. 2000: 41.

[8] The Liberal ministry enacted old age pensions in 1908, a system of labor exchanges in 1909, and trade boards in 1909; it further developed a national insurance scheme for health and unemployment in 1911, levied a minimum wage for miners in 1912, augmented the tax code to reflect earned and unearned income, and established progressive taxation in 1907. See Searle 1992: 97.

[9] The National Union of Women's Suffrage Societies was the largest organization, with seventy affiliated organizations by 1909 and 13,161 members. In 1914, these grew to 380 affiliated societies and over 53,000 members. The two other national suffrage organizations were considerably smaller: the Women's Social and Political Union (WSPU)—led by the controversial militant Emmeline Pankhurst—had eighty-eight branches in 1913, and the Women's Freedom League (WFL) had 4,000 members in the same year. See Pugh 2000: Table 8.4.

[10] The 1884 Representation of the People Act enfranchised 60 percent of the male population. Eligibility required paying an annual housing rent of £10 or possession of an equivalent value in land. The 1884 Act also eliminated a "multiplicity" of votes, meaning that one dwelling could not be associated with more than one vote. This enshrined the household as the basic political unit by effectively disenfranchising dependents, be they women or male domestic employees. Note, though, that "plural" votes still existed, so that an owner of multiple dwellings or businesses in different locales could cast ballots in several constituencies. Under some conditions a "lodger" could obtain the right to vote, but the legal process to do so was arduous. Tanner 1983.

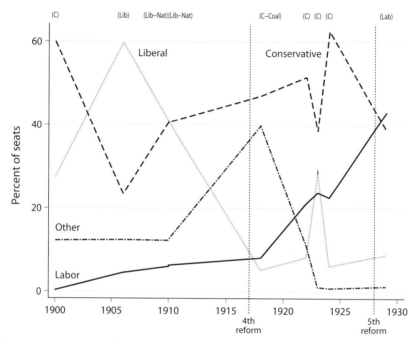

FIGURE 3.1. Seats Held by the Largest Parties in the House of Commons, 1900–1930. The figure shows the percentage of seats held by the Tories (C), Liberals (Lib), Labour (Lab), and Other parties. The top of the figure gives the location of each general election and indicates which party was in power. Lib-Nat indicates that the Liberals and Nationalists could overpower the Conservatives, while C-Coal indicates a conservative coalition. The vertical lines indicate the two instances of women's enfranchisement, 1918 and 1928.

Indeed, for most suffragists the enfranchisement of women was inconceivable until the Liberals swept the general election of 1906. In that year, their hopes were renewed not only because many of the Liberal MPs were openly sympathetic to suffrage, but also because their position was shared, at least privately, by the new prime minister, Sir Henry Campbell-Bannerman. The Campbell-Bannerman ministry enjoyed a clear majority: with the Liberals' 400 seats, even the combined power of the Unionists (157 seats), the Irish (83 seats), and the Labour representatives (30 seats) could not have prevented a government-sponsored suffrage bill from clearing the House of Commons.[11] (Figure 3.1 shows the percent of seats held by each party from 1900–1930.)

[11] The House of Lords is another issue. The Conservative-dominated Lords may well have rejected a democratic bill for women's suffrange.

But owing to poor health, in April 1908 Campbell-Bannerman resigned. His replacement was Herbert Asquith, a liberal imperialist long notorious among the suffragists because of his anti-suffrage attitudes. While we can only speculate as to whether Asquith's misgivings on the suffrage issue stemmed from deep-seated antipathy toward women's emancipation, he certainly had sufficient political reason to keep women from the vote.[12] To begin with, because British electoral law still allowed owners of multiple residences to vote more than once ("plural" voting), enfranchising women on the same terms as men would likely have benefited the wealthier voters of the Conservative Party. As in France, many in the Liberal camp also believed that religious convictions would make women more conservative voters than men. Hence a strategic Liberal leadership should not have sponsored a women's suffrage bill.[13] Thus, even though the Liberals had the power to pass a reform bill, there would be no motion under the 1910 ministry.

The Liberals' position worsened after the December 1910 general election, which left them tied with the (conservative) Unionists, with 272 seats each. Asquith formed a government with the support of the Irish Parliamentary Party (84 seats), who had sided with the Liberals since William Gladstone made "home rule" a cornerstone of Liberal policy in 1885,[14] and Labour (42 seats), which had been committed to the maintenance of Liberal rule since it formed a pact with them in 1903. Under this configuration of power, on matters of policy the Liberals could suffer defection from Labour so long as they maintained the wholesale support of the Irish Parliamentary Party. With the Irish as the veto group, the barriers to suffrage reform were higher in 1910 than they had been in 1906.[15]

[12] Asquith's cabinet was divided on the issue. He, Harcourt, and McKenna continued their opposition after 1910, whereas Grey, George, Birrell, Runciman, Burnes, Haldane, and Gladstone all seemed to support suffrage under some conditions. See Jones 1972; Blewett 1965.

[13] Conservative Prime Minister Arthur James Balfour might have supported suffrage by this logic, but at the time his claim was that the majority of women did not want the vote. Pugh 2000: 169. In fact, even after the turn of the century many conservative women were anti-suffrage.

[14] Home rule united the Liberal Party after 1885. Searle 1992: ch. 2. After that, Liberal support came from religious non-conformists, radicals, and industrial backers. In 1895 and 1900 they lost more than 90 percent of seats in the major industrial centers. In 1885 and 1892 they were dependent on the Irish as the pivot. Searle 1992: 52.

[15] Opinions about Irish independence also divided suffragists in Ireland (see Kelly 1996 and Ward 1982). The Irish suffrage societies had strong links to those in England, with militant groups affiliated with the WSPU and the Irish Women's Suffrage Society affiliated

TABLE 3.1. Options for Electoral Reform, c. 1900.

		Abolish Plural Voting	
		No	Yes
Enfranchise	No	A – Status Quo	B – Manhood
Women	Yes	C – Limited "Spinster"	D – Universal Franchise

Obstacles to Reform in Asquith's Parliament

To understand how the impediments to suffrage reform might be over-come, it is necessary to consider the set of relevant policies that could have been enacted and the preference rankings of the parties over this space. A man who owned several domesticities could have recourse to several votes, but men who resided in a household owned by someone else—sons, servants, and borders—generally did not have easy access to parliamentary franchise. Electoral law could be amended by abolishing the sex qualification, by moving toward manhood suffrage (and away from plural voting), or by a combination of the two.

Table 3.1 arrays these possibilities. Under option A, the status quo of a limited male franchise, which featured plural voting and was restricted by residency requirements and taxpaying, would remain.[16] Option B would relax these requirements, abolish plural voting, and move toward manhood suffrage. Policy C, often called "spinster" suffrage, would maintain limited franchise rights but allow women to vote on the same terms as men. Finally, D would abolish both plural voting and the sex qualification, allowing for one-person-one-vote in a universal suffrage regime.

It is relatively straightforward to predict parties' preferences over these different policy options. The Liberals preferred the status quo. They held a plurality of seats and were concerned that giving universal franchise to

---

with the NUWSS. Both John Redmond (the leader of the Nationalists) and Edward Carson (an Irish Unionist leader) were opposed to women's suffrage (Kelly 1996: 34). In 1912 the WSPU took a strong stance against the Nationalists, arguing that if the Nationalists defeated women's suffrage, the suffragettes would oppose home rule. But many Nationalist women in Ireland did not want to work against the greater goal (Foster 2014: 1782–83), and even once home rule was acceded in September 1914, the unstable political situation in the country leading up to the 1916 "Rising" led the suffragists to subordinate and eventually abandon the call for suffrage (Ward 1982: 34). In spite of the movement's disintegration, women in the newly independent Ireland were granted the franchise in 1922.

[16] These requirements remained in local government on the British mainland until 1948 and in Northern Ireland until 1969.

men would empower Labour to break their general election pact, which would have had the effect of returning the Conservatives to power.[17] Liberals ranked the widows and spinster suffrage option last because they thought that, on average, women were more conservative than men and would be more likely to vote for the Conservatives. Winston Churchill illuminated this logic in a statement he made to the House of Commons while debating a widow/spinster suffrage bill in 1910:

> I think it very creditable to the Unionist party opposite... that so many of them should resist a measure which I have not the slightest hesitation in saying would be a great party and electoral advantage to them. ...I am bound to say when I see a Liberal Member or a Labour Member voting for provisions like this I feel he must either be very innocent or must have been intimidated.[18]

Churchill believed it would be foolish for members of the Labour and Liberal parties to vote for a bill that enfranchised property-owning women, as this would surely harm them and help the Conservatives. In the words of Lloyd George, a limited female suffrage "spells disaster to Liberalism; and unless you take it in hand, and take it all at once, this catastrophe is inevitable."[19] Thus, Liberals ranked the more robust measure of universal suffrage higher than the limited widow/spinster suffrage.

Labour, for its part, was concerned about increasing its own national standing. An outsider party in 1910, Labour leaders could not have reasonably hoped to form a government under the current electoral rules, not only because of their pact with the Liberals, but also because of the nature of the franchise.[20] Many among the 40 percent of men still excluded from voting were presumed to be potential Labour voters, hence

[17] The Liberals feared manhood suffrage. The first Asquith government presided over many progressive reforms (see above), but although many in the working classes voted with the Liberals, their largest base was among farmers, shopkeepers, and publicans. The party's finances, tight in that era, still overwhelmingly came from businessmen. Thus policy oriented toward the working class likely would have alienated them on two sides. See Searle 1992: ch. 3, p. 97.

[18] House of Commons Debates, 12 July 1910.

[19] Lloyd George in a letter to the Chief Whip, Master of Elibank, on the subject of the 1911 Conciliation Bill. Passing the bill would "be playing straight into the hands of the enemy... [it would] on balance add hundreds of thousands of votes throughout the country to the strength of the Tory Party." Quoted in Blewett 1965: 55.

[20] In 1906, most seats offered to the Labour Party were ones that the Liberals did not contest in 1900. If Labour wanted to break into more areas, the Liberals would have to stand down. Searle 2000: 74.

a manhood franchise would have given the nascent party more bargaining power with the Liberals if their general election pact continued.[21] On the other hand, if the Labour party thought that working-class women were more conservative than their husbands, they may have been ambivalent between universal suffrage and the status quo.[22] The widow/spinster suffrage was arguably the worst for Labour because, applying in large part to wealthier women, it would have benefited the Conservatives and perhaps some Liberals, but would not likely fall in Labour's favor.

The Unionists did not want independence for Ireland nor the possibility that the Liberals would win with more votes from the working classes. The perception that women were on the whole more conservative than men should have allowed them to support some forms of franchise reform over others. In a letter to Mrs. Nicholson of the London Society for Women's Suffrage (which was a National Union affiliate), J.R.P. Newman, a Conservative MP from Enfield confided:

> In order to get over the fact that the Liberal Party are afraid of treating women as equal to men—and, by so doing, increasing the number of Conservative votes in the country—this Conciliation Bill proposes that only a select few women, who, the Radicals think, will be more inclined to vote for their Party, shall be given the vote, while the great mass of women, who would naturally be Conservative, are excluded.[23]

Newman is suspicious of the limited terms of the Conciliation Bill because he thought that the Liberals must have had some private information driving them to support the limited over the universal provision. It is likely that the widow/spinster suffrage would have favored the

---

[21] Historians still debate the size and demographics of the male disfranchised before 1919. McKibbin (1974: 86) writes that the restrictive franchise was likely "peculiarly unfavourable" to Labour and was a chief reason the Liberals were sluggish on bringing a Reform Bill. Whereas others, including Tanner (1983), claim that this exclusion was not mainly borne by the working class but by lodgers and migrants.

[22] Marxists, socialists, and labor organizations have a long and uneven history with the women's movement. Generally women's rights were thought to be a bourgeois preoccupation that took away from other goals. Nevertheless, several Labour leaders including Keir Hardie and Arthur Henderson were ardent supporters of suffrage. See Hirshfield 1990: 185; Liddington and Norris 1978; Pugh 1985. In the US, Jewish supporters of the socialist movement were the main supporters of suffrage in New York City. Lerner 1981.

[23] TWL: 2LSW/C/3/F153/1. 5-July-1910.

TABLE 3.2. Party Preferences in House of Commons over Options for
Suffrage Extension.

	Liberals	Labour	Conservatives	IPP
A – Status Quo	1	3	1	1
B – Manhood	2	1	4	2
C – Widows Spinsters	4	4	2	4
D – Universal Suffrage	3	2	3	3

Note: The table presents a hypothesized logical ranking of preferences of the four British parties over the different options for voting reforms in 1910. A "1" is the best, a "4" is least preferred. See text for rationale. As the Irish Parliamentary Party (IPP) was the pivotal party in the parliament elected in December 1910, deviations away from the status quo are nearly impossible. When, in 1912, the Labour Party conference resolved not to support any suffrage extension to men unless some provision was made for women's suffrage, their preferences changed to D > B > A > C.

conservatives, but perhaps they would have been ambivalent between C and D. Worst off is male franchise, which the Conservatives should have ranked last.

When adding the Irish Parliamentary Party (IPP) to table 3.2, the status-quo bias of the Parliament is clear. The IPP tended to vote against the several private member bills for suffrage, but their "true" preferences are difficult to glean. Some scholars have argued that the IPP voted against suffrage because they heard rumors that it would destabilize the government.[24] Another contends that the Irish voted against women's suffrage because they wanted more of the parliament's time to be devoted to the Home Rule Bill.[25] Though single-minded focus on home rule undoubtedly added to their reticence, in my reading, the Nationalists were much less concerned with giving time to debate suffrage than they were with the *consequences* of extending voting rights to women.

An article in the *Manchester Guardian* that discussed John Redmond's (the leader of the Irish nationalists) opposition to suffrage claimed that "it is necessary for the Irish Party in the interests of Home Rule to save

[24] See, for example, Wingerden (1999: 134). She does not explain what I do here, namely that the instability of the Asquith regime after enfranchisement would not be because of a lack of confidence in the government, but rather that the new voters would likely not be his partisans.

[25] McLean 2001: 106.

the Liberal ministry from the disruptive effects of women's suffrage."[26] English suffragists knew their chances were slim without the support of the Irish, and they understood that this support was driven by how it affected home rule.[27] In a letter to the Labour leader Arthur Henderson, National Union strategist Catherine Marshall wrote:

> The same considerations which led those Irish members who are Suffragists (the majority in their party) to oppose the Conciliation Bill would lead those who are not suffragists (the minority) to support a Women's Suffrage Amendment to the Reform Bill if they believed that the interests of Home Rule were best served by that course. Mr. Redmond himself said the other day that he was not personally opposed to Women's Suffrage.[28]

In other words, Marshall believed that the Irish were voting on women's suffrage strategically: they voted against the Conciliation Bill because they believed home rule would be compromised if women's suffrage upended the Liberal's position in Westminster.

Marshall could not look to Irish suffragists to solve the problem, especially because the Irish nationalist suffragists hesitated to press their claim too strongly, lest it compromise the greater goal of independence. In the words of one member of the Newry Suffrage Society, "we must do nothing to endanger the sacred cause of Home Rule. Therefore we must be doormats and feather cushions, and so make everything pleasant and easy to enable the men of Ireland to win their freedom ... but Ireland with her womanhood enslaved will not be free." A member of the Munster Suffrage Society concurred: "I put Ireland first ... . Three years more in our very exceptional circumstances will not hurt us."[29] Marshall would have to look for other allies in the fight for the vote.

A final player in this game was the House of Lords, which exercised veto power over the Commons until 1911. The conservative upper chamber may have faced a similar strategic landscape as the Tories.

---

[26] Quoted in Kelly 1996: 34.

[27] For the suffragists' need of the Irish vote, see correspondence between Millicent Garrett Fawcett and Kathleen Courtney, another National Union leader (Manchester Archives and Local Studies (hereafter MLS): M50/2/357. 8-Apr-12).

[28] The Labour History Archive and Study Center (hereafter LHA): LP/WOM/12/31. 5-Jul-12.

[29] Quoted in Kelly 1996: 35.

Thus, they may have vetoed a manhood suffrage bill put forward by the Liberals, while allowing for a "spinster" suffrage should such a measure receive government sponsorship.[30] As the Lords, too, were liable to act strategically, the Liberals and the Irish, who were trying their hardest to guarantee that the Conservatives did not end up in the majority, would neither support the women's limited "Conciliation" bill nor push through a measure for a broad-based franchise.

Preferences and Roll-Call Votes

If the arguments I have made about party preferences over suffrage are correct, they should be reflected in roll-call votes. From 1907 through 1913, the House of Commons debated seven private-member bills on women's suffrage, three of which would have given women national-level voting rights.[31] Table 3.3 provides a general sense of the resistance toward suffrage reform in the House of Commons. It tallies the share of each party that supported or abstained in roll-call votes on two such bills. The first roll call, in 1908, would not have altered the rules regarding plural voting but instead included women on the same terms as men, making it a "widow/spinster" bill. The second roll call transpired in 1909. It would have abolished voting in multiple localities (hence abolished plural voting) and extended the right to vote to all men and women above a certain age, making it a "universal" bill.

---

[30] That the Lords might not veto a wealthy women's suffrage bill could further explain a curious turn in British politics in 1912, when a proposed government Reform Bill which would have brought suffrage to all men and most women was "torpedoed" by Lloyd George. George, himself a government minister and an active promoter of the bill, had made promises to the National Union to get the Irish on board, yet personally ensured it was never taken to a vote (TWL: 6B/106/2/NWS/A4/4. 21-Mar-12). He was and is notorious for saying things hastily and not delivering.

[31] The 1908 "Stanger" Bill, the 1909 "Howard" Bill, and the 1913 "Dickinson" Bill allowed for parliamentary franchise for some portion of women. The latter two are known as "Conciliation Bills," because they were sponsored by the Conciliation Committee composed of fifty-four MPs, including twenty-four Liberals, seventeen Conservatives, six Irish Party members, and six Labour MPs. The Conciliation Bills were limited suffrage measures that were basically option C: rich unmarried women or widows would have suffrage if they were a householder of a dwelling with more than £10 annual rent. Husbands and wives could not vote on the same property, so any woman who was not rich enough for her own property, or any husband who could not give his vote from a second property to his wife, would not be allowed to vote. The text of all of these bills is available in Appendix II.

TABLE 3.3. Partisan Support for Two Types of Suffrage Bill in the House of
Commons, 1908–1909.

	Limited Measure (Stanger Bill, 1908)			Universal Measure (Howard Bill, 1909)		
	% yea (voters)	% yea (all MPs)	% abstention (total)	% yea (voters)	% yea (all MPs)	% abstention (total)
Liberal	0.80	0.52	0.35	0.70	0.30	0.58
Conservative	0.51	0.18	0.64	0.00	0.00	0.55
Nationalists	0.60	0.25	0.58	0.91	0.24	0.73
Labour	0.97	0.55	0.43	1.00	0.55	0.45
Socialist	1.00	1.00	0.00			
Average	0.75	0.41	0.45	0.56	0.24	0.58

Note: The 1908 measure was a limited bill, often called a "widow" or "spinster" suffrage bill, while the 1909 bill would have allowed for universal franchise. The averages reported in the bottom row are weighted by the number of MPs in each party. The designation of "Nationalist" for some members of the IPP comes from the National Union's analysis of the roll-call votes, TWL: 2LSW/C/3/FL153/7/May-1912.

As can be seen in table 3.3, the within-party roll-call votes track quite well to the theorized preferences in table 3.2. Of all the parties, Labour was the most amenable to reform, while the Unionists were generally the most resistant. None of the Labour Party voted against suffrage, but more than 40 percent abstained in both roll calls, and a few voted against the spinster suffrage option. Among the Liberals, 80 percent supported the limited measure while 70 percent supported the universal bill. Voting patterns for the Irish Parliamentary Party reflect the argument made in these pages quite closely: 60 percent support the limited measure while 91 percent support the universal measure. Finally, while 51 percent of the voting Conservatives supported a widow/spinster suffrage, nearly 100 percent voted against the bill for universal suffrage. Because in UK politics private-member bills carry little weight without government backing, and because most MPs in the House of Commons could be confident that Herbert Asquith was not going to propose a suffrage bill in that Parliament, the preferences in table 3.3, are likely truthful representations. With the Irish Parliamentary Party in the pivotal position, a simple road to suffrage without changing the entire electoral code was unlikely. Under these conditions, the National Union of Women's Suffrage Societies embarked on a period of strategic innovation that, they hoped, could finally break the opposition to women's suffrage.

SUFFRAGISTS AND THE LABOUR PARTY

We have at last got a real sword in our hands
instead of a foil with a guarded tip.[32]

A distinctive feature of British politics is a strict set of regulations governing election finance. Under the Corrupt Practices Act of 1883, which restricted the amount that could be spent on campaigns, the parties have came to rely heavily on volunteers to conduct elections, many of whom have been women.[33] In fact, one of the primary activities that occupied suffragists of all political persuasions in each election cycle was the provision of administrative and logistical support to candidates. Generally this aid was contingent on candidates' support for suffrage measures, but it was hard for the organizations to punish the politicians if they reneged or dragged their feet. This put Liberal suffragists, in particular, in a difficult situation. They knew that suffrage had to emanate from the government, and believed the Liberals, on the whole, to be the party most sympathetic to suffrage.[34] Thus, they preferred the election of sympathetic Liberal MPs over anti-suffrage MPs. But, once these purported allies were elected, the suffragists had no way to force them into action.

This powerlessness was something that was understood quite early on by many in the movement. For example, as early as 1905 the Women's Liberal Federation refused to undertake canvassing and organizational work for Liberal candidates who produced insufficient answers on a questionnaire related to women's issues. In a more extreme reaction, the Women's Social and Political Union actually began to campaign against the Liberal Party in 1906, believing that the party's ouster was the only way to compel reform.[35] The National Union came somewhat later to this realization. Led by Millicent Garrett Fawcett, whose late husband Henry

[32] Catherine Marshall, 12 July 1912. Cumbria Archive Center (hereafter CAC), Carlisle, UK: DMAR/3/54.

[33] The Corrupt Practices Acts of 1854 and 1883 limited the amount of money that parties could spend on campaigns, Salmon (2009: 267), obliging candidates to rely on volunteers, especially women's organizations, to run elections. Volunteer groups included the Women's Liberal Federation (Liberal Party), with 150 thousand members circa 1900. The Primrose League (Conservative Party) boasted of 500 thousand members in 1900. These groups canvassed, assisted in tracing the local registers, and got people to the polls. Hirshfield 1990.

[34] Whereas in the United States the executive rarely proposes bills and these are rarely passed, in the United Kingdom it is the reverse.

[35] Pugh 2000: 22.

had been a Liberal MP from 1865 to 1884, the organization held out hope that the Asquith government would sponsor suffrage reform.[36] But after three consecutive private members' bills failed to gain the government's backing, the leaders of the National Union sought a new plan.

In early 1912, several months of debates between Catherine Marshall, Fawcett, and Labour leaders led to the founding of the Election Fighting Fund, an organization that raised capital to support Labour candidates in upcoming by-elections. By-elections are special elections that arise due to death, promotion, resignation, or elevation to the House of Lords. Having no official alliance with the suffrage movement after the Pankhursts broke with the party in 1903, several Labour MPs who served on the Conciliation Committee had formed relationships with leaders of the non-partisan National Union. Together, they agreed that because Labour was the only party to put women's suffrage on its platform, the party deserved suffragist support. The organizations agreed that the National Union would provide both money and administrative assistance to official party candidates that had "acceptable" views on suffrage, so long as the opponent was not a "tried friend" of women's suffrage. In other words, any Liberal candidate with a bad record on suffrage stood a chance of facing a well-funded Labour opponent. In return for this funding, Labour leaders, with the backing of their members, agreed not to support electoral reform if women were excluded.[37]

For the suffragists and for the Labour Party, the EFF policy was novel and contentious. It was explicit in its intention to support Labour against Liberal candidates in by-elections, even if doing so would end in a Conservative victory. This fact made many of the women uneasy: several members of the National Union voiced concerns that such an aggressive strategy might debase their cause in the eyes of the Liberal Party. Moreover, they feared what would happen under the policy if

[36] The NUWSS was technically a "non-party" organization, but many of its leaders were affiliated with the Liberal Party. Nevertheless, EFF organizers Esther Roper and Eva Gore Booth were leaders of various working-class suffrage organizations. Liddington and Norris 1978.

[37] The Labour Party had a mixed record of official support for suffrage bills. At the National Conference of the Labour Representation Committee in 1904, it had affirmed a limited suffrage bill, but in 1905 it rejected this support on the grounds that such a limited bill would benefit middle- and upper-class women while so many men remained disfranchised. But, at their 1912 conference held on January 23–26 in Birmingham, a resolution was adopted which said a government reform bill that did not include women would be unacceptable. (For the official language of the resolutions, see Harmer 1999.) The 1906 measure passed by a large majority (TWL: 6B/106/2/NWS/A4/4).

a general election were held. Was it worth maintaining a harsh stance against the Liberals if it would empower the Conservatives? Ultimately it took a few visionary women to persuade the majority of National Union members that the Election Fighting Fund was their only chance to force the hands of the Liberal government.[38]

Primary sources reveal the Labour Party's objectives in forming the alliance. Several leaders of the party stated in letters and in speeches that they believed in the principle of women's suffrage, but the party's refusal to put it on their platform before 1912 and its acceptance thereafter indicate that principle was not the only factor guiding the party's stance. Internal documents show that the idea for the alliance came out of communications between Labour MPs and the National Union surrounding the failed Conciliation Bills in 1910 and 1911.[39] The internal documents point to four ways in which Labour stood to gain from the alliance.

First, the Labour Party would have the money to run more candidates. Second, they would have the ground forces of the National Union at their disposal to do the arduous (and costly) work of maintaining and adding to the electoral register. Third, in utilizing the grassroots network of the suffragists, the Labour Party would not only help to mobilize working-class women, but also potentially turn some of the Liberal suffragists into Labour voters in the future. Finally, the Labour Party might be able to use the threat of standing in more constituencies as a way to force the Liberal Party to grant them more and better seats to contest in the next general election. This latter prospect would play directly to the interests of the National Union, too, as it was not inconceivable that Labour could someday provide the critical pivot in the House of Commons.

The financial and organizational support that the National Union could offer Labour was not trivial. The Labour Party had only just begun to emerge on the national stage in 1910. They contested fifteen constituencies in 1900 (and returned two MPs), fifty constituencies in 1906 (returned twenty-nine), seventy-eight in January 1910 (returned forty), and fifty-six in December 1910 (returning forty-two).[40] It would be difficult for Labour to contest more seats in the next general election not only because of their

---

[38] The policy, especially in regards to the general election, was contentious within the NUWSS.

[39] In several letters between members of the National Union, the EFF is referred to as "Mr. Brailsford's plan" because Henry Noel Brailsford, a radical journalist, Labour MP, and member of the Conciliation Committee, was instrumental in its foundation. Brailsford's wife, Jane, was a member of both the National Union and the "militant" WSPU.

[40] Rallings et al. 2000: 79.

pact with the Liberals, but also because theirs was not a rich organization. They lacked the type of wealthy donors who supported candidates in the other parties, and their members were not flush with personal wealth. The lack of finances was a real problem for a party with national aspirations. Candidates had to fund their own elections, and were bound by tradition to show generosity to local clubs. If a candidate were lucky enough to win, he had to pay the cost of moving the loser home, which could cost upward of £300.[41] One estimate puts the total cost of an election as between £500 and £1,000 to fight an urban borough and twice as much to fight a rural county seat.[42] Moreover, MPs were not paid for their service until after 1911, and even then the income was not large. Running and serving were both costly endeavors and likely prevented many aspiring Labour candidates, who were generally of the working classes, from running.

In addition, while the Conservatives and the Liberals could and did rely on unpaid female labor to perform administrative political work in constituencies between elections, many women that the Labour Party might attract were themselves paid laborers with little free time to volunteer.[43] With gross riches standing around £32,000 and members totaling more than 42 thousand across 410 branches in 1912, the National Union was in a position to help Labour remedy its financial and organizational disadvantage.[44]

One final benefit of the alliance stemmed from the increased bargaining power the Labour Party might gain if the Liberals feared that their general election pact would dissolve. The historiography of the demise of the Liberal Party and rise of the Labour Party speculates considerably about Ramsay MacDonald's intentions for the Liberal-Labour pact in the event of a 1915 election. The consensus among historians is that the pact would

---

[41] From 1906 to 1910 the average fees for the returning officer were £308. Rallings et al. 2000: 121. This is around $40,000 today.

[42] Searle 1992: 70. The cost of running in an urban borough would be between 65 and 130 thousand US dollars today.

[43] This is evidenced in meeting requests made by working women's suffrage organizations, which implored MPs and even the prime minister to pick a time at night so that women could come without missing a day's work (LHA/LP/PA/14/1/383/12-Jun-14). In the New York suffrage movement, executive committee meeting times during the day and on Saturdays meant that key bases of support for the movement—working women and Jews—were often unable to attend and therefore could not hold leadership positions. See Lerner 1981.

[44] Pugh 2000: 256 and table 8.4.

have gone on, but that it would have been more advantageous to Labour in the future.[45] The research here points to the possibility that the EFF would have contributed to the rising bargaining power of the Labour Party in the context of the Lib-Lab pact, though no major history of the period, save Pugh's (2000) tract on the suffrage movement, mentions this possibility.[46] The commanders of the Election Fighting Fund, on the other hand, saw the potential clearly. Catherine Marshall states the possibility succinctly:

> Our enemies in the Liberal camp have uneasy doubts as to how much we are concerned in the revolt of the Labour Party and what mischief we may be up to next. There is just that feeling of uneasiness that we want to create both in the House of Commons and in the daily press. In the present political situation the government cannot afford to run any risks and they are at last beginning to feel there is some risk in putting off demand for Women's suffrage.[47]

Trenchant words from the strategy's key architect, but what remains to be seen is whether the EFF would prove effective.

Impact of the Election Fighting Fund

The Election Fighting Fund provided for cooperation between the National Union of Women's Suffrage Societies and the Labour Party during by-election campaigns in which Labour fielded an official candidate.[48] What is still unknown is whether the policy could have a great enough impact to sustain cooperation between the organizations into the future, thereby allowing Labour to credibly commit to its side of the bargain. In other words, were the effects of the EFF alliance strong enough to compel Labour to maintain its promise?

---

[45] Searle 1992: 116.

[46] By some accounts, if a general election had been held in 1915, the Labour Party would have wanted to field between 120 and 150 candidates. In fact, in the election after the signing of the Armistice on December 1918, Labour ran 288 candidates and was awarded sixty-three seats. Searle 1992: 122. In a classic text on the Liberal Party's demise after WWI, Dangerfield 2011 does point to women's suffrage as a primary driver of the party's collapse.

[47] Report of the Election Fighting Fund Committee Private Council Meeting, CAC/DMAR/3/54/12-July-1912.

[48] A "by-election" is a special election in a parliamentary constituency, a jurisdiction that is similar to US congressional districts. Some British constituencies had multiple representatives, whereas congressional districts in the US are single member. Under the 1885–1918 constituency boundaries, however, the vast majority of districts were single member. See Craig 1972.

To demonstrate the potency of the policy, I evaluate three outcomes before and after the policy was implemented: whether the EFF increased the scope of and support for the Labour Party; whether it was effective in initiating three-cornered contests against anti-suffrage liberals; and whether it allowed for a turnover of seats.[49] The study window begins with the first by-election after the December 1910 general election, held on 11 February 1911. It stops with the end of the year 1914. In all, the analysis covers ninety-three by-elections.

The study window ends with 1914 because, due to the onset of World War I, political work by the National Union was disrupted, and the parties had agreed to suspend competition, making later elections a poor comparison group for those that happened before the war broke out.[50] For example, whereas before the war began 22 percent of by-elections for seats outside of Ireland were uncontested, in 1914 this reached more than 50 percent and grew to above 70 percent during the war. The apex was reached in 1915, when 80 percent of seats outside of Ireland went uncontested. Because new political forces ushered in by the war were already evident in late 1914, ending the sample at the close of the year is a conservative choice that, if anything, would bias against finding an effect of the EFF policy.[51]

The date that divides the set of by-elections into pre- and post-EFF implementation is 20 June 1912.[52] This is the date of a by-election in Holmfirth, the first in which Labour fielded a candidate after the policy was announced. Table 3.4 reports summary statistics before and after the

---

[49] In the Westminster system, by-elections serve to take the temperature of the electorate and are not considered trivial events. If the government loses several of the "byes" it could be cause for early dissolution. See Cox 2005: 139ff.

[50] The first Electoral Truce, signed 28 August 1914 and effective until 1 January 1915, agreed to halt by-election competitions among the parties. An amended version signed 5 February 1915, and renewed every three months until the end of 1916, declared that in the case of resignation, the three parties could confer over whether candidates could compete. Craig 1987: 361.

[51] For example, one thesis I examine is whether Labour contested more elections (or a greater proportion of elections) after the EFF was implemented. Extending the sample window to the end of 1914 increases the post-policy denominator and thereby decreases the fraction of contests. This drives test-statistics toward the null of no difference before and after the policy was implemented.

[52] National Union leaders Millicent Garret Fawcett and Catherine Marshall began to negotiate the contours of the EFF with Labour leaders Arthur Henderson and Ramsay MacDonald early in 1912. Both organizations were committed to the policy by May of that year. The specifics were announced in a "special council meeting" attended by representatives of more than 370 affiliated suffrage organizations on May 16, but the policy did not come fully into effect until the Holmfirth contest. LHA/LP/WOM/12/19.

TABLE 3.4. Overview of By-Election Results before and after the Election Fighting Fund, 1910–1914.

	Pre-EFF	Post-EFF
By-elections, n	45	48
Uncontested, percent	0.24	0.27
Two-way, percent	0.60	0.42
Three-cornered, percent	0.16	0.31
Labour Contested, n	4	13

Note: Though the number of elections before and after the alliance is formed is similar, the characteristics are changed by the policy. Labour fields more candidates than before, and, while a similar fraction of contests are uncontested, a much larger share are three-cornered after the policy is implemented. Numbers are rounded to the nearest decimal. Data on number of candidates and the parties that fielded them have been coded from McCalmont et al. 1971.

EFF was implemented. The table shows that while the fraction of seats that were uncontested remained relatively constant across both periods (24 percent before and 27 percent after), the fraction of contests that were two-way fell by sixteen percentage points, while the fraction that were three-way rose by fifteen points. Table 3.4 also shows that the number of contests in which Labour fielded a candidate rose in the aftermath of the EFF. This difference is statistically significant at the 5-percent level. (See table 3.5.) Thus, in terms of the goal of helping Labour to contest more seats, the EFF policy produced fast results.

Examining differences in election outcomes before and after the alliance was formed, table 3.5 presents Pearson χ^2 coefficients from an analysis of two categorical variables: whether Labour fielded a candidate in the election (in the first row) or whether the seat changed hands (in the second row). These tests reveal that turnover was more likely after the EFF was implemented than before: 54 percent of seats changed hands after the policy began versus 20 percent before ($p = 0.027$). This is especially true when we compare elections where the policy was and was not operative. In three out of thirteen elections where Labour fielded a candidate after 28 June 1912, the EFF was not active. They abstained once because a "tried friend" of women's suffrage was chosen as the Liberal candidate, and twice because the Labour Party announced a candidate too late for the women to send their ground forces.[53] In the two cases where Labour

[53] Northwest Manchester, which held a by-election on 8 August 1912, was not an EFF constituency because the incumbent was a "tried friend" of women's suffrage. In two other cases, the East Carmarthenshire election on 22 August 1912 and Keighley on 11 November 1913, the Labour party decided to enter too late for the EFF to be

TABLE 3.5. Effect of the Election Fighting Fund in By-Elections, 1910–1914.

	Pre-EFF	Post-EFF	Pearson χ^2	Fisher's Exact p
Share Contested by Labour	0.09	0.27	5.14 $(p = 0.023)$	0.031 (1-sided $= 0.021$)
Seat Changed Hands	0.13	0.31	4.26 $(p = 0.039)$	0.049 (1-sided $= 0.034$)

Note: The null hypothesis tested using the Pearson χ^2 coefficient is that the probability of Labour contesting an election, or of a seat changing hands, is the same before and after the EFF policy was implemented. Since some of the cells have few observations, the final column presents *p*-values for Fisher's exact test, which is less sensitive to sample size. One-sided *p*-values are appropriate because the alternative hypothesis is that both the fraction contested, and the probability of a seat changing hands, is higher after the EFF is implemented.

entered the contest too late, the "potential outcomes" are not independent of the suffragists' decision, so I hesitate to make too much of those cases.[54] Yet, where the EFF was operative, seven out of ten times the seat turned over. Though the sample size is small, if we consider that out of all of the by-elections that Labour contested before the EFF was operative, turnover happened in only one case (25 percent), whereas after the EFF was operative, seats turned over in seven cases (54 percent), then we can conclude that, on the most basic level, the EFF was successful in helping Labour to force seat turnover.

Inferential Concerns

In drawing firm conclusions about the effect of the Election Fighting Fund, it is important to consider whether unobserved or unobservable attributes are actually driving the results. If this is the case, the before-elections may not be a relevant counterfactual group for those elections that came after. As a step toward allaying this concern, I briefly consider a few potential sources of confounding and bias.[55]

---

implemented. (TWL/6B/106/2/NWS/B1/2; TWL/NU Minutes/8-Jan-1912, 9-Dec-1912; CAC/DMAR/3/54.)

[54] This approach is cautious. The difference in the timing of a nomination announcement that would have allowed the EFF to help is necessarily small. Section 19 (5) of the Representation of the People Act, as Amended in 1985, specifies that by-elections can be drawn out over no more than nineteen working days from the date of announcement. Nominations must be announced between days four and nine, and polling between days thirteen and nineteen. See Craig 1987: 363.

[55] On the problem of confounding variables for causal inference, I draw here on Dunning 2012.

First, we might worry that the date of the first EFF election was strategically timed. If the EFF began in a period when Labour already expected to contest more seats, or when turnover was already more likely, the inference that the policy drove these changes would be invalid. From my reading of the archival sources on the EFF, it is clear that once the policy was hammered out and agreed to by both the National Union and the Labour Party, it was implemented in the first election in which Labour fielded a candidate. If either group had taken longer to secure the consent of their adherents, or if both had hastened the process of negotiation, the EFF could easily have been implemented sooner or later, implying that the date of implementation is not a likely source of confounding.

Concerns about strategic timing would also arise if the Liberal Party manipulated the by-elections by scheduling them at an earlier date to avoid three-candidate contests. To examine this potential source of bias, we have to consider the reasons that by-elections arise in the first place, which include death, resignation, promotion into the government's cabinet, succession to a title, or elevation into the House of Lords.[56] Table 3.6 tabulates the reasons that by-elections arose before and after the EFF was implemented, and figure 3.2 shows the timeline of events. If politicians strategically manipulated the timing of these elections we should observe imbalances in the two types of by-election where timing is more likely to be malleable: those because of elevation and those because of promotion.

Imbalance across the before and after period might arise if the Liberal Party attempted to avoid three-cornered contests by promoting or elevating MPs early, so as to avoid facing a third candidate in the contest. For by-elections because of elevation, table 3.6 reveals an imbalance insofar as seven MPs were elevated to the House of Lords before the EFF was implemented and only one was implemented after.[57] Visual inspection of figure 3.2 allays the concern of strategic manipulation: all of the pre-policy elevations took place in 1911, long before the EFF was conceived. Thus there is no evidence that the Liberal Party manipulated elevations

[56] Promotion to a cabinet position required that a re-election be held after 1832.

[57] Elevation to the House of Lords happens when a new peerage (or position in the house) is created. This is not common, but after 1910 there were many elevations because of negotiations carried out between Asquith and King Edward, followed by his son, in the wake of the Lords' veto on Lloyd George's budget. Asquith demanded that more peers be made so that the conservatives could not control public policy merely because they controlled the hereditary House of Lords.

TABLE 3.6. Causes of By-Elections before and after the EFF was Implemented, 1910–1914.

	Pre-EFF	Post-EFF	Row Total
Promotion	12	12	24
Death*	10	23	33
Resignation	10	10	20
Succession to Title	3	2	5
Elevation to Peer	7	1	8
Void	3	0	3
Column Total	45	48	93

Note: Coded from McCalmont et al. 1971. Elections for Great Britain only included.
* When death is excluded from the cross-tabulation, the p-value for Fisher's Exact test of balance across treatment and control is 0.201.

in response to the Election Fighting Fund. The incidence of promotion into the government's cabinet seems numerically balanced across the two groups and does not appear to cluster just prior to the reform. The only category that drove more by-elections after the EFF policy came into effect is death. Even though death was more common in the post-EFF period, it is hard to imagine MPs strategically choosing to end their lives with the EFF in mind. In sum, it is unlikely that the Liberal Party strategically scheduled the by-elections to avoid three-candidate contests.

A second inferential concern would arise if attitudes toward the Liberal or Labour parties were changing over the period in question in a pattern that was itself driving the changes that I attribute to the EFF. While it is true that the Liberal Party grew in disfavor as the war progressed, the period in question was likely too early for these effects to be felt. As for the Labour Party, the growth of trade union membership in the years before the First World War does not support this concern.[58] From 1910 to 1911, membership grew at 22.5 percent. From 1911 to 1912, the rate was 8.8 percent. From 1912 to 1913, it was 21 percent, and from 1913 to 1914, it grew only 0.23 percent. Given these figures, if Labour's popularity drove the party's ability to field candidates in new constituencies, the effects on Labour should have shown up earlier than when the Election Fighting Fund began.

[58] See McKibbin (1974) on the rise of the Labour Party.

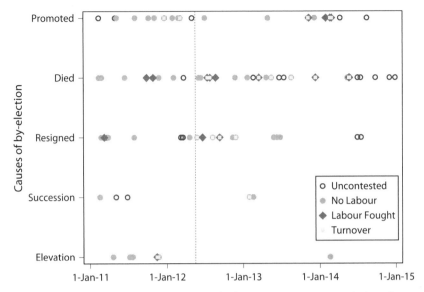

FIGURE 3.2. Timeline of By-Elections and Their Outcomes around the Election Fighting Fund Cut-off. Each dot on the graph represents a single by-election. The x-axis lists the exact date of the contest, from January 1911 to January 1915, and the y-axis lists the reason that the seat became open. Hollow circles indicate that a by-election was uncontested. A filled circle indicates that it was contested but Labour did not participate. A diamond is a by-election where Labour fielded a candidate, and a square indicates turnover.

In sum, I have argued that the Election Fighting Fund provided sufficient financial and organizational incentives to the Labour Party to allow the party to credibly commit to support women's suffrage in the House of Commons. Its commitment—to refuse support for any electoral reform bill that did not include some provision for women's suffrage—was bolstered by four features of the EFF: access to the wealthy coffers of the suffragists allowed Labour to field candidates in more constituencies; the large grass-roots network of National Union members provided the free labor the party needed to trace the electoral registers and organize elections; in mobilizing women for Labour candidates, the party hoped to win the allegiance of women from all classes; and, finally, in contesting more elections, Labour hoped to improve its hand in negotiations with the Liberal Party regarding which seats Labour could contest in the general election. In an empirical analysis of by-election contests before and after the EFF was implemented, I demonstrated that the policy allowed Labour to contest more seats, that it increased the number of three-cornered contests, and that it increased turnover as a result of its alliance with the suffragists.

1918: THE THIN END OF THE WEDGE

On 19 June 1917, Clause Four of the Representation of the People Act was put to a "free vote" in the House of Commons.[59] The clause, which passed 387 to 57 votes, would enfranchise a large cohort of British women once the king signed the Act into law. It is my contention that Labour's alliance with the National Union of Women's Suffrage Societies, under the aegis of the Election Fighting Fund, was key to women's inclusion in that bill.

Before making this case, however, it is necessary to confront a compelling alternative thesis that claims that women won the vote because of the First World War. The close timing of the war's end and women's suffrage in the UK is impossible to deny, and there are several reasons to think that wartime activities contributed to women's emancipation. From charity and relief work to filling soldiers' vacated jobs, the large-scale participation of women in the war effort has been credited with changing public opinion on the issue of suffrage. Yet there are both comparative and context-specific reasons to question a simple, deterministic relationship between the war and the franchise. In comparative context, the variation in wartime mobilization and extension of the franchise to women is not consistent across sides in the war or levels of mobilization. Furthermore, in the particular context of the United Kingdom, a simplistic view that the war changed public opinion, leading to women's enfranchisement, is difficult to sustain.

My contention is not that the war had no influence on public opinion; perhaps it did.[60] The claim, rather, is that a change in public opinion was not strictly necessary to get women onto the Representation of the People Act. Since private members' bills for women's suffrage had received majorities on the floor of the House of Commons several times prior to 1914, all that was really needed was for opinion to remain the same but

---

[59] In other words, the clause was voted on separately from the entire Act, so even if it failed this would not doom the rest of the bill.

[60] The suffragists believed public opinion changed earlier. An NUWSS Council meeting reported, "Press support for Women's Suffrage seemed to be gaining ground rapidly everywhere. Of the 566 papers now overlooked, 244 were favourable, only 47 being anti-suffragist while the rest were neutral or unclassified." TWL: 7MGF/A/1/Box 1/80/23-May-1913.

for the government to support the bill. Indeed, the roll-call division taken in 1917 on Clause Four, with 385 MPs for and 55 against, is only slightly more favorable for suffrage than a division taken in 1913, which passed 283 to 112.[61] The difference between these two bills is that the 1917 bill was a government bill which, in the British parliamentary context, had a good chance of becoming law. In order to understand why women were enfranchised in 1918, then, we need an account of why the government bill included Clause Four in the electoral reform bill.

Clearly, a change in the configuration of power in the House of Commons might have led to government sponsorship. Because the Labour Party evinced the highest levels of support for women's suffrage before the war, such a change may have resulted if a general election brought Labour into a pivotal position (see table 3.2). A general election was not held until after the Representation of the People Act was passed, however, and so the Labour Party as a whole did not become pivotal in the interim. Yet Labour did come to occupy a different position after the war, not so much in terms of seats, but rather in the person of Arthur Henderson, a Labour leader who was appointed to the multi-party wartime cabinet.

I submit that it was the close relationship that the suffragists had forged with Arthur Henderson that secured the presence of a provision for women's suffrage in the government's reform bill. An MP from 1903 to 1935, in that time Arthur Henderson wore many hats. He was the chief whip of the Parliamentary Labour Party; Treasurer, Chairman, and Secretary of the National Labour Party; President of the Board of Education; Home and Foreign Secretary; and he was also the first Labour politician to serve in the government. Henderson was, moreover, the highest-ranking member of the Labour Party to serve on the EFF committee. He helped craft the suffragist strategy vis-à-vis parliament and by-elections, and helped sell the EFF to the Labour Party elites and their general public.[62] At some points he was in near daily communication with Catherine Marshall, the key architect of the EFF within the National Union. Most importantly, it was Henderson who became the chief champion of women when a government reform bill began to be discussed in 1916.

On 14 March 1916, a confidential government memorandum entitled "The Revision of the National Register is Essential" was leaked to the

---

[61] Dickinson's was an amendment to the 1913 Government Registration and Franchise Bill, which would have allowed for the "dual" vote—every woman married to a male elector would have a vote, as would single women over twenty-five with the requisite householder qualification.

[62] See Vellacott 1993: ch 9, 181ff.

Times of London. The memo specified the need to overhaul voter registration procedures to allow returning soldiers, who would be disfranchised because of the country's strict residency requirements, to vote. At this point Millicent Fawcett began to suspect that a government bill was on the horizon.[63] She wrote to Labour leaders Henderson and W. C. Anderson to shore up their alliance, announcing that, despite earlier prevarications about the future of the EFF since the war commenced, in the event of an election under the "three-party" system the EFF alliance would continue as before.[64] Testing the waters with the government, Fawcett also wrote a concerned letter to Prime Minister Asquith, inquiring about the possibility of electoral reform for soldiers and not women. Without addressing the leaked report, Asquith dissimulated, assuring her that no such legislation was currently under consideration.[65]

Just five days later, on 12 May 1916, Arthur Henderson wrote a detailed, confidential memo to the Wartime Cabinet, of which he was a member, outlining a series of revisions to the electoral law.[66] In it he discussed the need for electoral reform to address four issues: 1) revise the electoral registers to allow returning soldiers to vote who do not meet the current residency requirements; 2) address the malapportionment of seats across the British Isles; 3) discuss the abolition of plural votes; and 4) consider the issue of women's suffrage. He wrote:

> What form the extension of the suffrage to women ought to take is a question for further consideration. I do not personally think that anything less than adult [i.e., universal] suffrage could be regarded for more than a very short time as a final settlement but the argument which is based on the resulting disproportion between male and female electors could, I think, be met by making twenty-five the age at which the suffrage could be exercised in the case of women. I have reason to believe that this solution would be acceptable to the women's organizations.[67]

---

[63] Runciman to Asquith, Oxford Bodleian Library (hereafter OBL) (MSS.16.89-94/14-March-1916). The report, issued by the Committee of Reserved Occupations, discussed the need for an overhaul of the electoral law to allow returning soldiers to vote.

[64] Fawcett to Henderson & Anderson, and their favorable replies (TWL/7MGF/A/1/118/6, 14, 17-April-1916).

[65] Fawcett to Asquith: TWL/7MGF/A/1/119/4-May-1916; and response: TWL/AL C9/01/1111/7-May-1916.

[66] National Archives, UK Cabinet Papers (hereafter CAB): 37/147/31/12-May-1916.

[67] Ibid.

In drafting this memorandum, Henderson established a blueprint for electoral reform that would in fact form the basis of the 1918 Act. But, where all parties agreed to points one, two, and three, there was considerable resistance to including women in the bill.

The language of the Representation of the People Act grew out of a special committee, commissioned in October 1916, to evaluate the issue of electoral reform. Led by the conservative speaker of the house, J. W. Lowther, it became a "Speaker's Conference."[68] All parties were keen to allow soldiers and volunteers returning from the front to vote, and Prime Minister Asquith believed that appointing a diverse committee to study the issue and make recommendations was the likeliest way to ensure a bill's passage. Neither Asquith nor most members of the conference had intended for women's suffrage to be among the proposed reforms. Indeed, in allowing Lowther to run the committee, Asquith contrived to weight the conference toward the Conservatives to guarantee that a limited measure would be secured rather than a wholesale reform of the franchise.[69] Upon seeing the committee's appointments, certain suffrage sympathists wrote to Asquith to protest the cabinet makeup, which, given the appointment of well-known anti-suffragists from the Conservative camp, was also stacked against suffrage.[70] Yet, as correspondence between Asquith and Conservative Walter Long reveals, it was precisely in an attempt to ensure a limited measure that the committee was structured as it was.[71]

At several points during the conference's negotiations, the opposition to women's suffrage waxed. This prompted Henderson, along with his

[68] A Speaker's Conference is the UK's device for an all-party commission that is not controlled by the government. The opening session was held on October 12 1916. Thereafter, thirty-two members held meetings twice weekly. Decisions were made by majority rule. To avoid sinking the whole bill, the conference addressed women's suffrage last. Unfortunately, no official papers of the conference were recorded, so I rely here on letters between members instead of minutes. Rolf 1979; 44.

[69] Walter Long to Asquith: "If we cannot get these thorny questions considered and decided by a conference of some sort ... it... will open the door to a wholesale reform of the franchise and may easily land us into an extremely difficult position." OBL/MSS.17.85-86/17-Sep-1916.

[70] John W. Gulland, Liberal MP from Edinburgh, to Asquith: OBL/MSS.17.79-80/13-Sept-1916.

[71] Walter Long to Asquith: 17 September 1916, OBL: MSS.17.85-86. Long later writes to Asquith that if the Cabinet actually prefers Henderson's scheme and takes women's suffrage as a priority, he has misunderstood its wish. OBL/MSS.17.126/29-Oct-1916.

unlikely Conservative bedfellow, Lord Robert Cecil, to threaten to resign from the Cabinet if women were not included on the bill.[72] In a letter to Asquith they confess to being

> put in a very difficult position if Carson [the anti-suffragist conference leader and leading opponent to Irish home rule] is allowed to bring the soldiers vote before the House in such a forum as will preclude the discussion of Women's Suffrage.[73]

In the nuances of parliamentary correspondence, the reminder of their difficult position stood as a warning to Asquith that the cabinet members might be forced to resign, an act which would likely bring the whole government down. Behind closed doors, members of the Speaker's Conference agreed that because there was disagreement on the issue of suffrage, they themselves should vote over the particular recommendations.

In the end, fewer than half of the members of the Conference assented to an equal suffrage clause, while fifteen of twenty-one agreed to a measure which imposed an age floor of thirty on female voters.[74] These vote tallies do not evince the type of dramatic shift in public opinion that would have made suffrage "inevitable" at the close of the war. Instead, the votes mirror earlier divisions in the House of Commons. Yet since the result of the Speaker's Conference was a set of recommendations for a government reform bill, passage of the limited measure for female voters within the committee meant the suffrage clause had a spot on the bill. This, thanks in large part to the early initiative taken by Arthur Henderson in the drafting stage, and to the threat that he and Robert Cecil made ahead of the conference's general discussions. Though all of British womanhood was not included in the 1918 measure, Clause Four proved to be the "thin end of the wedge," which, once inserted into electoral law, opened inexorably to universal suffrage in 1928.

---

[72] Cecil had long advocated in the House for suffrage. See Hansard 1912. 23-Nov-16, OBL: MSS.17.155. Pugh (1974: 358–374, 383) agrees with this interpretation.

[73] Henderson and Cecil to Asquith: OBL/MSS.17.155/23-Nov-1916.

[74] Ibid.: 362.

THE END OF THE STORY: 1928

As we have seen, the relationship formed between the Liberal suffragists and the Labour Party brought women's suffrage to the government agenda in 1916 and resulted in women's inclusion in the 1918 Representation of the People Act. But various political factors led to the reform remaining only a partial victory for women, as those under thirty, and those over thirty who did not pay taxes, were excluded. It is hard to see these factors in anything but a strategic light: to the degree that the male constituency was depleted during the War, women would have had a numerical advantage in the electorate, a fact which concerned the Liberal Party. Moreover, in earlier roll-call votes the Conservative Party was more supportive of suffrage measures that truncated the female electorate by age or property status. Both of these concerns suggest that the parties had prior beliefs about how including women would affect their electoral positions.

In the period after the Fourth Reform Act of 1918, Labour rose to a position of national prominence. Forming a minority government, from 1922 to 1924, Ramsay MacDonald became the first Labour politician to serve as prime minister. The 1924 election brought yet another change in electoral fortunes: the Liberals lost 151 seats while the Conservatives gained 161, allowing Tory Stanley Baldwin to become the country's prime minister. Perhaps it was in an attempt to solidify these gains that Baldwin and his party removed the last restrictions on female voters. Baldwin may have felt the way about women that Disraeli had about the lower classes in 1867—that they were "naturally conservative in temperament but also naturally Conservative in politics."[75] Yet, Baldwin seems to have read the tea leaves incorrectly.

The 1928 franchise extension, which removed the last barriers to women's equal participation in British elections, did not have huge effects on standard measures of political competition, but it benefited the Liberals at the expense of the Conservative Party. In places where the share of registered electors grew the most, Liberal Party support surged. In the greater scheme of things, this increase in support may not have mattered much, as Liberals gained a mere 19 seats in 1929. On the other hand, Labour picked up 137 seats, returning 288 members of parliament over the Conservative's 260. Although it is difficult to attribute these changes to the

[75] Himmelfarb 1966: 113.

effects of younger women voters (the problems of "ecological" inference described by social scientists), contemporary observers may have seen the Liberal revival as due in part to women's votes. If this interpretation is correct, the Conservative Party may have been right in the postwar period to insist on the age floor in 1918, as removing the floor may have hurt their party's performance most of all.[76]

CONCLUSION

The Election Fighting Fund, a curious and clandestine agreement brokered by Liberal leaders of the National Union of Women's Suffrage Societies and the Labour Party, paved the way for British women's enfranchisement. In just two short years the EFF helped Labour contest more seats, forced three candidate contests in by-elections, and resulted in higher rates of seat turnover than before the policy was implemented. These striking results resonated with members of the Liberal camp, including Philip Whitwell Wilson, a former MP and parliamentary correspondent for the London Daily News. In 1914 he warned the Liberal Prime Minister Herbert Asquith and his ministers that ignoring women's suffrage would be to their peril. The suffragists, "saying little that appears in the press, are in every direction reinforcing Labour and influencing the balancing vote on which depends the fate of Governments."[77]

The alliance between the suffragists and Labour proved crucial to winning women the vote. The importance of the Election Fighting Fund to the end-game politics for women's suffrage in Britain has been suggested by historian Sandra Stanley Holton, but discounted by Martin Pugh, the only other scholar who treats the issue, albeit in only a few pages.[78] Holton hints that the EFF was more important than the war in shaping the outcome in 1918, but her contribution rests on the description of the program more than the reasons that it provided the party with a

---

[76] A counterfactual possibility is that if the Conservative Party had grown out of favor with the rest of the electorate, it may have been even worse off without the reform. This would justify Baldwin's choice in 1928, but further probing of the issue will need to be saved for future research.

[77] P. W. Wilson's article appears in the April 1914 edition of The Englishwoman (TWL: 6B/106/2/NWS/A4/4).

[78] Holton 1986: ch. 4. See, too, Holton 1996: ch 10.

credible threat against the Liberal Party. For his part, Pugh argues that the alliance was problematic because the suffragists and the Labour Party had divergent preferences about which constituencies they should contest.[79] He further questions the degree to which Ramsay MacDonald would have been willing to break the general election pact with the Liberals if it allowed the Conservatives to take hold of Westminster.

These concerns may have been particularly relevant before 1916, as the Liberals, Labour, and the Conservatives agreed to several gentlemanly pacts to forego competition for seats in by-elections during the war. Yet in 1916, as the war drew to a close, the Labour Party refused to re-sign the electoral truce. In response to Pugh's objection, I would note that in order to gain leverage in their negotiations with the Liberals, the Labour Party need not actually break their electoral pact. Instead, all that was required was a credible threat that signaled their willingness to defect. The strategic impact of the alliance was well understood by Catherine Marshall, who, in a private council meeting of the Election Fighting Fund proclaimed:

> There is no doubt that this new development of our policy is going to prove a very effective weapon. We have at last got a real sword in our hands instead of a foil with a guarded tip.[80]

The credibility of the Labour Party's threatened revolt that Marshall alludes to was made possible thanks to the National Union's administrative and financial support of the party, which was bolstered, in turn, by the party's promise not to support electoral reform that excluded women. Labour's promise was put to the test and reaffirmed during the events that surrounded the 1916 Speaker's Conference on electoral reform, when, in the course of the committee's negotiations, Arthur Henderson threatened to resign from the cabinet if women were not included in the government bill. Above all, this history demonstrates the power of an innovative electoral strategy in shaping electoral reform in a context marked by political volatility. By forming a crosscutting alliance with

---

[79] Pugh 2000. In reality, the suffragists did bend to the party's wishes, sponsoring every election that the party contested after 1912 except three. Two of these were scheduled too close to the election for the EFF to become involved, and the third was fielded against a pro-suffrage Liberal, driving the suffragists to abstain as in line with the conditions of the alliance.

[80] Report of the EFF Private Council Meeting. CAC/DMAR/3/54. 12-Jul-1912.

the Labour Party, the suffragists were able to take advantage of a shift in the political opportunity structure which brought the Labour Party into a more prominent position in order to secure the vote for a large share of women in the UK. The question that remains is whether shifts in the competitive landscape were also important for establishing women's suffrage in other contexts.

4

Remember the Ladies: Competition and Mobilization in the United States

In a well-known letter written to her husband, then a delegate to the 1776 Continental Congress, Abigail Adams implored the future president to "remember the ladies and be more favorable and generous to them than your ancestors."[1] She meant, by this, that the congressional delegates should remember the many sacrifices that women had made for the sake of their country's independence, and therefore reward women with more freedom under the new regime than they had enjoyed under the old.

Despite Abigail Adams's exhortation, the constitution written down by the founders after the Revolutionary War was won made only two provisions for the electoral franchise, neither of which made full citizens of American women. Article I, Section 2 established that whoever was eligible to vote for the "most numerous" office in each federal state would be allowed to vote for the national House of Representatives;[2] and Article II, Section 1 established that state legislatures had the power to choose the president's electors. After the founding, nearly 144 years passed before an amendment was ratified by the federal government that declared that voting rights could not be withheld on the basis of sex.

Decentralized authority over voting rights in the states prompted early activists to pursue a multi-faceted strategy: from school boards and municipal councils to state legislatures and branches of the judiciary, suffragists sought the right to vote at all levels of government.[3] Carrie Chapman Catt, the architect of the successful push for the Nineteenth

---

[1] 31 March 1776. Quoted in Butterfield et al. 2002: 121.

[2] Under the state legislature's discretion a person who could vote for the state House could vote for the national House. Until the Seventeenth Amendment provided for "direct" election in 1913, national senators were chosen by state legislatures.

[3] Note that the term "suffragist" refers to movement activists who used legal means to pursue reform, while "suffragette" is generally reserved to describe militant activists. Over time, specific organizations and members could cross or straddle these boundaries.

Amendment, recalled that to get the word "male" out of the US constitution required:

> fifty-six campaigns of referenda to male voters; 480 campaigns to urge Legislatures to submit suffrage amendments to voters; 47 campaigns to induce State constitutional conventions to write woman suffrage into State constitutions; 277 campaigns to persuade State party conventions to include woman suffrage planks; 30 campaigns to urge presidential party conventions to adopt woman suffrage planks in party platforms, and 19 campaigns with 19 successive Congresses.[4]

These thousands of appeals for suffrage at the state level gave policy-makers ample opportunity to reform or to resist voting rights expansion. Along with many other suffragists, Catt saw political parties as a key obstacle to women's inclusion. She continued, "During this long stretch of time, the dominant political parties, pitted against each other since 1860, used their enormous organized power to block every move on behalf of woman suffrage."[5] In other words, the dominant parties did everything in their power to prevent changes to the status quo.[6] In addition to resistance by political parties, a vibrant anti-suffrage movement worked to prevent women's political inclusion.[7]

It is tempting to think that state leaders were either for or against women's enfranchisement, and that this stance applied in all realms of participation. But in fact the landscape of suffrage expansion for women in the United States is as diverse as the country's terrain. Many of the states that denied women voting rights at the national level gave women lower forms of voting rights, such as the school board franchise. The timeline in figure 4.1 sets out these state level patterns. For every five-year interval from 1840 to 1920, the timeline indicates whether women could vote in school board elections, municipal elections, presidential elections, or had full suffrage rights. If two types of right were granted in the same year, the timeline depicts the highest level granted. When a state joined the union after 1870, figure 4.1 presents the year of statehood.

---

[4] Catt and Shuler 1923: 107.

[5] Ibid.: 108.

[6] Not one of the national parties took suffrage on its platform until both did in 1916.

[7] Work on anti-suffrage mobilization includes Camhi 1994 and Marshall 1997. Due to foot-dragging, complicated registration procedures, and Jim Crow laws, American women in some states did not get to vote in the 1920 election.

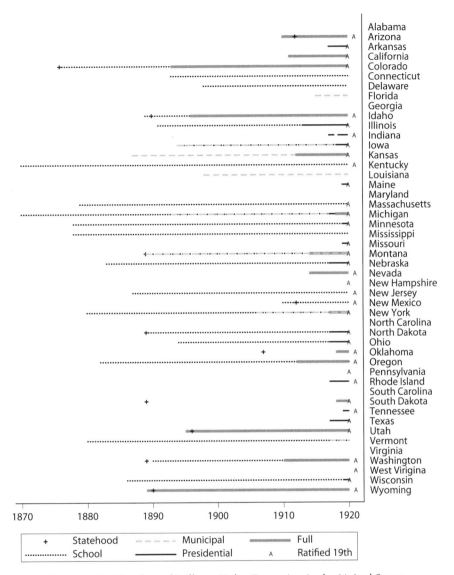

FIGURE 4.1. Timeline of Suffrage Rights Expansion in the United States.

As the timeline in figure 4.1 shows, a mere ten states withheld all forms of voting from women before the Nineteenth Amendment. In the Northeast, only New Hampshire and Pennsylvania showed such reluctance; the other eight holdouts were in the South. Occupying a middle ground between states that extended no franchise rights to women and places

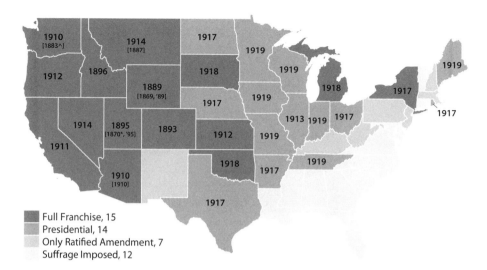

Full Franchise, 15
Presidential, 14
Only Ratified Amendment, 7
Suffrage Imposed, 12

FIGURE 4.2. Map of National Suffrage Extensions in the United States. The darkest shade represents states that gave women full voting rights on the same terms as men. The intermediate shade depicts the presidential franchise. States in the lightest shade did not give women national voting rights before the Nineteenth Amendment.

where women could participate equally were three groups. Those states that granted only school board suffrage: Connecticut, Massachusetts, New Jersey, Maine, Delaware, Kentucky, and Mississippi; those states that allowed municipal suffrage but no higher levels of participation: Florida and Louisiana; and states that allowed for the presidential franchise but nothing else: Illinois, Missouri, Maine, Rhode Island, Arkansas, Tennessee, and Texas. The final group of fifteen states gave women the vote on equal terms as men prior to the Nineteenth Amendment.

Figure 4.2 shows the geography of national suffrage rights for women. The darkest shaded states gave women suffrage in the full gamut of elections, on equal terms as men. The states in the middle allowed women to vote in presidential but not congressional or state legislative races. The dates of the extension as a state are listed in the center, and territorial enfranchisement is listed in brackets. As can be seen, there is a clear pattern of full suffrage rights, with western states emerging as early adopters long before any eastern or southern states extended such rights.[8] Yet even among the fifteen states that gave women voting rights

---

[8] Although there are debates about which states were "southern" in this period (Texas, in particular, is debatably "western")—I define regions here in a conventional way according to the census classification.

on equal terms as men, there is considerable variation: the Wyoming territory admitted women as early as 1869, while California, Oregon, and Washington followed nearly forty years later.[9] Early enfranchisement in western states and the lack of voting rights in many forms in the South provokes a question as to why women in the United States were successful at gaining access to voting rights in some states and unsuccessful in other states. Is the regional pattern in figure 4.2 reducible to things like political culture on the frontier? To male resistance to temperance politics? To partisanship? To suffrage mobilization? This chapter takes up these themes by exploring the articulation of the women's suffrage plank and the political forces that gave way to suffrage within and across states.

The American "woman suffrage" movement, as it was called by contemporaries, is arguably the most studied women's movement of all time. To understand the breadth of historical work on which this book draws, interested readers can look to the footnotes for histories of the movement as a whole, for regional analyses, and for state-specific treatments.[10] In addition to the extensive work by historians, a robust social science literature has long debated why the movement was more successful in some contexts than in others. Explanations have focused on the difficulty of overcoming state amendment procedures, the "gendered" opportunity structure that made men in some states more receptive to suffragists' arguments, the direct-action tactics adopted by movement leaders in some states but not in others, and the importance of male constituents' preferences in providing a justification for parties to support suffrage.[11]

[9] In a first hand account of the passage of suffrage reform in Wyoming, one Justice Kingman wrote that the author of the Wyoming suffrage bill persuaded Democratic representatives to vote for the bill by claiming the governor would veto it, "insisting at the same time, that it would give the Democrats an advantage in future elections" by burnishing their liberal bona fides and bringing notoriety to the state. Quoted in Grimes 1967: 57; and "The Woman Voter of the West," *The Westerner*, Aug. 1912: 4. Also see Morgan 1972.

[10] First is a rich historiography of the women's suffrage movement that includes the writings of suffragists themselves as documented in the *History of Women's Suffrage* (HWS), Carrie Chapman Catt's memoirs of the movement, and the pioneering work of suffrage historians such as Eleanor Flexner (1995) and Ellen Carol Dubois (1987, 1998). The historiography includes, too, excellent state- and city-level accounts of suffrage mobilization, accounts of suffragists' relations to the Democratic and Republican parties, details on Woodrow Wilson's initial resistance to and later advocacy for suffrage, and a new wave of work on the role of race and anti-suffrage mobilization in stalling (white) women's political inclusion. On the western suffrage movement, see Mead 2004; on interactions between suffragists and parties: Morgan 1972, Gustafson 2001; on Wilson: Morgan 1972, Behn 2012; on race: Davis 2001, Free 2015, Green 1997; on anti-suffrage: Camhi 1974 and Marshall 1997.

[11] State-level electoral reform generally required a state constitutional amendment, which, in every state but Delaware, was subject to passage by a popular referendum. To further

Although most suffrage scholars see women's activism as critical for the state and national level reforms, quantitative relationships between the strength of the movement and women's enfranchisement have not always been detected, and there are questions about whether suffragists mattered more for setting the political agenda or for actually seeing legislation through to the end.[12]

Ultimately, much of the social scientific work comes to two important conclusions about suffrage across the states. First, although suffrage politics were deeply partisan in any given state, suffrage itself could not be attributed to any single party.[13] Across all of the US states, there were seventy legislative sessions in which a bill for women's suffrage on equal terms as men passed both houses of a state legislature.[14] Among these, the Democrats had control of both houses in 11 percent of cases and the Republicans were in power in 64 percent of cases. Although there are more instances in which Republicans passed suffrage bills, they were also more likely to be in power and thus had more opportunities to pass such legislation.[15] In addition, partisanship has been found to be a weak predictor of support for suffrage in national congressional roll-call votes and in patterns of referendum voting in the states.[16] This does not mean that partisan logic was unimportant, but rather that the electoral conditions that drive an incentive to extend the franchise, and popular conceptions of women's future behavior may have been different in different states.[17]

---

complicate the matter, through what became known as the "Illinois" loophole—because it was first implemented in Illinois—state legislatures could bypass the referendum process and enfranchise women as presidential electors. McCammon et al. 2001; McCammon and Campbell 2001; Banaszak 1996b; 1998; McConnaughy 2013. Marilley 1996.

[12] Banaszak (1996b: table 4) finds that in the US, movement strength is correlated with some but not all measures of women's suffrage at the state level, while McConnaughy (2013: tables 6.5 and 6.7) finds quantitatively small, but statistically significant, relationships between state membership in the largest suffrage organization and suffrage reform. See, too, King et al. (2005) on the efficacy of the movement in different stages of the legislative process.

[13] There is, in addition, an argument that urban male residents were less receptive to suffrage in referendum voting. McDonagh and Price 1985: 431.

[14] These calculations are all my own using the King et al. (2005) database described herein.

[15] Republicans held power in 42 percent of the state sessions in the relevant period of suffrage reforms, while the Democrats held power in 31 percent of state sessions.

[16] McDonagh 1989; Teele 2018; McDonagh and Price 1985.

[17] This echoes the discussion in a recent book on women's political behavior after the Nineteenth Amendment in which Corder and Wolbrecht (2016) argue that women in any given state (like men) tended to vote with the dominant party in that state. Since regional patterns of partisanship are important for understanding women's actual vote choice, we might suspect that parties would have made different predictions about women's likely votes in different regions.

The second major finding among social scientists is that third parties played an important role in galvanizing suffrage, particularly in the western states.[18] Although third parties only controlled the legislature in 4 percent of cases where an equal suffrage bill passed both houses, the electoral threat that they posed may have driven the Republicans or Democrats to sponsor electoral reform.[19] What has been less emphasized is the fact that in 20 percent of cases where a full suffrage bill passed both state legislative houses, a different party controlled each branch. This is remarkable given that supermajorities were often necessary to change state electoral laws. The varied basis of party support for suffrage across the states suggests that something more than partisan identification or ideologies related to women's role in society was at work in driving women's enfranchisement in the US.

As in the book as a whole, I contend that suffragists' ability to form a broad movement influenced their success in states that were more competitive. Under the US's winner-takes-all electoral rules, which often produces two-party competition, a threat from a third party or a divided legislature is a strong indication that the political landscape is competitive. In most states, politicians initially resisted reform, claiming there was not enough evidence that women actually wanted the vote. Suffragists responded to this criticism first by trying to rally more middle-class women to the movement and then, after 1910, by reaching out to working classes in key urban areas such as New York City and San Francisco. The formation of a broad coalition of women, symbolized by growing membership in a large non-partisan suffrage organization, in combination with competitive conditions in state legislatures, was crucial to securing politicians' support for women's suffrage in the states.

This chapter substantiates the book's central argument in three ways. first, it gives a broad overview of the phases of the US suffrage movement, arguing that the salience of political cleavages related to race, ethnicity, nativity, and class influenced the type of movement suffragists sought to build. After many losses and with the infusion of new ideas, especially about class, in the early twentieth century, the movement expanded to

---

[18] Grimes 1967; Mead 2004. McConnaughy (2013: 215, 257ff.), also shows that electoral vulnerability often rose just prior to women's enfranchisement in the states. King et al. (2005) show that the number of parties is positively correlated with the introduction of suffrage bills and passage in at least one legislative chamber. However, cf. McCammon and Campbell (2001), who do not find a correlation between third-party presence and final date of state enfranchisement in their event history analyses.

[19] McConnaughy 2013: 257ff.

include women from the working classes and adopted new strategies of raising awareness and new forms of organization that proved critical to state legislative change. After charting this history I turn to describing the political geography of the Gilded Age, showing how the diversity of political competition and party organization that characterized the several regions mirrors the pattern of women's enfranchisement across the states.

Although many social scientists have theorized that the local electoral context mattered for women's suffrage, I develop a multifaceted approach to measuring competition—both by drawing on old data to construct new measures and by creating new data related to the presence of political machines in the states over time. Political machines, which presided over urban politics from Trenton to San Francisco, were run by bosses and subscribed to by clients under a currency of patronage. An indicator of machine strength in the states is useful because, as several historians and political scientists have argued, machines sought political monopolies based on the lower-class male vote, and often strenuously resisted women's enfranchisement.[20] After describing these measures, I turn to a quantitative analysis of the relationship between the suffrage movement's strength, the level and form of political competition, and support for women's suffrage in state legislatures. In combination with women's mobilization, low competition (conceptualized by large majorities and political machines) is associated with a lower probability of enfranchisement, while high competition (conceptualized by a close runner-up) is associated with a higher probability of reform. The quantitative section also investigates the interaction between competition and mobilization—that is, whether the probability of supporting suffrage, which is higher when women's mobilization is higher, rises even more when competition is more robust. I argue that such an interaction does exist at the highest levels of competition.

Finally I construct a number of indicators that can be thought of as forming "alternative" hypotheses about the expansion of the franchise to women in the United States, including measures of progressive political reforms; indicators of gender egalitarianism within the states; and a battery of measures related to temperance politics within states, including an original measure of membership in the Women's Christian Temperance Union (WCTU). None of these alternative measures explain

---

[20] Women's organizations often claimed that female voters would help to clean up politics, giving political machines specific reasons to resist women's enfranchisement (Buenker 1971; Flexner 1995: 309).

more of the variation in state level enfranchisement than the competition and mobilization variables, and including them in the analysis does not overturn the main findings. Hence there is good evidence that political competition and women's mobilization were important in the moments that led to women's suffrage in the states.

State-level politics mattered, not only to women within the states, but also because the federal structure of US political system meant that state legislative change was paramount for passing the Nineteenth Amendment in 1920. Article V of the US Constitution requires that constitutional amendments receive two-thirds support in both the House and the Senate or, alternatively, that two-thirds of the states call a convention. Thereafter, three-quarters of the states have to ratify the amendment. This high hurdle meant that it would have been nearly impossible to get a national suffrage amendment without considerable support in the states and without support of national congressmen. Thus state delegations to the national chambers needed some incentive to support reform. As more states adopted suffrage, national representatives' fates were chosen, in part, by female voters. The increased pressure from suffragists within states, as well as the national parties' concerns that they would lose women's votes in the states with suffrage if they failed to support an amendment, paved the way to the national reform.

THE SUFFRAGE MOVEMENT IN FOUR ACTS

Reading the early writings of suffragists themselves, newspaper accounts, Carrie Chapman Catt's papers, classic accounts of the movement, newer local histories of mobilization, and recent studies on the anti-suffrage movement suggests that the US suffrage movement can be periodized by four moments. The years after 1848 mark an early phase in which a very small segment of bourgeois women, many of whom were part of the abolition movement, drew heavily on natural rights discourse to argue for women's inclusion.[21] Second is the post-Reconstruction phase in which racist, xenophobic, and classist arguments were more

---

[21] There is a big historiographical debate about Aileen Kraditor's early claim that natural rights discourse was fully replaced by racialized discourse after the Civil War. Most historians now think that both strains were prevalent in different periods, but that as the character of the movement changed and it grew, the strategic deployment of racialized arguments became more common before 1900 and less common thereafter. See Green 1997, Kraditor 1981, Wheeler 1995, Mead 2004.

prominent, but where sectional splits among bourgeois suffragists produced different strategies of reform—with one organization focusing on a national amendment and another focusing on a "states rights" approach to suffrage.[22] During the third period, beginning in the mid-1880s, a broader, but still exclusionary, coalition was formed using "expediency" arguments—that politics itself would benefit from women's input—to draw more middle-class women into the fold. This period also marked the growth in the elite anti-suffrage movement. Finally, after 1900, and especially after 1910, mobilization of the working class became an explicit part of suffrage strategy through which important victories in California and eventually New York were achieved through assiduous mobilization of the working classes in the major cities.

As in American history more generally, race, nativity, and region, and ideas about the proper role of these elements in politics, were dividing forces in the suffrage movement. After Reconstruction, white bourgeois suffragists, even those who had been staunch abolitionists, focused their energy on mobilizing women that were educated and relatively well-off into their ranks. Hoping to prove to the public that the majority of women did want the vote, suffragists generally formed non-partisan organizations. Their recruitment became more successful when they began appealing to ideas about "republican motherhood" and "municipal housekeeping." While anti-suffragists argued that voting would put an undue burden on women without having any obvious social benefit, suffragists claimed that society needed educated women to vote because these women would be the antidote to the poison of popular participation and immigrant, poor white, and black male voting rights. The suffragists' line of reasoning was so powerful that by the 1890s, even those women not particularly keen for the vote admitted that they would do their duty to cancel out the votes of the ignorant and unworthy groups. In forming such a coalition, and by maintaining a non-partisan stance, suffragists were able to claim that women were not mere partisan actors, and to hint thereby that the vote choice of women was not a foregone conclusion. The flexibility afforded by this strategy allowed suffragists to seek alliances with parties where they saw advantage: from the populists in Colorado, Democrats in Kansas, socialists in New York, and Republicans in midwestern states, suffragists put their weight behind

---

[22] Dubois (1998) is one authoritative account of the split in the suffrage movement after reconstruction.

whichever group seemed the most supportive of suffragist demands. This proved particularly effective in states that were more competitive.

Race, Class, and the Suffrage Coalition

In the popular imagination, a woman's convention held in 1848 in Seneca Falls galvanized the struggle for the female franchise. In the tiny town in upstate New York, a group of precocious white female activists, many of whom had cut their teeth as Garrisonian abolitionists, came together to proclaim women's rights. The conference delegates were involved in several days' debate which culminated in a proclamation, *The Declaration of Sentiments*, that promulgated rights for women by documenting the "repeated injuries and usurpation" by men toward women. The list of injuries is long, and includes women's lack of the vote, lack of voice in the laws that they must obey, their legal dependency (particularly after marriage), their unequal access to education, and psychological subjection associated with women's inferior status.[23] But if Elizabeth Cady Stanton, Quaker minister Lucretia Mott, and Susan B. Anthony, among others, ultimately won the day with a resolution for women's suffrage, the decision was highly contentious, hardly unanimous, and failed to catalyze a major movement for suffrage in the convention's aftermath. For that moment we must fast-forward about twenty years, to the Reconstruction debates after the Civil War.

As the country began to recover from devastating internecine conflict, Radical Republicans in Congress argued for provisions for a black franchise in the decimated South. Having worked for abolition and stumped around the country with the likes of Frederick Douglass, suffragists including Susan B. Anthony were hopeful that whatever decision was reached on the black franchise would include provisions for the female franchise. But the women's hopes were dashed in the name of the "negro's hour"—the idea that in that particular moment the only essential reform entailed enfranchising black men—and so by law (if not in fact thereafter), black men attained the vote and white women did not.[24] Anger and indignation followed for many of the suffragists. All arguments made in defense of the black franchise, they countered, could just as easily apply to women's suffrage. Like black men, women had distinct interests that

[23] For a first-hand account, see Anthony et al. 1969: 70–71.

[24] See Flexner (1995: chapter 8), and Keyssar (2000: 180ff), who writes: "nowhere did the enfranchisement of women seem likely to vest Republicans or Democrats with any discernible partisan advantage," hence the parties had no incentive to reform.

could not be represented by the current government; like black men, many women had provided invaluable service during the civil war; like black men, the enfranchisement of women boiled down to a matter of justice.[25] These arguments fell on deaf ears. Ultimately, what Anthony and others failed to grasp, or, more likely, refused to accept, was the political— rather than solely moral—basis of the Radical Republicans' decision to emphasize the negro's hour instead of the woman's hour.

Politicians in the national legislature, however, understood well the electoral implications of extending the vote to black men while simultaneously excluding white women. In December of 1867, as the United States Senate debated the introduction of the franchise for black men in the District of Columbia, the issue of women's suffrage was raised in Congress for the first time. The debate is instructive, as its blunt and fine points highlight all the issues of the day, including whether women could reason (many thought they could), whether they could exercise the vote responsibly (yes), whether they wanted the vote (less clear), and whether it was just. On this latter point, a few thought the justice apparent and would vote for suffrage on that alone, while others claimed justice was beside the point entirely. Virtue and political interest should determine the scope of the franchise.[26]

Although the bill on debate was primarily about the black male franchise, Senator Edgar Cowan (R-PA), in what was perceived to be an attempt to sink the black male vote, proposed an amendment that would strike the word "male" out of the original bill and thereby grant women in the District voting rights. Cowan faced considerable opposition within the chamber, and the amendment ultimately failed, but he proclaimed that the outcome would have been different if it were electorally expedient: "If [women's enfranchisement] became necessary in order to elect a dozen Senators to this body this winter, ... then I should have great hopes of carrying my amendment." Looking toward future elections and the composition of southern delegations, abolitionists and southern Republicans purposefully wanted to restrict the reform to black men

---

[25] Chapter 6 in Free (2015) does an excellent job of recounting the history and arguments made by suffragists against the reconstruction amendments. See especially p. 160ff for the point here.

[26] *Congressional Globe*, 39th Congress, 2nd Session, 11 Dec. 1867: 58. In the lengthy debate, some senators, like George Williams (R-OR) argued that women did not need the vote because they were not slaves and did not constitute a distinct class, but that in order to protect black men he would support that group's enfranchisement (p. 56). Henry Anthony (R-RI) countered that although the time had not yet come for enfranchisement, it would be coming soon and he would therefore vote for it (p. 56).

and exclude white women. They "had their eyes fixed on a windfall of 2,000,000 potential male Negro voters in the South, which they had no intention of jeopardizing by stirring up an unnecessary tempest over woman suffrage."[27]

Several disgruntled suffragists, including the eminent Stanton and Anthony, refused to concede a greater urgency for black men and the vote, and turned toward protesting the Reconstruction amendments.[28] In 1867, Stanton and Anthony broke with the Equal Rights Association (a group that had worked for black and female suffrage rights) and founded the National Women's Suffrage Association (NWSA). In the same year, southerners Lucy Stone and Henry Blackwell formed the American Women's Suffrage Association (AWSA).[29] Stanton and Anthony's National Women's Suffrage Association advocated for many causes related to women's well-being, but it worked foremost for a national amendment. Stone and Blackwell's American Women's Suffrage Association, on the other hand, eschewed a broad women's rights agenda and instead set its sights on pursuing suffrage at the state level.[30] The distinction between the national approach and the state-based approach within these two organizations was not only one of strategy—it was in part whether going for states first was the best route to the national amendment—but also of tension regarding the ultimate reform.

Many advocates for the strategy of state-led suffrage reform were patently against pursuing a national suffrage amendment. A prominent argument was that unlike a federal amendment, which would theoretically enfranchise all women regardless of race and nativity, state laws could be written in such a way as to enfranchise white women while still preventing women from other groups from voting.[31] The social concerns that drove the southern exclusionary strategy can be understood in the terms laid out in chapter 2—that the challenge of forming a broad feminist consciousness rises in the presence of extreme levels of inter-group inequality.[32] The social distance that existed in the South between

27 Flexner 1995: 145–146.
28 Ibid.: 148.
29 Ibid.: 155.
30 Ibid.: 156.
31 Green 1997; Behn 2012: 191.
32 Kraditor (1981) and Wheeler (1995) both stress the importance of white supremacy in the southern movement. Green (1997) gives a thorough treatment of race and class in both the suffrage and anti-suffrage movements in the South. Susan Marshall (1997) has described this as the "gendered class" privilege of some white women, and argues that this is the basis of women's activism against suffrage.

formerly enslaved people and whites led southern Democrats (the majority party across the south) to resist expansion of the franchise to black men, and formed a barrier between white suffragists and black women. Many white women benefited from the racial hierarchy in the South, and so aligning along the dimension of race could emerge for some as more important than aligning on the dimension of gender.

As evidenced by the state-based strategy of the American Women's Suffrage Association, the racial hierarchy led southern suffragists to articulate the demand for reform in a narrow way. Some southern white women wanted the vote, but only if they could avoid enfranchising black women and thereby dodge the subsidiary effects of a broad reform. An illustrative passage comes from Elna Green's comprehensive treatment of suffrage and anti-suffrage movements in the South. Kate Gordon, a vehement states' rights suffragist, remarked "if Louisiana employs an understanding clause to preserve white supremacy and will grant woman suffrage, then I will not have a word to say against it."[33] Gordon did believe in suffrage for women like herself in the south, but when the national amendment was on the horizon, Gordon and others worked to try to defeat the federal amendment: "white supremacy is going to be maintained by the South by fair or foul means."

Statistical rationales were trotted out to bolster southern suffragists' narrow delineation of the suffrage demand. First piloted by Stone and Blackwell, the argument that white women would "cancel out" the votes of the newly enfranchised blacks because whites were statistically more numerous became a recurring theme in suffrage debates in the press and on floors of legislatures. In 1867, Blackwell penned what is now a famous pamphlet, entitled "What the South Can Do," which entreated southern Democrats to recognize that the votes of emancipated men could be overcome by the ballots of "your four million Southern white women."[34] Specifically, Blackwell argued that since the Radicals of the North were fixed on "negro suffrage," and since another civil war should be avoided, a compromise should be reached on the adjustment of the franchise that was "acceptable to both sections." He estimated that of the 12 million inhabitants of the slave states, there would be 1.6 million white male voters, 1.6 million white female voters, and 800 thousand black voters of each sex. The way to bolster southern white power, at the same time as gaining more representation in national politics (as black people would

[33] Green 1997: 131.
[34] Quoted in Free 2015: 149.

no longer count as three-fifths of a person), would be to give women the vote at the same time. "Suppose all the negroes vote one way and all the whites the other, your white majority would be 1,600,000—equal to your present total vote."[35]

The statistical argument and its implications were perceived to be important for convincing white women to join the movement. Not only would women's suffrage reinforce white hegemony in the South, but also would end the question of regional fanaticism and push the North out of southern politics. Widely circulated around the 1870s, the statistical argument was also repeatedly invoked as a reason that legislators should agree to women's inclusion in the moments leading up to the national amendment.[36] But for a party that already considered itself secure, which could suffer defections of all black men and still win, there was little need to include women. What is more, including women might actually have impinged on the southern Democrats' electoral strategy. Said a Mississippi senator in the 1880s, "We are not afraid to maul a black man over the head if he dares to vote, but we can't treat women, even black women, that way. No, we'll allow no woman suffrage. It may be right, but we won't have it."[37] In other words, because black men's votes could be suppressed violently, Democrats could win a bigger share of the vote with just black men voting than if all men and women could cast ballots.

Shifting Suffrage Alliances

That many southern suffragists wanted state control of voting rights so that they could continue to exclude black voters is well known, and that southern white women's political consciousness would hew to the racial cleavage instead of the gender dimension is perhaps obvious. But what is remarkable about the post-Reconstruction period is that it marks the beginning of a moment in which even northern and former abolitionist suffragists employed racist, xenophobic, and classist rhetoric to argue that poor, ignorant, and black people were less deserving of political

[35] The pamphlet is reproduced in HWS, volume II, ch. XIX.

[36] For example, in the discussion surrounding the Nineteenth Amendment, Senator James Phelan (D-CA) assured his southern comrades, "So by extending the suffrage to women you do not change the present condition, deplorable as it may be in the eyes of the men of the South. You simply increase the electorate by the addition of women; and if they are less literate than the men, or if they hold no property . . . there is very little likelihood of their ever exercising the suffrage . . . The amendment, I am told, will increase by 20 per cent the voting white population in the South as a whole. So the South will be stronger. Where, then, is the danger?" Quoted in Behn 2012: 241.

[37] Quoted in Morgan 1972: 84.

rights than wealthy, educated, white women. The dark underbelly of suffragist history has been given good treatment as a normative issue and historical phenomenon in many works, including by Angela Davis and Rosalyn Terborg-Penn.[38] But the racist, nativist turn in the northern suffrage movement also deserves study as an example of how suffrage organizations could strategically employ exclusionary rhetoric to attempt to form a coalition across white cleavages.[39]

As historian Laura Free's recent book recounts, in the wake of Reconstruction, Stanton and Anthony were desperate to find an inroad to press the suffrage claim. Although their ultimate goal was a national amendment, they attempted to form coalitions with Democratic leaders in states where suffrage was up for discussion. After their abandonment by the Republican Party, Stanton later reflected, "We saw that our only chance was in getting the Democratic vote."[40] In 1868 they found a backer in George Francis Train, a Democrat, who gave them enough money to start a new suffrage paper, *The Revolution*. In an early issue, Stanton describes a possible reasoning behind a newfound alliance with Democrats: "the party out of power is always in a position to carry principles to their logical conclusions, while the party in power thinks only of what it can afford to do; hence, you can reason with minorities, while majorities are moved only by votes."[41]

Here, Stanton hints at the logic of women's enfranchisement: those in power are constrained by what they can afford to do—what I have called the need for additional voters. Those out of power, on the other hand, may be convinced to sign on to the movement if they think the issue through logically. The "logical conclusions" that she alludes to are about the effect of including black men but not women in the franchise. By being reminded of the potential benefits of women's enfranchisement—for electoral fortunes, white supremacy, and policy—an out-of-power party can come to support suffrage. In truth, the Republicans were aware of the logical conclusion of including white women. In the Northeast and Midwest, early suffragists hailed from the groups—native, white, Protestant—that formed the key Republican constituencies. Giving women the vote in those places may not have threatened the Republican Party, but it might added some uncertainty into elections because not all white women

---

[38] Davis 2011: chs. 4 and 7; Terborg-Penn 1998; Free 2015; Green 1997.

[39] This argument echoes those made about Margaret Sanger's adoption of eugenicist rhetoric to bring white men around to the idea of birth control. See Roberts 1994: ch. 2.

[40] Free 2015: 150.

[41] Stanton writing in *The Revolution* in 1868, as quoted in Free 2015: 156.

in the Northeast and Midwest were Republicans. Moreover, since the Democratic Party was dominating the South with a white supremacist platform, the only place where the Republicans could conceivably lose the majority of white women's votes was the South. Hence convincing the Republicans to support suffrage was a non-starter at the national level. This presented the suffragists with a double bind: Republicans could not be convinced to undermine their interests in the South, and Democrats in the rest of the country could not be convinced that women outside the South would vote for them in large enough numbers to support reform.

In the 1870s, then, suffragists and politicians faced one another in a stalemate. Many politicians claimed that women simply did not want the vote, and balked at the idea of including women without some evidence of support for suffrage within the various states. In order for the suffrage demand to move from parlors to the sphere of practical politics, suffragists had to form a mass movement and get some political backing for the cause. After few successes, in the 1880s the suffragists began to employ two forms of argument: that women's domestic role gave them unique moral positions on political matters, and that moral women voters would provide the antidote to the poison of certain types of male participation. Seeking a broad constituency, they strategically adopted racist, classist, and nativist language that became prominent in public conversations about the impact of the women's vote. The shift from natural–rights based arguments to what historian Aileen Kraditor called "expediency" arguments was a key innovation that transformed suffrage from a fledgling idea to a broad movement.[42] As McCammon and Campbell have shown, invocation of expediency arguments was highly correlated with women's suffrage success in the West.[43]

Elite Women as Antidote to the Country's Ills

In the early days of suffrage activism, opponents of women's inclusion made two big claims: first, that women simply did not want the vote— so why should they get the right in a national amendment?—and second, that without one single state adopting the reform, there was no evidence that national leaders would support it. This much was said on the floor of Congress, in the popular press, and by anti-suffragists.[44] To combat

[42] See footnote 21 in this chapter.

[43] McCammon and Campbell 2001.

[44] The claims that women did not want the vote were pervasive. For example, in a Democratic convention in South Dakota in 1890, a congressional candidate named Miller

these two ideas, suffragists sought to form a broad (white) coalition for voting rights and to secure support for the female franchise among state legislators.

Several histories describe well the elitism of suffrage rhetoric and the importance of exclusionary arguments for the advancement of the movement. Recently these ideas have been interpreted in a strategic light, with authors arguing that gendered class interests drove both suffrage and anti-suffrage strategy.[45] What is important to note is that the twin ideas—that women would be a salve to the nation's ills and that women's vote could be used to counteract the baser elements of politics—were circulated both among those women specifically interested in politics, as well as those who were less keen on formal political rights. Take, for example, a lengthy segment published in the *Indianapolis Journal* in 1888 called "Would the Women Vote?" in which more than twenty "prominent" women wrote to discuss plans for electoral participation.[46] The article is instructive both because of the range of opinions it displays and because of how the writers' constructions of arguments against or in favor of the vote displays the exclusionary logic forwarded by suffragists.

Among the respondents, only two women suggested they would not vote under any circumstances, but about half of the writers claimed that although they had not personally seen the need nor agitated for suffrage, they would consider it a duty to participate if given the vote. Several women cited an aversion to being mixed up "in mere machine politics," "wrangling and wrestling" at the polls, or mingling in the "political cauldron," and some suggested that their hesitance sprang from deeper misgivings about popular voting more generally. One Jenny June wrote, "I have never worked for suffrage because I do not believe in it for all men any more than for all women," and Sarah Orne Jewett claimed, "I believe it would have been better to carefully restrict the voting of men by high educational and certain property qualifications." June intimated that she would vote so as not to be debased vis-à-vis men in the republic—the "brutal and ignorant" to whom the country opens its arms—while Jewett claimed that women would not increase the "ignorant" vote but that "there will be a larger proportion of conscientious and unpartisan votes

---

declared that no decent women wanted the suffrage (25 July 1890, *Wessington Springs Herald*, South Dakota p. 1). Note that in this same year, under a Republican legislature, the South Dakotan legislature did pass a suffrage bill in both chambers but a referendum in that year failed.

[45] Free 2015; Marshall 1997; Green 1997.

[46] Kate Sanborn "Would the Women Vote?" *The Indianapolis Journal*, 28 Oct. 1888.

than are cast now." Similarly, Adeline Whitney did not want women to lose their essential, external place in society, but "might vote if pressed into the necessity by the voting of all sorts of other women." And finally, as Olive Thorne Miller wrote:

> Whatever my opinions as to the importance of desirability to women of the ballot, if the polls were opened to them I should feel obligated to vote, for the same reason that I insist every man should vote now; namely, that the intelligence of the country shall be represented as well as its ignorance.

Among those women who did not explicitly want the vote, the arguments suggest a balancing mentality was at work that specifically accounted for the impact of their votes relative to the votes of other groups. Many of these women voiced concern that the male franchise was already too expansive, but since they could not control that, if women were to be included, they would consider it a duty to vote in order to cancel out the bad effects of other voters.

On the other hand, those female writers who were more explicit in their desire for the vote had positive instead of negative reasons for wanting to vote. They cited "the justice of equal pay for equal work," for the sake of "women who have wrongs to right," and because women would "introduce a refining influence into politics." Departing from many anti-suffragists, the suffragists believed that women had political interests that were separate from interests of male relatives. Mary Booth argued that "facts show that voters alone have their interests properly guarded," while Frances Willard suggested that "for one-half the race to be wholly governed by laws made and administered by the other half is not fair play." Further, suffragists often argued that women's unique role in society—as mothers and carers—would be an important moral force in politics.

From these accounts we can glean distinctive political philosophies among women. Suffragists argued that women have unique interests that make women's participation in politics necessary and just. Non-suffragists did not have the same view of women's interests, but many would begrudgingly vote as their duty commanded. Both, however, referred to the female vote as a way to cancel out the bad effects instantiated by the choices of undesirable voters.

Women as an antidote to the poison of mass politics was invoked not only by the large suffrage organizations, but also by the Women's Christian Temperance Union. The WCTU, led by Frances Willard, emerged in the 1880s as a big (if potentially damaging) agitator for suffrage.[47] Willard believed that the many broad social goals of the organization related to education, health care, and food quality, among others, would be easier to gain if women had the vote. But she drew many women into the organization by explicitly wielding the moral valence of temperance.[48] For example, at the South Dakota state convention of the Women's Christian Temperance Union, the president of that chapter, a Mrs. Parker, claimed that women could help the government kitchen by "cleansing its pollution and putting to rights its disorder, ere the constantly increasing tide of filth, brought in from foreign lands shall render such a step necessary as our only hope of governmental salvation."[49] The path toward respectable suffrage politics was paved by fear of the "ignorant" votes. It was in light of these ideas that a mass constituency was formed.

The Growth of the Movement

The National and the American Suffrage Associations, after decades of division and failure, merged in 1890 to form the NAWSA. In that same year, the Women's Christian Temperance Union adopted a suffrage plank. Both organizations saw tremendous growth in the last quarter of the nineteenth century. Figure 4.3 shows membership information for these two organizations. The top panel plots the evolution of NAWSA membership in the US using data from Banaszak (1996b). The data summarize the number of members, per thousand residents in a given state, averaged by region. The bottom panel presents data that represent membership in the WCTU, and looks at the average value of dues paid per capita in a given region. The data were collected using minutes of the WCTU from various years. Although a raw membership figure was present in the organization's minutes in some years, this was often missing, and so dues, which were supposed to be allocated to a state based on membership, are used instead.

In both organizations, membership was generally highest in the Northeast and lowest in the South. However, for the NAWSA, there were

---

[47] The worry for non-WCTU suffragists was that women and women's votes would be rejected because of the temperance issue. This was the assessment of Abigail Scott Duniway, the pioneer suffragist from Oregon, who pinned an early Oregon loss on the temperance issue (Flexner 1995: 187).

[48] Willard believed that ordinary women could become more receptive to a women's rights agenda if they became involved with her organization. Early on, she argued that women could really only achieve their goals if they had the right to vote.

[49] *Wessington Springs Herald,* 25 July 1890, South Dakota, p. 1.

(a) National American Women's Suffrage Association membership

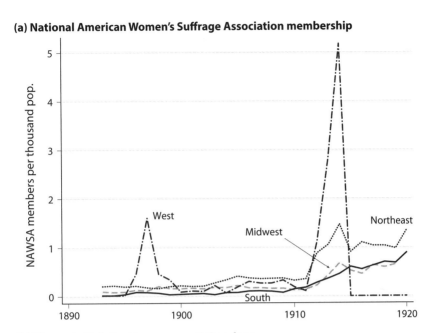

(b) Women's Christian Temperance Union dues

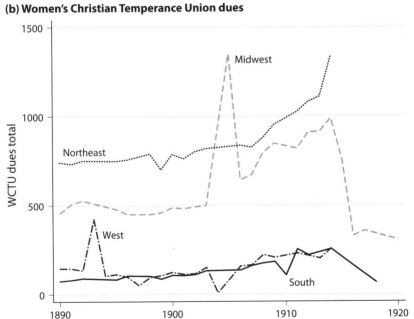

FIGURE 4.3. Membership in Two Major Suffragist Organizations. Source: Banaszak 1996b and WCTU, various years.

several moments of heightened activity in the West vis-à-vis the other regions.[50] Midwestern women were the second most mobilized group in each organization. These patterns in membership are mirrored in legislative activity related to suffrage. Figure 4.4 displays the entire history of suffrage bills in state legislative chambers across the period. Using data from King et al. (2005), I have coded suffrage bills into four broad categories of extension, which are depicted on the graph: full suffrage (F), municipal voting rights (M), school board suffrage (S), and presidential elector suffrage (P). The number of bills of each type are aggregated for the previous decade. In other words, a point corresponding to 1889 on the x-axis adds all proposals in a given category from 1880 to 1889.

Figure 4.4 shows a takeoff in the number of full suffrage proposals after 1870. Bills that would extend municipal and school-suffrage rights began to grow after 1880. Presidential suffrage bills gained steam after 1900, and, when Illinois became the first state to extend this form of right in 1913, suffragists in the National Association of Women's Suffrage Societies began to push for this type of bill elsewhere. In the universe of 1,124 suffrage bills, 514 were for limited suffrage and 610 were for full suffrage. "Partial" suffrage bills were more likely to restrict which women would have the vote than bills that would have allowed women to vote in all realms. Overall, though, exclusionary clauses in the bill language were rare—fifty three partial suffrage bills had one exclusion (10.3 percent), and only thirteen of the full suffrage bills had one exclusion (2.1 percent).[51] The most common form of restriction for limited suffrage constrained the eligible electorate to taxpayers or property owners only. Aliens were excluded in only one bill, and non-whites were excluded in five bills. The decades surrounding the Civil War and Reconstruction, from 1860 to 1880, marks the greatest exclusionary period. In that period, around 68 percent of all partial suffrage bills proposed that only taxpaying women should be included. This, in spite of the fact that taxpaying had been eliminated from white male franchise requirements after the 1840s. The necessity of exclusions likely fell once Reconstruction collapsed and Jim Crow laws were in force. Thus, although early on many of the partial

---

[50] For example, Nevada saw membership surge just prior to a bill's passage by a third party legislature in 1895, and again after 1910 when two consecutive sessions of a split legislature finally passed and referred the bill. The referendum, the state's first, succeeded in 1914.

[51] For detailed breakdowns, an online appendix to Teele (2018) is available at doi:10.7910/DVN/EVYI2H.

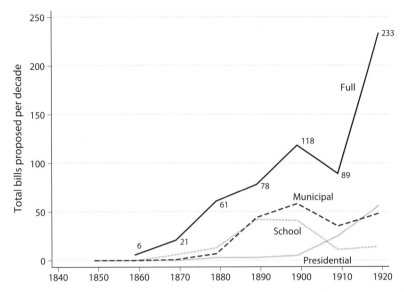

FIGURE 4.4. Suffrage Bill Proposals in State Legislatures in Previous Decade, 1840–1920.

suffrage proposals would have restricted the vote to only some women, the presence of these restrictions fell throughout the era.

Generally speaking, full suffrage proposals did not carry restrictions on the types of women that would be included. There are two intuitions for why this is so. First, suffragists may actually have supported universal suffrage but simply used exclusionary rhetoric to try to grow their coalition.[52] Second, since there were, in the late nineteenth century, few restrictions on men's right to vote in state and national legislative elections, exclusions for women in this realm may have been difficult to justify and write. Writing a partial suffrage law, on the other hand, which would exclude women from particular elections, may have squared better with excluding some women at the same time.

The rise of more inclusive proposals for women's suffrage beginning around 1910 reflected a transformation in the suffragists' strategy described above. In 1909 the National American Women's Suffrage Association circulated a pamphlet arguing that "the people who are

[52] Lerner (1981) makes this argument about NAWSA propaganda and interpretation of the New York win in 1917, where the leaders knew they had to mobilize the Italian garment workers and the Upper West Side Jews to get the referendum through, but where they gave credit to the Upper East Side WASPS.

fighting for industrial freedom who will be our vital force at the finish." The "daughters" of the suffrage movement, which metaphorically included a younger generation of suffragists and literally included the daughter of Elizabeth Cady Stanton—Harriet Stanton Blatch—were responsible for ushering in this new ideology of suffragism after the turn of the century. Ellen Dubois credits Blatch with the shift in suffragism that opened organizations up to working-class women by integrating concerns of these women (including wages and working conditions) into their mobilization strategy. Having studied under the Pankhursts in England, Blatch introduced more "militant" street tactics, including open air meetings and boisterous rallies. She also worked "insider" channels to put more pressure on politicians.[53] Blatch believed that there were common interests that could unite the rising professional class of female workers and industrial workers, and she worked to mobilize garment workers and their husbands in the push for the New York State referendum.

Though the suffrage movement in New York had been active for more than sixty years, a re-organization by Blatch, Carrie Chapman Catt, and others after 1914 sought not only to mobilize new women, but also to get men on board with women's votes.[54] The much-anticipated New York state referendum in 1915 failed, but the tireless activity and a precinct-by-precinct grass-roots strategy that was set into motion around that time pushed the 1917 referendum to victory with the help of working-class male voters. Precinct-level returns showed the importance of immigrant votes in securing the New York state victory. The Italian workers on the Lower East side and the Jewish workers in Harlem and the Upper West side came out for suffrage, while the predominantly Irish Greenwich Village and Anglo-Saxon precincts of Upper East side, along with the Germans and Slavic immigrants in Yorkville, voted against.[55]

As we have seen, the suffrage movement grew tremendously after the 1890s and especially after 1910, but suffragists were not as successful in all states as they were in some. The work of historians, which has documented the changing social bases of the suffrage movement, has

---

[53] See Dubois 1987: 36, 38, 50. Quote on p. 52.

[54] Lerner 1981: 23.

[55] Lerner 1981: 142–43. In spite of the obvious role played by working-class women and working class men in the big city victories, mainstream suffrage propaganda attributed the victory to the conversion of men of the white-anglo variety. Although Lerner (1981: ch. 3) does not use the expression "respectability politics," her argument is that this type of narrative was strategically employed by the NAWSA so as not to disturb the coalitions being built for suffrage in the Midwest. See Neuman (2017) on the role played by New York's fashionable socialites after the turn of the century.

been complemented by the work of social scientists, which shows how diversity and divisiveness in the movement led to tactical innovations that drew more people to the movement.[56] Broad mobilization was crucial for securing some states, but did not work as well in others. Consider the difference between California and Massachusetts. In California, after a failed referendum in 1896, sometimes credited to the urban machines in Sacramento and San Francisco, the movement re-grouped, gained working-class support, and won the 1911 referendum.[57] In Massachusetts, on the other hand, despite a fourfold growth in the number of suffragists from 1900 to 1914, reform was not forthcoming. Members of the Women's Trade Union League who were suffragists argued that women would support progressive candidates to bolster factory legislation.[58] But the entrenched Republican Party, which had defeated factory regulation, child labor, and temperance, also successfully resisted suffrage. Thus the Massachusetts referendum was defeated in 1915 and was not resuscitated thereafter. To understand why strong movements, which were a feature of both of these states, led to victory in one but not the other, we must turn to how politicians responded to women's entreaties for the vote.

POLITICIANS AND THE WOMEN'S VOTE

Why were suffragists successful in some states but not in others? In the following section I will explore quantitative sources that record support for suffrage reform at the state level, and show that suffrage support was higher in states where power was less entrenched and competition was more robust. But first, drawing on qualitative sources, I document the strategic nature of the conversation about suffrage by providing evidence that politicians were concerned with the nature of the women's vote. Often, political support for suffrage depended on individuals or party actors, suggesting that suffrage would help their group politically. Although few thought that women would vote as a bloc, both party elites and suffragists expected the female vote to tilt toward the Republican Party.[59] In fact, it was often the anti-suffragists who argued that women's

[56] McCammon 2003: 805.

[57] Englander 1992.

[58] Strom 1975: 304.

[59] Gustafson 2001: 133–4; Corder and Wolbrecht 2016: 131–135. This argument goes against some previous claims about women's enfranchisement—made in passing by Acemoglu and Robinson (2000: 1186), but in greater depth by McConnaughy (2013)—that politicians expected women's votes would not matter at all for electoral outcomes.

votes would merely double support for each party because, they claimed, women and men shared the same interests. If this were the case, the long denial of this right to women does not make much sense. It is precisely because politicians were concerned that women and men had different interests, and that women were not a sure bet for their party, that they resisted reform.

Expectations for Women's Votes

To understand whether elites expected women's votes to merely replicate men's, it is important to put the suffrage movement—or more precisely, the suffrage movements—into context. Women's moral purity and their positions as mothers were often claimed to give women unique purchase on political problems and justified women's enfranchisement. This moral argument was capitalized on by suffragists—as described above—and was successful in drawing adherents to the movement. It was bolstered by women's prolific civic activism on social issues, such as temperance, compulsory education, child welfare, the eradication of child labor, and labor protection for women. In the words of one advocate who was "Interested in all topics of the time: education, religion, politics, the liquor questions, social purity," she would gladly go to the polls "to exert an influence in the direction of progress and reform."[60] In the late nineteenth century, the female vote was often thought to be anti-saloon, verging on prohibitionist, and therefore closely linked to the Women's Christian Temperance Union and the Republican Party.[61]

The fear that women were more likely than men to support prohibition caused the liquor lobby to mobilize against women's inclusion in many states.[62] At a Democratic convention in South Dakota in 1890, where certain women urged the party to support suffrage, anti-suffrage protestors won the day with signs that read "we are against prohibition and Susan B. Anthony. We want our beer, and the men do the voting."[63] Suffrage history is rife with organized liquor's attempts to forestall reform: in 1895 in California the Wholesale Liquor Dealers' League beseeched saloonkeepers, hotels, and grocers to vote against suffrage claiming, "It is in your interest and ours to vote against this amendment. We request and urge you to vote and work against it and do all you can to

---

[60] Kate Sanborn, "Would the Women Vote?" *The Indianapolis Journal*, 28 Oct. 1888.
[61] Grimes 1967: 68; McDonagh and Price 1985: 418.
[62] Catt and Shuler 1923: ch. 10.
[63] *Wessington Springs Herald*, 25 July 1890, South Dakota, p. 1.

defeat it."[64] And, fearing that women represented the "dry" vote, the head of the United Liquor Dealers personally went to fight against suffrage in Illinois in 1913.[65] Even on the eve of the ratification of the Nineteenth Amendment in Tennessee (after the prohibition amendment was in force), liquor companies plied state legislators with whiskey in an attempt to sway the decision against suffrage.[66] Because women were often linked to temperance, and the temperance issue was so closely linked to the Republicans, women were often expected to lean Republican.[67]

Nevertheless, the association of women with the Republican Party does not necessarily hold up across regions, or throughout the seventy year period during which the suffrage battle was waged. In the South, the expectation was that white women would vote Democratic to preserve racial hegemony. In fact, Southern suffragists notoriously argued that they should be enfranchised precisely because adding their numbers to the electorate would shore up the white majority.[68] Yet it was not only in the South where Democrats may have seen some potential advantage in the women's vote. In the early twentieth century, as nativist fears were sparked by a large influx of immigrants, women's votes, even among immigrant groups, were hailed as a salve to the votes of the less scrupulous men. In a House judiciary committee on suffrage in 1908, progressive Senator Robert Owen (D-OK) said he would have been willing to give the ballot to lower-class immigrant women "because the vote of the male immigrants is largely dominated by the saloon and brothel influences and the vote of the women would counteract the votes of this class of males."[69] As we will see with the debate over the Nineteenth Amendment below, many progressive Democrats claimed that they came around to the issue of suffrage because of the supposedly moral force women were to exercise on politics.

In addition to harboring an intuition that women would vote distinctively, politicians debating whether to enfranchise women often hinted at the strategic considerations that sustained their choice, and at times

---

[64] Grimes 1967: 86.

[65] NAWSA 1940: 87.

[66] Catt and Shuler 1923: ch 10.

[67] As Corder and Wolbrecht (2016: 131–135) argue, although in 1920 the Democratic platform contained more planks advocated by the League of Women voters and did reach out to women, Republicans are seen to have had a stronger pro-suffrage claim in that election.

[68] Morgan 1972: 15–16.

[69] "Woman's Suffrage Discussed Universal Suffrage Advocated by Senator Owen of Oklahoma," *The Idaho Statesman*, 4 March 1908.

suggested that enfranchising women would help (or hurt) them in particular ways. In a firsthand account of the passage of suffrage reform in Wyoming, one Justice John W. Kingman wrote that the author of the Wyoming suffrage bill persuaded Democratic representatives to vote for the unlikely bill by insisting "that it would give the Democrats an advantage in future elections" by burnishing their liberal bona fides and bringing notoriety to the state.[70]

Depending on the state being considered, contemporary observers had different intuitions about the fate of the female vote. Many thought women would vote for the issues espoused by the emerging progressive movement. In this sense, women's enfranchisement was not expected to merely double the electorate for each party, but to operate in particular ways in different states. This meant that state-specific political environments would be crucial to determining which parties would support women's suffrage.

Electoral Politics in American Political Development

In what is known as the Gilded Age, the regions of the United States had distinctive political landscapes. Whereas voters in the North exhibited strong partisanship and were unlikely to switch parties (only 3.2 percent of voters switched parties from 1876 to 1900), voters in the West were more likely to do so (10.7 percent switched parties in the same period).[71] Westerners were also much more comfortable splitting their votes to support members of different parties in the same election than their northeastern counterparts. In the West, 12.1 percent of all ballots were "split" tickets, contrasted with 1.7 percent in the East.[72] Parties also had different lifespans across the regions, with southern Democrats maintaining power much longer than any one party out west. Moreover, minor parties were especially featured in the Midwest, West, and parts of the South.[73] The existence of minor parties is relevant under plurality rules because it can be an indication that competition is not so tight as to preclude entry by new groups and because these parties' electoral strategy was often premised on mobilizing those who were not already committed to the major organizations.[74] As Shortridge (1978: 34) emphasizes, minor

---

[70] Quoted in Grimes 1967: 57; and "The Woman Voter of the West," *The Westerner* Aug. 1912: 4. Kingman suggested that most people expected the governor to veto the bill.

[71] Kleppner 1983.

[72] See Gimpel 1993: table 1.

[73] Goodwyn 1978; Postel 2007.

[74] Rosenstone et al. 1996; Shortridge 1978.

parties often sought to gain entry into legislatures by courting new and unattached constituencies.

Finally, there is the issue of party organization. As several scholars have pointed out, political "machines" were a distinctive feature of urban politics in many cities around the turn of the twentieth century. Machines are a type of traditional party organization run by bosses and subscribed to by clients under a currency of patronage, and which would have generated disincentives to reform. Women's organizations often claimed that female voters would help to cleanup politics, giving political machines specific reasons to resist women's enfranchisement.[75] In most accounts of referendum voting, urban men were less amenable toward suffrage than their rural counterparts.[76] A placard from the era perfectly captures these tensions, claiming "Machine politicians do not want equal suffrage for *woman*, too much *truth, honesty* and *purity* applied to *the machine* would demolish it."[77] Because political machines sought to create and maintain political monopolies through tight control of the electorate, their presence should signal a heightened resistance to women's enfranchisement.[78] All of the studies cited describe a distinctive politics in the western US that may have driven women's early enfranchisement.

DID MOBILIZATION AND COMPETITION DRIVE SUFFRAGE EXPANSION?

To evaluate the correlations between competition, mobilization, and suffrage expansion, I constructed a panel dataset that contains state level decisions related to franchise extension, women's mobilization into the National American Women's Suffrage Association, and the several indicators of political competition described above. My analysis will begin in 1893, the first year for which data on mobilization into the NAWSA are available, and end in 1920, when the Nineteenth Amendment enfranchised women nationally.[79] Overall, there are forty-five states

---

[75] Buenker 1971; Flexner 1995: 309; Scott and Scott 1982: 26.

[76] McDonagh and Price 1985: 431.

[77] http://www.lib.udel.edu/ud/spec/exhibits/fifty/suffrage.html.

[78] See Trounstein (2009) on machines as monopolies.

[79] If a state joins the union after 1893, its observations begin in the year of statehood. The observation period for a state ends if full suffrage is adopted for women, typically after a public referendum.

under consideration, fifteen of which fully enfranchised women ahead of the Nineteenth Amendment.[80]

The unit of analysis in this dataset is the state legislative session. This means that every time a legislature gets replaced (which happens after an election), a new row appears in the dataset for the new legislative session. Because each state legislature was bicameral in this period, each competition variable is measured as the average level across both houses in a given state legislative session.[81] On average, the data contain almost eight legislative sessions per state, with a minimum of four for earlier enfranchisers like New Mexico and Arizona, and a maximum of twenty-seven sessions for late enfranchisers like New York or non-enfranchisers like Massachusetts and New Jersey. Using the legislative session instead of an individual year as the unit of analysis sets this study apart from others that consider women's suffrage. Although a bill may pass in a specific year, the partisan composition of the legislature often does not change. So if the question is how changes in the composition of the legislature affects support for suffrage, then it is important that the unit of analysis reflects the possibility of change. Since measures of legislative power do not change between elections, the only logical possibility is using each session.

Measuring Suffrage Support

The dependent variable—the outcome I am trying to explain—is suffrage support in state legislatures. I operationalize this concept as the passage of a bill for "full suffrage" in both houses of a state legislature. Full suffrage is defined here as voting rights granted to women on the same terms as men, meaning that any age, literacy, and property requirements are not distinguished by gender. Since all state legislatures

---

[80] Although there were 48 states in this period, Arizona, Wyoming, and Utah entered the union as franchise states and so do not appear in the dataset.

[81] Data from Burnham (1986) do not incorporate special elections, so competition data does not change between elections. All state legislatures were bicameral in this period (Moschos and Katsky 1965), so a state's legislative sessions incorporated information across two chambers. By 1890, most states had adopted an early November election schedule (see state entries in Dubin 2007). Most legislature data in Burnham (1986) begin on even-numbered years, which I infer is the election year. Since most elections were in November, I assume that the newly elected do not take office until January in the odd year. Thus if a state had elections in 1880 and 1882, the years 1881 and 1882 would represent one legislative session and hence a single row of the dataset, and the years 1883 and 1884 would similarly constitute another row. In the collapsed dataset, 98 percent of the state sessions cover a period of one or two years.

were bicameral, suffrage support takes the value of one in each state session in which both houses pass a full suffrage bill. The dependent variable is zero in all other session years.

Importantly, the dependent variable can take on the value of one in several session years because a state might have had to pass a bill several times before it became law.[82] There are four reasons for this. First, because all US states except Delaware required a referendum vote after the legislature approved of a constitutional amendment, if the referendum failed, the legislature would have had to re-pass and re-refer the amendment. Idiosyncratic legislative rules could also prompt legislatures to pass suffrage bills multiple times. Nevada, for example, required proposed constitutional amendments to pass in two consecutive legislative sessions (McCammon et al. 2001: 65). Others, such as Arkansas, only allowed three amendments to be referred per year.[83] Finally, a governor's veto could drive the process to begin again. Governors vetoed full suffrage bills in North Dakota (1885), California (1893), Arizona (1903), and Wisconsin (1913). Although we might worry that politicians could approve suffrage bills knowing the bill would fail down the line, this strategy would have been risky because four of the first states to grant women voting rights—Wyoming, Utah, Idaho, and Arizona—did so in their first referendum. Events in the state legislature mattered, then, because they might stick.

Defining the outcome of interest in this way has several benefits. Banaszak (1996b), McCammon and Campbell (2001), and McConnaughy (2013) conduct analyses of the final date of enfranchisement, which, for all states but Delaware, occured in the year a referendum was approved by the voting public.[84] This is less than ideal analytically and theoretically because of the small sample size, and because the values of the independent variables related to competition, if measured in the year of final passage, may not reflect the composition of the legislature that actually approved the change prior to the referendum. The measurement strategy I use instead provides the closest link between the argument—which focuses on the incentives of politicians in legislatures—and the dependent variable. Among the forty five states in the sample, the average number of times a full-suffrage bill passed both houses is 1.29 with a standard

---

[82] This variable comes from King et al.'s (2005) *Database on Women's Suffrage*. Complete details on the coding process are in the online appendix to Teele (2018), available at doi:10.7910/DVN/EVYI2H.

[83] Arkansas's HJR 7 passed both houses in 1915 but was not referred for this reason.

[84] Vote tallies on state referenda were notoriously fraudulent (Catt and Shuler 1923: chs. X, XIV, XV).

deviation of 1.49.[85] The maximum number of times a single state passed a full suffrage bill in both houses is four. The minimum is zero.

Measuring Competition

Figure 4.5 presents the average values for three measures of political competition for each geographical region. The variables are ordered from indicators of low competition in the top to indicators of high competition in the bottom. Indicators of low competition include a measure of *majority surplus*, defined as the fraction of seats that the largest party holds over 50 percent. When majority surplus is high, the dominant party is less vulnerable (David 1972). If the party with the largest share of seats holds a plurality instead of a majority, majority surplus can take on negative values. To construct this measure I took the average over both houses. In the dataset, the average value of majority surplus is 0.27 with a standard deviation of 0.14. At the mean, the largest party controls 77 percent of the seats. A 1 standard deviation increase would give the largest party 91 percent of seats. Over the whole period, as seen in figure 4.5, majorities had the largest margins in the South and the lowest in the West.

Population under machines (%) is another indicator of low competition. This measure divides the total population living in machine-dominated large cities within a state by the state's total population to construct an annual measure of the intensity of machine politics in urban areas.[86] Drawing on the large literature on Gilded Age urban politics, each large American city has been coded annually based on whether or not it was run by a political machine. Large cities are considered to be those with

---

[85] From 1848 to 1920, there were 560 full suffrage bills introduced in state legislatures, and 71 instances in which a suffrage bill passed both houses of the state legislature. The empirical portion of this analysis looks only after 1893, when movement data become available. In this window there are 56 instances where a full suffrage bill passed both houses of the state legislature. Note that the published version of King et al. (2005) studies 67 instances in which a full suffrage bill passed both state legislatures. They begin their study only in 1860, thereby dropping a few cases.

[86] The online appendix to Teele (2018: 4–8) has full details of this variable's construction. To generate this longitudinal measure of machine presence in US states, I, along with a research assistant "blind" to the question in this book, independently coded the rise and fall of urban machines in US cities from 1850 to 1950. My coding hews closely to the definition of "Traditional Party Organization" developed by David Mayhew (1986), which measures hierarchical party and non-party organizations that attempt to get preferred candidates on the ballot and that use patronage as a way to reward constituents. A political machine, by my definition, has the following four characteristics: 1) Is a patronage-based organization with an identifiable political boss. 2) Must be active for at least two election cycles. 3) Must be in a city with a population greater than 25,000 in 1900. 4) Local bosses could promise to deliver large blocks of votes.

(a) Majority surplus

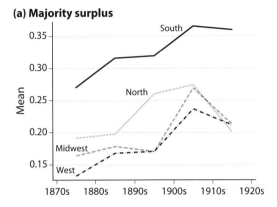

(b) Population in machine cities (%)

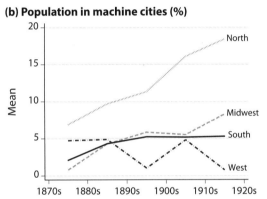

(c) Runner-up/Winner

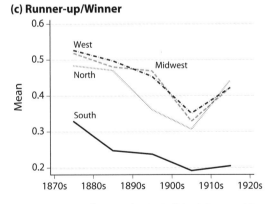

FIGURE 4.5. Regional Variation in Political Competition, US.

more than 25 thousand residents circa 1900. In 1900, 160 cities had more than 25 thousand residents. Overall, 38 of the then 48 states had a city this large, and the average number of cities of this size in the states which had at least 1 was 4.21. Within the group of 160 cities, 30 had a machine circa 1900. The machine data have been collected from 1850 to 1950, but only the years in the sample (1893–1920) are used herein.

Finally, the *ratio of runner-up to winner* is an indicator of high competition. This indicator measures the fraction of the winner's seats held by the next closest party, averaged over both houses. A ratio closer to one indicates that the ruling party is vulnerable to a competitor, making suffrage reform more likely. Note that when third parties have seats in the legislature, the runner-up-to-winner ratio and majority surplus are not generally linear transformations of each other. Overall, the runner-up is farthest from the winner in the South.

As can be seen in figure 4.5 there was significant regional variation in political competition in the era of women's suffrage. Parties had the longest lives in the Northeast and the South, and the Southern parties had much larger winning margins than parties in the rest of the country. In population terms, the Midwest and the Northeast had larger shares of their residents living in machine-dominated cities. The West stands out as a place where power was more likely to be split across houses and where third parties gained more access. On the other hand, the South had larger runner-up-to-winner margins. Overall, most of these statistics conform to prior knowledge of party politics in the Gilded Age. More importantly, the various measures of competition exhibit regional variation consistent with the pattern of women's enfranchisement in the US. Given the variation in political competition and suffrage mobilization across the US, what evidence do we have that these factors mattered for women's suffrage?

Plots of Changes

As a first step in exploring whether competition and mobilization are correlated with women's enfranchisement, consider figure 4.6 which plots the average level of mobilization, the average level of majority surplus, and the average ratio of runner-up to winner for all states that enfranchised women ahead of the Nineteenth Amendment. These graphs center their averages around the date of suffrage, demarcated by zero on the x-axis. The averages are measured at the number of legislative sessions before and after suffrage.

The top panel in figure 4.6 plots the average growth of the suffrage movement prior to state legislative passage of a suffrage bill. On average,

(a) NAWSA Membership

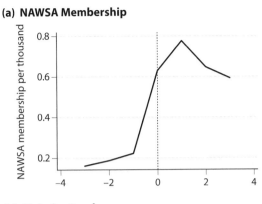

(b) Majority Surplus

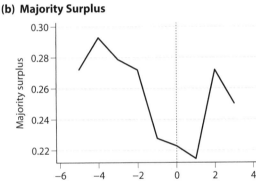

(c) Runner-up/winner

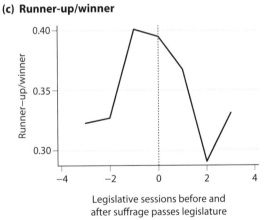

Legislative sessions before and
after suffrage passes legislature

FIGURE 4.6. Trends in Mobilization and Competition Surrounding US Suffrage.

there is an almost two-fold growth in the size of the movement from two legislative sessions prior to the year of passage. Note that the size of the movement continues to grow thereafter likely because, as described above, all states but Delaware required a legislative referendum to approve the electoral reform. Suffragists might therefore have pushed for more members ahead of referendum campaigns.

The middle panel looks at the trends in majority surplus for all states that passed a suffrage bill in both houses of the state legislature. Here we see that several legislative sessions prior to the bill's passage, majority surplus was much higher, and hence competition much lower, on average. Notably, there appears to be a decline in majority surplus, and hence an increase in competition, one session before passage, and then a jump up in the year of passage. In figure 4.6 the average majority surplus in the year of passage is 0.23—more competitive than average—which would have given the largest party about 73 percent of seats.

The bottom panel of figure 4.6 plots the ratio of runner-up to winner in the years before and after suffrage bills passed in state legislatures. Here we see that it was about 0.44 two sessions before suffrage—ten points higher than the average value in the dataset as a whole. At this level, in a two-party system, the winner has just less than 70 percent of seats. The graphs of changes suggest that the movement was growing, and competition was higher on average, in the years just prior to suffrage passage.

Plots of Interactions

To investigate the interaction between competition, mobilization, and suffrage, first I outline theoretical predictions for the direction of correlation, and second present raw data plots of the average level of suffrage support conditional on different levels of political competition and women's mobilization. The theoretical argument in chapter 2 suggests that no matter the level of women's mobilization, if a party is completely secure in its power, it should not support reform. Hence when competition is very low, women across the range of mobilization levels should be unlikely to get the vote. On the other hand, if competition is high, women's mobilization should increase the probability of reform. If there are diminishing returns to the information politicians gather when women mobilize, we should not necessarily expect that the relationship between competition and suffrage support increases at an increasing rate.

The raw data plots in figure 4.7 provide a useful way to look at the three-way correlations between competition, suffrage mobilization, and

(a) Majority surplus

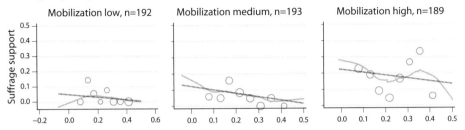

(b) Population in machine cities, frac.

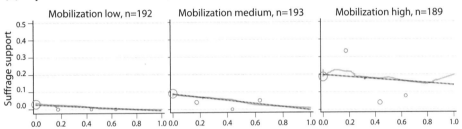

(c) Runner-up/Winner

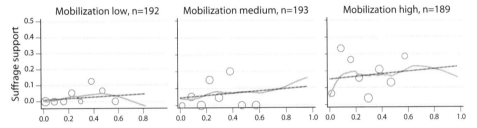

FIGURE 4.7. Raw Data Plots of the Interaction between Competition and Mobilization Surrounding Suffrage Expansion. The figures show the relationship between the average level of suffrage support (y-axis) across deciles of the competition variable (x-axis) for terciles of mobilization. The markers are proportional to the number of observations for a competition decile in the whole sample at that level of mobilization. A linear fit and Lowess curve also appear on each graph.

legislative decisions, and they can help to detect potential interaction effects which might be present if, for example, mobilization has a larger effect when competition is high.[87] When the competition variable is continuous, the raw data plots will present the average level of suffrage support along the y-axis against different levels of the competition

---

[87] Here I am following a technique recommended by Hainmueller et al. (2017).

variable on the x-axis at different levels of mobilization, as depicted in separate graphs. Practically speaking, the measure of suffrage support is the average number of times legislatures at a given level of competition and a given level of mobilization pass a bill that would give women "full suffrage." The levels of competition are sliced into ten evenly sized groupings (deciles), and the mobilization variable is sliced into three evenly sized groupings (terciles). The mobilization variable is labeled "Low," "Medium," and "High" for the terciles beginning at the 33rd, 66th, and 99th percentiles.[88] When the competition variable in question is binary, the raw data plot will present the average support for suffrage in state legislatures (y-axis) against decile bins of women's mobilization for each level of competition.

Theoretically, I expect that the interaction coefficient on longevity of the ruling party and mobilization is zero.[89] This is because longer rule is associated with less incentive to reform, independent of the level of mobilization. On the other hand, as the runner-up to winner grows, we should expect this to positively interact with suffrage as competition is increasing. I find that there is no interaction between the longevity of the ruling party and suffrage mobilization. Also as expected, there is a positive interaction between the strength of the runner-up to winner and mobilization, but only at the highest levels of mobilization. These graphs and associated analyses in Teele (2018) provide evidence that the probability of women winning the vote when a party had been in power for a very long time was low even when mobilization of women was high. Thus even a strong suffrage movement was unlikely to see returns if the party in control was entrenched. On the other hand, when the runner-up was close on the heels of the incumbent, suffrage became more likely if the movement was larger.

[88] The mobilization variable is right-skewed: the 25th percentile still contains zeros while the 76th to 99th percentile contains extreme values (which include states with 2.23 to 9.97 members per thousand in the NAWSA).

[89] In general, the Lowess curves seem to be quite close to the linear fit, suggesting that the worries of Hainmueller et al. (2017) regarding non-linear interaction effects are not a huge problem here. Using the kernel density estimator suggested by Hainmueller et al. (2017), as expected I find that there is no interaction between the longevity of the ruling party and suffrage mobilization. Also as expected, there is a positive interaction between runner-up to winner and mobilization, but only from the 95th to 99th percentiles of mobilization. (The online appendix to Teele (2018) contains the full set of results.)

CULTURE, EGALITARIANISM, AND TEMPERANCE

In addition to competition and mobilization, can other features explain women's enfranchisement in the United States? The study of women's suffrage benefits from a long tradition of historical and theoretical work that can inform this question. In unpacking why western states enfranchised women first, some scholars have pointed to the culture of the West—a pioneer society which, because its economy required its women to toil alongside their men, tended to think of women as equals and rendered distinctions between the sexes less salient.[90] Others have similarly argued that the western states had a unique "gendered" opportunity structure that was more amenable to the arguments made by suffragists of the day.[91] And still others have contended that because women were scarce in the West, policies favorable to women might encourage their westward migration, which was seen as beneficial to marriage and thereby society at large.[92] I take up each of these themes in turn.

Gender Egalitarian Policies. If pioneer culture or attempts to attract settlers to the frontier promoted a culture of equality for women, this should be visible in the package of rights offered to western women. But the data do not exhibit the dramatic differences in policy that we should expect to see if the West were courting women by offering them a better package of rights.[93] Table 4.1 tabulates three policies by region: *Property Rights* are state-level provisions for the right of a married woman to own property; *Earnings Laws* likewise provide for women the ability to retain subsequent wages; and *Sole Trader Laws* allow women to be the sole proprietors of businesses.[94]

---

[90] Flexner 1995: 160; Larson 1970; Beeton 1986; Mead 2004; Postel 2007.

[91] Kraditor 1981. McCammon and Campbell (2001: 63) find that the western states were particularly amenable to what they call "expediency arguments": when suffragists argued that women have special skills that could temper corruption, increase humanitarian activities, and improve public education, women were more likely to win the vote.

[92] Grimes 1967. Note that while Braun and Kvasnicka (2013) find evidence that a male-heavy gender ratio is correlated with early adoption in the US, as I show in figure 2.4, this pattern is not as strong on the world scale.

[93] Specific policies to woo migrants, such as the Oregon Land Donation Act of 1850, which gave 320 acres to women and 640 to married couples, would have been difficult for women to capitalize on without a partner, typically male. Flexner (1995: 164).

[94] Property rights, earnings laws, and sole trader dates come from Khan (1996) and Hoff (1991). Georgia's secret ballot date comes from Novotny (2007). Mothers' pensions do not appear in table 4.1 because the first state that implemented such a policy did so only in 1911 (Skocpol 1992: table 10).

TABLE 4.1. Regional Differences in Women's Rights before Suffrage.

	Property Rights		Earnings Laws		Sole Trader	
	No	Yes	No	Yes	No	Yes
Midwest	0	100	16.67	83.33	33.33	66.67
Northeast	0	100	11.11	88.89	11.11	88.89
South	18.75	81.25	56.25	43.75	37.5	62.5
West	18.18	81.82	27.27	72.73	9.09	90.91
Total	10.42	89.58	31.25	68.75	25	75
Pearson χ^2						
(p-value)	3.34	(0.23)	7.62	(0.05)	4.19	(0.24)
First State	ME	1844	ME	1857	OH	1811
Last State	UT	1895	GA	1943	UT	1895

The cells in table 4.1 list the fraction of states in each region that had implemented each policy prior to the date in which it extended voting rights to women. The table also includes information on the first and last state to grant such a law and the year that this occurred. In general, the table does not provide evidence that policies were more favorable to women in the West.

Progressive Political Culture. Another alternative explanation of women's enfranchisement, advanced in both the political economy literature and in American political development, theorizes that would-be political reformers push to extend voting rights to the disfranchised because those groups will support their preferred policies. More generally, progressive reformers want to include the masses in the electorate because the masses will support the progressive policy agenda.

This idea finds a close analog in the literature that describes US regions' differential tendencies toward reform, sometimes described as a region's "receptivity" to reformist agendas.[95] A host of policies were considered progressive reforms around the turn of the century, including the adoption of the *Australian ballot*, where votes are secretly cast; the shift to *direct primaries*, where citizens and not party elites decide which candidate will represent the party in the general election; and the adoption of *initiative rights*, which allows specific legislative proposals to be put to vote by plebiscite.[96]

---

[95] Bridges 1997 and Shefter 1994. Note that Trounstein (2009) locates reform coalitions in American cities where the poor were a minority, while machine coalitions operated in cities where the poor were a majority.

[96] Harvey and Mukherjee (2006) study the introduction of the secret ballot. And Smith and Fridkin (2008) study initiative rights. Data for the Australian ballot come from Katz

TABLE 4.2. Regional Differences in Progressive Reform before Suffrage.

	Australian Ballot		Direct Primary		Initiative Rights	
	No	Yes	No	Yes	No	Yes
Midwest	0	100	8.33	91.67	50	50
Northeast	11.11	88.89	44.44	55.56	77.78	22.22
South	18.75	81.25	43.75	56.25	81.25	18.75
West	36.36	63.64	63.64	36.36	63.64	36.36
Total	16.68	83.88	39.58	60.42	68.75	31.25
Pearson χ^2						
(p-value)	5.72	0.126	7.77	0.051	3.6026	0.308
First State	MA	1888	MS	1902	SD	1898
Last State	SC	1950	UT, AR, NM	1921	MA	1918

Table 4.2 shows that there are no statistically significant regional differences in the adoption of the Australian ballot or initiative rights before suffrage was extended to women.[97] There are statistical differences in the move to direct primaries: the West exhibits a *lower* propensity to have adopted this reform prior to the date of enfranchisement. Yet this is a specious comparison, as the first state to extend initiative rights did so in 1902, after several of the states in the West gave women voting rights.

It is worth pointing out, finally, that the progressive movements themselves were not necessarily the origin of gender egalitarian policies. Intuition might suggest that the ideologies of progressive organizations should point to more support for women's freedom, but, for the most part, women were still subordinated to men within these movements. For example, women were invited to participate in particular activities within the populist movement, but they were not allowed to be dues-paying members like their husbands. Often, their sole responsibilities consisted in coordinating the luncheons that accompanied the meetings.[98]

---

and Sala (1996). Other reforms popular around the turn of the century, such as the move to non-partisan city governments, have been revealed to be quite anti-democratic, rather than progressive. See Bridges (1997) and Shefter (1994).

[97] Banaszak (1998) finds no relationship between the existence of initiative rights in a state and successful petitions for women's suffrage.

[98] Leaders of The Grange took a "separate spheres" approach to women's involvement, creating segregated positions for participants of different genders. On the other hand, the Farmers' Alliance allowed women to speak and hold office just like men. Yet the Farmers' Alliance supported suffrage only within the bounds of a traditional view of women, supporting school board voting rights but never taking suffrage on its platform. Postel 2007: ch. 3.

In summary, while the West may have been earlier adopters of pro-gressive reforms, these reforms came *after* the key moments of suffrage in those states. Moreover, the reform movements themselves were not neces-sarily drivers of the egalitarian changes. In my view, progressive reforms, and the acceptance of women in states where progressivism was stronger, may themselves stem from the factors that drove franchise reform, namely, increased political competition vis-à-vis the other regions.[99]

Temperance Forces. Finally, we might consider one specific reform proposal which may have divided electoral groups on the suffrage ques-tion: the issue of temperance. Citing the role of the Women's Christian Temperance Union (WCTU) in pursuing both prohibition and suffrage, many scholars have suggested a link between resistance to prohibition policy and resistance to suffrage reform. To the extent that women's enfranchisement might bring temperance to a state, "wet" interest groups and voting blocs are believed to have resisted the suffragists.

In the Gilded Age the largest organization of American women was the WCTU. It was established in order to promote temperance in both the private and the legislative realms, and its members sought the vote as a means to this end. Figure 4.3, presented at the beginning of the chapter, arrays *per capita dues* paid to the organization from 1884 to 1914.[100] It is clear from the figure that per capita contributions were highest in the Northeast, followed by the Midwest, West, and finally the South. While the higher payments in the Northeast may explain the resistance to suffrage in that region, the low contributions of the South do not explain why those states avoided franchise reform. The same can be said for the Midwest, whose states began to extend voting rights around the time that WCTU contributions were on the rise.

Probing the issue further, the *fraction of dry counties* in a given state, averaged over region, does not exhibit variation that is consistent with explaining franchise extension as a reaction to temperance.[101] In the era before suffrage rights were extended, the West and Northeastern states were "wetter" than those in the Midwest and the South.[102] Thus regional

---

[99] There is, further, the possibility that early enfranchisement of women supported these reforms. See Miller (2008) with reference to public health policies.

[100] Dues, which were regularly recorded in the minutes of the organization's annual meetings, provide one indicator of the WCTU's size.

[101] Sechrist 2012.

[102] In the country as a whole, on average 33 percent of counties in each state were "dry." In the West this figure was 24 percent, in the Northeast 31 percent, in the Midwest 38 percent, and in the South 40 percent.

variation in prohibition policy does not exhibit a correlation consistent with the pattern of franchise reform for US women.

This correlation might be explained by arguing that northeastern men feared their states becoming drier still, but why would it have been different for men in the West? Since the western states enfranchised women earlier than others, it is possible that anti-prohibition forces in the other regions saw that temperance policies sprung up after suffrage, and as a result resisted such reform in their own locales. But I do not find evidence that enfranchising women actually did lead to more pro-temperance policies.

Figure 4.8 plots the fraction of dry counties in states that extended early voting rights to women, along with a vertical line indicating the date of suffrage. There is no consistent pattern between suffrage reform and prohibitionist policy in the States. Just after suffrage passed, both California and Washington saw slight increases in the fraction of dry counties, but in Oregon and Montana the fraction of dry counties fell. There were no discernible changes in the fraction of dry counties in Colorado, Idaho, Kansas, Nevada, and Utah after women won the vote.[103] Hence men had little reason to suspect that temperance policy would change dramatically as a result of women's enfranchisement.[104]

Overall, the alternative explanations for the early expansion of women's suffrage in western states explored here, including political progressivity, gender egalitarianism, and the fear of prohibition, do not appear to be a better fit for the question at hand.[105] Rather than focusing solely on what is unique about the West, my analysis provides an explanation for the differential timing of franchise reform both across and within regions: the competitive landscape and the scope of women's mobilization for the vote were crucial to securing state level reform. This translated into the federal amendment through a similar process of forceful strategizing by suffragists, politicians' strategic calculations about the reform, and a propitious national condition in which Wilson feared losing Congress without supporting reform.

[103] Carrie Chapman Catt details the efforts of the liquor lobby to prevent suffrage all over the country, including the West (Catt and Shuler 1923: ch. X), though she does not think that the liquor interests were strong sources of resistance in New York State.

[104] See, too, García-Jimeno (2012: supplementary appendix), who does not find a relationship between suffrage and temperance.

[105] A thorough quantitative treatment that examines these potentially confounding variables in time-series cross-sectional regression analysis is available in Teele 2018 and the associated online appendix.

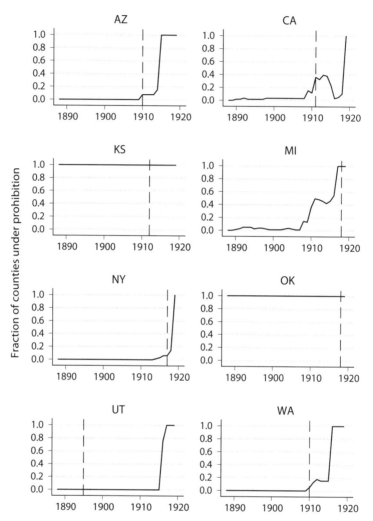

FIGURE 4.8. Prohibition and State Suffrage. The pictured states gave women national voting rights ahead of the Nineteenth Amendment (the suffrage year is indicated by the vertical line). The graphs show the fraction of counties that had adopted temperance laws, i.e., "dry counties" in each state before and after franchise extension.

THE NINETEENTH AMENDMENT

What has come to be known as the "Anthony Amendment," for the relentless female activist Susan B. Anthony, who first imagined women's suffrage as a possible political outcome, was proposed and debated

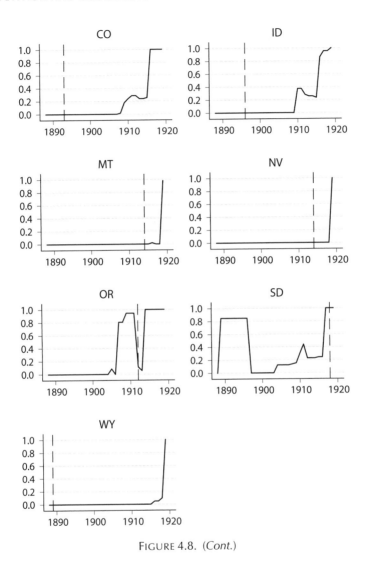

FIGURE 4.8. (*Cont.*)

numerous times in Congress before it was sent to the states for ratification in 1919.[106] Anthony's vision always entailed a federal amendment as the Holy Grail for women's political rights, but many women who believed

---

[106] See Flexner 1995. The first senator to propose a suffrage amendment was S. C. Pomeroy of Kansas in December 1868. The "Anthony Amendment" proposed by Senator A. A. Sargent of California in 1878 held: "The right of citizens of the United States to vote shall be denied or abridged by the United States or by any state on account of sex." This language was later incorporated into the Nineteenth Amendment. In 1882 both houses had committees on woman suffrage, which they reported on favorably. In 1886 Henry W. Blair of New

in the justice and utility of the female franchise simultaneously argued that election law was best left to the states. The strategies of the major organizations that fought for the female franchise reflected this division, with some organizations advocating and pursuing a state-based approach to suffrage laws, while others set their sights on the national amendment. Although an umbrella organization was formed in 1890 to encompass all of these organizations, at every single stage of the battle over the Nineteenth Amendment there was a vociferous group that argued against the federal path. Resistance to suffrage was often clothed in the rhetoric of states' rights, but partisanship, exclusionary racial politics, and a preference for the status quo ultimately provided the largest barriers to reform. Yet buried within the federal system was also a contradiction: federal legislators could exclude women writ large from voting, but they could not stop the women in suffrage states from casting ballots for the House, Senate, and the presidency.

In light of the growing number of suffrage states, the partisan benefits of enfranchising women were on the minds of progressive Democrats as the country geared up for the 1916 election. Woodrow Wilson, a longtime opponent of women's suffrage, underwent a political "conversion" on the issue that began with his decision to vote for the New Jersey suffrage referendum in 1915. Judge Bledsoe of the Los Angeles district court wrote to congratulate Wilson on his change of heart: "Your declaration at this time will serve to win support for us in the suffrage states whose 62 electoral votes...will be most helpful to us in 1916."[107] Wilson thereafter worked hard to secure suffrage, often stressing the strategic benefits it would bring the Democratic Party. In May 1917, he urged Representative Edward Pou (D-NC) to appoint a committee on the subject, suggesting that "it would be a very wise act of public policy" to consider the issue in the House.[108] In August 1918, when Wilson was struggling to get the last votes in the Senate necessary to pass the suffrage amendment, he wrote to Kentucky Governor Augustus Stanley regarding a recently vacated Senate seat, stating "It would be of great advantage to the party and to the country if his successor entertained views favorable to the pending

---

Hampshire called a suffrage bill, which failed thanks to solid southern opposition, 16 to 34, with 26 absent, in a 25 January 1887 vote. This amendment was continually reintroduced with each congressional session until 1896, then fell out of discussion until 1913 (p. 176–178).

[107] 5 Oct. 1915, quoted in Morgan 1972: 81.

[108] Carrie Chapman Catt Papers, Box1/3/14-May-1917, New York Public Library.

constitutional amendment."[109] Similar calls were made from the floor of the House of Representatives: Representative Jouett Shouse (KS-D) called on Wilson to make a public statement to urge Democratic senators to vote for suffrage, arguing that a defeat of the bill in the Senate would harm the re-election bids of Democrats in suffrage states.[110]

To learn about the political preferences of the newly or soon-to-be enfranchised women in America, politicians kept a close eye on women's organizations. In a letter to a newspaper editor penned by US Representative J. T. G. Crawford (D-FL) in 1919 to defend a vote taken in his name in support of the suffrage resolution, he wrote:

> I do not know where you obtained the figures you use in your state-ment that "less than 5 percent of the women of Florida are actually in favor of the suffrage amendment to the federal constitution," as the Federation of Women's Clubs, the Woman's Christian Temperance Union, the State Teachers' Association, and other organizations com-posed largely or wholly of women, have endorsed the amendment. [Even] if there were no other reason for endorsing the amendment, common sense dictates that course to any one desiring to see the Democratic party saved alive, and as the representative of that party in Florida I consider it my duty to at least render what assistance I can to continue the party's existence as a political factor in the nation.[111]

Crawford was well aware of which women were mobilized for the vote, and believed that to reject them at this stage would be a disaster for the party. Contrary to the standard narratives which argue that women's enfranchisement would have led to a doubling of the electorate or which argues for ideational as opposed to strategic reasons for enfranchisement, the evidence presented above suggests that elites in several states and over time voiced opinions that women would exercise their votes in a distinctive manner, and it shows that politicians did think strategically about how women were going to vote.

---

[109] Quoted in Behn 2012: 236.
[110] Quoted in Behn 2012: 231.
[111] "Equal Suffrage Department: Mr. Crawford Explains," *Ocala Evening Star*, Florida, 15 March 1919.

CONCLUSION

In response to his wife's appeal for ample rights for women in the new republic, John Adam's response was unequivocal: "We know better than to repeal our Masculine systems ... which would completely subject Us to the Despotism of the Peticoat."[112] Whatever fears that Adams or later politicians may have had about petticoated despots, there were, in time, political conditions in which they were willing to try their luck with female electors.

This chapter shows that the interaction between political competition and the strength of the reform movement is key to understanding the pattern of women's enfranchisement both across and within the US states. Parties in western states were more vulnerable to new entrants and were more likely to split power across the legislative branches than parties elsewhere. This made politicians in the West open to the entrepreneurial task of recruiting new supporters, including women. In this context, a small number of mobilized women were able to successfully press for their demands, and received voting rights earlier than women elsewhere in the US. On the other side of the country, single-party rule in the South translated into large legislative majorities and little need for new constituents to bolster Democratic control. Southern women could lobby day and night without making a difference until something in the political winds indicated a changing of fortunes. Finally, though the northeastern states had higher levels of competition than states in the South, the dominance of certain parties within states allowed leaders to ignore, for nearly seventy years, the pleas of the well-funded and highly subscribed women's suffrage movement. As new political groups began to mount viable challenges to the Republican and Democratic strongholds around 1910, the women's movement searched for a broader coalition of women, and was at last able to capitalize on decades of groundwork and bring victory to a few of the northeastern states.

The answer to the puzzle at the heart of this chapter about why western states enfranchised women earlier than states in the East is because their political landscape was more competitive. Although most suffrage scholars have assumed that this pattern was curious because women's mobilization was relatively lower in the West, the data actually show that western suffragists were able to galvanize membership during key moments just prior to reform. Across the states, when higher mobilization

[112] Adams 1776. Quoted in Butterfield et al. 2002.

and competition occurred together, suffrage support in state legislatures rose. Given the logic of enfranchisement articulated in the second chapter, this interaction suggests that heightened mobilization can lead one party or another (or possibly multiple parties) to believe they would have an advantage in mobilizing women in future elections. In other contexts, where competition was high but powerful groups perceived a real threat should women vote, we would expect that politicians would be less inclined to extend the vote. As we will see, this is exactly what happened in the French Third Republic.

5
The "Clerical Peril" and Radical Opposition to Female Voters in France

If you knew our villages! At the present time, to give the right to vote to women in France would be to give the priest in each village the ballots of all the women.[1]

Though they were early innovators in the rights of man, when it came to the political rights of women, the French were not among the vanguard.[2] Around 1920, when women in more than twenty countries were entering the ranks of the voting public, France seemed like a natural place for women to triumph. As in the US and the UK, French women had formed and tended suffrage organizations, and many had devoted themselves fully to the war effort, taking over for fighting men in munitions factories and other manufacturing positions as needed. As in the other countries, the French political system was highly in flux, with members of the centrist Radical Party holding power through rotating coalitions with leftist and conservative republicans. In 1919, when a suffrage bill came up for debate in the French lower house, the stage seemed set for electoral reform. Why, then, were French women kept from formal participation until the end of the next great war? That is, why did suffrage fail in the Third Republic?

From the time of the suffrage debates until the present day, many have argued that the "French twist" can be attributed to the salience of the religious cleavage in French electoral politics.[3] The long-standing alliance

---

[1] Emile Darnaud, a male provincial feminist, in a letter to the Parisian newspaper *La Française*, 9 May 1914 (quoted in Hause and Kenney 1984: 60). At 64, Darnaud was a pensioned military officer who established a feminist committee in 1889. While he believed in equal justice for men and women, he was opposed to women's suffrage on the ground that it would not work in the provinces (ibid.: 61).

[2] Ironically, in spite of the fact that the very term *"féminisme"* was invented by French suffragette Hubertine Auclert. Offen 1994: 152.

[3] Offen 1994.

between the Catholic Church and the political right—which effectively was an alliance of monarchists against those who supported the Republic founded in 1870—emerged alongside modern French politics.[4] As Suzanne Berger writes, the French religious cleavage is not a rift between believers and non-believers, because the majority of people in France were and are Catholic, but rather a fierce disagreement about the proper role of the church in the state. Late nineteenth-century battles over this issue produced two camps of Catholics: the liberals, who did not resist the secularization of politics, and the integralists, who envisioned a society with Catholic principles enshrined in law.[5] From 1886 until the Second World War, integralists participated in the Catholic Action Movement as a way to organize collective action and influence elections. Combined with the Church's attempts to intervene directly in politics, and the republicans' insistence on a strict separation, the secular-confessional division became the dominant political cleavage in the Third Republic.[6] In this context, it has been argued that fear of the "clerical peril," the idea that French women, especially those in the countryside, would vote as the priests told them, emerged as a powerful narrative to keep women from the polls. This fear was particularly salient in the political atmosphere of the Third Republic, where political contestation centered not only on the question of who governs, but under what political system.

This chapter assesses the evidence for the role the religious cleavage played in hampering French suffrage politics.[7] Was Catholicism "decisive," as historian Pierre Rosanvallon claims?[8] I will argue that it was, insofar as the issues raised by the religious cleavage influenced

[4] Berger 1987: 112.

[5] Berger 1987: 119, 126.

[6] Berger 1987: 130. The legacy of the religious cleavage likely cuts even deeper: several scholars have shown that the cleavage-generated voting patterns of yore are remarkably predictive of French voting patterns into the late twentieth century. See Brustein 1988: 146ff.; Manow and Palier 2009: 149; Tackett 2014: 11–14.

[7] I draw information on the legislative system in the Third Republic from historians of the period including Campbell (1958), Sowerwine (2001), Tilly and Scott (1987), and Zeldin (1973). On the importance of religion in French political life I look also to the work of Berger (1974, 1987) and Tackett (2014). On the suffrage movement, I draw from English-language discussions of Hause and Kenney (1984) and Smith (1996), and in French the key sources include Du Roy and Du Roy (1994), Decamont (1996), Scott (1998), Rosanvallon (1992), and Bouglé-Moalic (2012), who provides rigorous content analysis of suffrage debates, including a long discussion of the final adoption in 1944. I draw, finally, on the parliamentary debates themselves, which are housed in the archives of the National Assembly.

[8] "Le poids du catholicisme serait déterminant, serine-t-on surtout," Rosanvallon 1992: 393.

both the incentives of leaders in the Radical Party and the motivations of women who were suffragists. As historian Paul Smith notes, what is peculiar about the suffrage debate in France is that it took place in a context where the regime itself was under threat.[9] The fact that the system faced many detractors meant that the stakes of women's enfranchisement (or any reform that would have empowered the right indefinitely) were perceived to be quite high. We can see this sentiment within the feminist movement itself—Léon Richer, founder of the largest and longest-lived of the feminist groups, the Ligue française pour le droit des femmes— declared in 1888 that "it would be dangerous—in France—to give women the political ballot. They are, in great majority, reactionaries and clericals. If they voted today, the Republic would not last six months."[10] And it cropped up in suffrage debates, where a senator who was instrumental in defeating suffrage in the upper chamber in 1922 portended that enfranchising women would amount to "sealing the tombstone of the Republic."[11]

As background information on the political structure in the Third Republic, the first part of the chapter delves into the rules governing electoral politics and the groups that were empowered throughout the period. After an 1885 electoral reform, seat malapportionment—where parties' seats in legislatures did not reflect their popular support—led to a situation in which elections to both houses of the French legislature favored voters in the countryside over those in the towns and cities. This malapportionment remained in spite of several major electoral reforms that are detailed below. Although the Radicals are believed to have been the prime beneficiaries from malapportionment, their position was vulnerable throughout the period due to high competition and a weakly institutionalized party system. If the distribution of voting preferences in rural areas changed—for example, by allowing a large conservative group of women to vote—then the Radicals' teetering position was certainly at risk.

In this volatile political environment, suffrage activists faced social, cultural, and logistical constraints on their organizational activities. The chapter's second section gives a brief introduction to the campaign for women's suffrage in France after 1870. Around the turn of the century, one organization boasted 21 thousand members; more than half a million

---

[9] Smith 1996: 4.
[10] Quoted in Bidelman 1976: 106.
[11] Alexandre Bérard, 1922, quoted in Hause and Kenney 1984: 240.

women were polled in support of the vote in 1914; and at least one large demonstration attracted two thousand or more supporters just before the First World War commenced. Though the scope of their actions were limited in some ways by the legacies of women's involvement in the French Revolution and the Paris Commune, French women were successfully working toward building broad organizations to agitate for franchise rights. Nevertheless, the 1914 march represented the last time that France's myriad suffrage organizations came together under a unified front.

The third section consists of an analysis of the failure of suffrage reform in the French legislature. In 1919, when a bill for women's suffrage was debated in the Chamber of Deputies, an amalgamation of Socialists, conservative republicans, some Radicals, and parties of the right brought it to a majority vote. But many among the Radicals, and nearly every member of Georges Clemenceau's cabinet, voted against the measure.[12] Analyzing roll-call votes, I show that opposition to suffrage was linked to the threat posed to the Radical Party by women's enfranchisement. On the whole, members of that party were more likely to vote against suffrage reform than members from the other parties, but there is also a crucial amount of *variation* in Radical members' votes. Using an historical proxy for the depth of the religious cleavage in French departments, I show that individual Radical politicians were unlikely to support suffrage reform if they came from highly religious constituencies, but more likely to support the measure if they represented more secular areas. In 1922, when the bill came up for discussion in the Senate, it was the Radicals that sent it to languish indefinitely in committee. Knowing the Senate would not budge, further attempts at passage in the Chamber were futile. This analysis provides support for the logic of women's enfranchisement: in the face of a long-standing political cleavage such as that posed by the religious divide in France, politicians make strategic choices about electoral reform. The implications of the strategic choice can be seen in national level political outcomes and in the individual incentives that drove roll-call votes.

The question that remains, and which is taken up in the final section, is how French suffragists responded to the Radical Party's fear of the clerical peril. Historians of the period have noted the plurality of "feminisms"

---

[12] Clemenceau's position itself was fairly clear. In 1907, while leading the country as Prime Minister, he authored a pamphlet that declared "if the right to vote were given to women tomorrow, France would all of a sudden jump backwards into the Middle Ages." Quoted in McMillan 1991: 56.

within French society, including socialist feminism, radical feminism, and even Catholic feminism. These factions have been labeled in different ways over time, but the major texts on the suffrage campaign agree that there was a substantive rift between the Catholic feminists and the secular feminists that undermined suffragists' abilities to form coalitions across cleavages. Unlike women in the United States and Great Britain, French women did not form non-partisan encompassing organizations that sought mass bases. This was problematic, because given France's manhood suffrage laws, the rules could not be written in such a way as to exclude large swaths of women from the electorate. Thus I suggest that secular suffragists chose to mobilize narrowly, even at the risk of not getting the vote, because the consequences of including all women were perceived to be too grave. Ultimately, the Senate's strong stance against suffrage in the 1920s, which was not challenged by a reinvigo-rated suffrage movement, would not be overturned until France's fourth republican project.[13]

THE FRENCH ELECTORAL SYSTEM AFTER 1870

In September of 1870, after Napoléon III suffered a humiliating defeat at the hands of the Germans in the Franco-Prussian war, the French monar-chy was once again stripped of its power, and the country embarked upon its third experiment with representative institutions.[14] The news of Napoléon's surrender caused the streets of Paris to erupt with protestors demanding the end of empire and the formation of a republic. By mid-month the Germans had laid a siege, encompassing the city's walls, and most of the city's elites decamped to the countryside. In the following spring, amidst the vacuum of power that grew as the siege wore on, a group of revolutionary workers, no small number of women, and the radicalized National Guard founded the Paris Commune to rule the city. After only fifty-four days, the army of Adolphe Thiers, which entered the city to "disarm the National Guard, repress popular activity, and restore state power," suppressed the Commune.[15] During one week of fighting, between 10 and 30 thousand Parisian communards were killed, ending, in

---

[13] Table A.4 in appendix IV presents a timeline of suffrage bills in France.

[14] France alone declared war on Prussia in July of 1870 because the latter, under the rule of Chancellor Otto von Bismark and King Wilhelm I, had annexed the previously (and presently) French territories of Alsace and Lorraine.

[15] Sowerwine 2001: 16.

a brutal show of force, what is known as Paris's last great revolution.[16] The government of the Third Republic, which emerged victor to this struggle, put into place institutions that, though revised through several major electoral reforms, sustained the Republic until the middle of the Second World War.

The Rules

The institutions of the Third Republic provided for an electoral system with a divided legislature, composed of the Chamber of Deputies and the Senate. This much remained constant throughout the entirety of the Republic. Members of the Chamber of Deputies were elected via direct ballot, open to all men, whereas Senators were elected indirectly by local councils. After 1913, with the advent of envelopes and voting booths, the ballot was secret.[17] The exact rules by which members were elected, including whether districts returned single members under personalistic voting procedures or multiple members via lists, changed several times in this period. Below I recount this electoral history as succinctly as possible, taking pains to highlight the perceived winners and losers under these sets of rules.

Under the electoral laws of 1875, the entire assembly would elect a president for a seven-year term. Deputies in the Chamber were normally expected to sit for four years, while most senators would sit for nine.[18] But if both the president and the Senate agreed, the Chamber could be dissolved ahead of schedule. If no candidate received an absolute majority of votes, the election went to the "second" ballot, where the candidate with the most votes (a plurality or a majority) could win.[19] Deputies were originally elected in single-member districts (*arrondissements*), three or four of which were contained in each of the country's ninety departments (*départements*), akin to US states.

Reforms established in the 1885 electoral law set departments up as multi-member constituencies, with the average department returning

---

[16] The sheer brutality of the repression is evident in comparison to the Jacobin's "Reign of Terror" under Robespierre, which took sixteen months to eliminate 2,600 Parisians. Sowerwine 2001: 24.

[17] Crook and Crook, 2007: 449.

[18] Campbell 1958: 73; Sowerwine 2001: 31.

[19] Interestingly, even candidates who had not stood on the first ballot could present themselves for the second ballot. The second ballot is still used today in France. It has been argued that the second ballot serves as a force for moderation in the French environment where extremist parties are quite well subscribed, because on the first ballot people vote their true preferences, but they vote strategically on the second. Campbell 1958: 44.

three deputies to the Chamber. The total number of seats varied with the population. The 1885 law allowed for one representative for every 70,000 inhabitants of French nationality, with an additional deputy if the remaining population summed to more than 35,000 French nationals.[20] Yet it also gave a minimum of three deputies to each department, leading to overrepresentation of the rural departments.[21]

The French Senate was composed of 300 members. The 1875 legislature elected 75 "life members," who were appointed until death or retirement.[22] The position was dissolved in 1885, but the last life senator was seated until 1919. The remaining 225 senators served nine-year terms, with one-third being elected every three years. (Seven of these senators came from Algeria and other colonies.) Depending on population, each department returned two, three, or five senators (and after 1885 with the multi-member districts, could have up to ten), who were chosen through department-level electoral colleges. These electoral colleges consisted of the department's deputies, members of a department's general council (*conseils généraux*), members of a department's municipal councils (*conseils d'arrondissement*), and, originally, one delegate from each commune council, regardless of commune size. In 1885, under the multi-member system, the more populous communes were given more delegates to the college, with Paris, for example, awarded thirty delegates.[23] This was reversed in February 1889, with the re-instatement of single-member districts. The single-member districts were maintained until September 1919, at which point another list system was introduced, only to be replaced, again, by single-member districts in 1928.

In spite of several reforms and reversals of those reforms in the rules regulating French elections, throughout the period, elections to both the Chamber and the Senate favored voters in the countryside. This is because a department's seats in the Senate and the Chamber were not determined solely with reference to population, and so seat shares were not allocated strictly as a function of vote shares.[24]

---

[20] Under the original electoral law of 1870 all inhabitants added to population counts, so the 1885 change took representation away from, for example, the populous industrial departments with lots of migrant workers. Campbell 1958: 76.

[21] The average department had three deputies. Campbell 1958: IV.

[22] Of these original life senators, 57 were republicans. Sowerwine 2001: 32.

[23] Campbell 1958: 139–40.

[24] Under the 1885 electoral laws it is believed that the Radicals were the beneficiaries of malapportionment at the expense of the Socialists, Communists, and Conservatives. Campbell 1958: 82–83.

Who Governed?

The question of who held decision-making power in France after 1870 has two components. The first relates to which factions were prominent, while the second relates to the parliamentary procedures that affected de facto power, allowing certain individuals or institutions to control the legislative agenda. During the Republic's early years, from 1870 onward, politics were dominated by the aristocracy, gentry, and supporters of the monarchy. The early fights among leaders of the Republic were over whether a republic was better than a constitutional monarchy, and about the proper role of the church in state affairs. Though monarchists, called "Conservatives," were divided over the church issue, republicans were united in the belief that church involvement in politics was inimical to a republican constitution.

Technically, the executive branch of government had considerable influence, insofar as the president had the constitutional power to dissolve the government. But after a strategic dissolution in 1877 that did not go as planned, no other Chamber was dissolved in the Third Republic.[25] Without recourse to dissolution, the executive of the French Republic was stripped of a key tool for shaping the agenda. Escaping a constant threat of re-election, deputies were freer to vote as they pleased. They were also vested with the power to bring down the cabinet if they felt it did not represent the general will, a tool which the deputies seem to have wielded with exuberance. Indeed, 70 years of the Republic saw 110 cabinets, with turnover reaching an apex in the interwar years, where 10 cabinets were installed in just 6.5 years.[26] The great instability of the governing cabinet brought to fruition a system in which legislation emanated from special committees in both legislative chambers.

When considering a piece of legislation, the chambers would send it to a commission, whose members, after studying the subject, would file a report. The *rapporteur* chosen to speak in the name of the commission was responsible for the fate of legislation. It was he who decided when to

---

[25] In 1873 a provisional government, elected by the assembly, brought to power a monarchist president for a seven-year term. The first legal elections of 1876 allocated 70.5 percent of seats to the republicans, but in 1877 the Conservative president, along with the Senate, dissolved the Chamber in the hopes of extracting an anti-republican majority from the voters. The strategy failed miserably: though their majority was not as large as before, the republicans secured 60.5 percent of the Chamber's seats. For the rest of the Third Republic, no other Chamber was dissolved in this way. Campbell 1958: 29.

[26] Campbell 1958: 28.

issue reports (or to stall), and how much support to give the bill ahead of roll-call votes (*scrutin*). Rapporteurs thus had considerable power, a fact that will emerge as important to the issue of women's suffrage.[27]

As to the social groups that dominated the legislature, landowners were quite powerful, but by the late nineteenth century more space was made for members of the professional classes. Only after 1900 did the lower-middle class begin to emerge as an important force in national politics. Thus, while in 1893, 56 percent of the Chamber's deputies were nobles or grand bourgeois, this number remained high, at 40 percent, by 1919. Throughout the era, it is safe to say that both chambers underrepresented the interests of industrial areas and the working classes in favor of the male peasantry and wealthy men.[28]

For reasons that historians and political scientists still debate, the Third Republic produced a party system that was relatively weak.[29] Only gradually, perhaps around 1900, did parties begin to emerge as coherent bodies. And even then, with the exception of the Communists and Socialists, they are said to have been parties more for legislative than for electoral purposes. Nevertheless it is possible to give a general sense of partisan "tendencies" in the legislature using legislator-level information. As figure 5.1 shows, prior to the First World War, the legislators with Radical leanings had the highest representation in the Chamber, though they never captured 50 percent or more of the seat shares. The Radicals, a group that voted left on political issues but right or center right on social and economic issues, tended toward coalition with the left before WWI, but were pushed toward a coalition with the right until 1923, when the "Cartel des gauches" again gained control of the government.[30]

A key fact to take away from a legislative history of this era is that although the Radicals were predominant in the Chamber and in the Senate, their hold on power during most of the Third Republic was never secure enough to engender complete confidence that their own power or the Republic more generally was insulated from attack. At first, it was the

[27] Smith 1996: 107.

[28] Campbell 1958: 22.

[29] The failure to develop strong parties is perhaps best explained by the fact that the Radical group of legislators, who formed part if not all of the ruling coalition for more than forty years, were united on political issues but divided on social and economic matters. The Radicals were able to coordinate on policies deemed crucial to the maintenance of the Republic—especially in the realm of education and the separation of the church and state—but its leaders were wary of too much disruption of the social order that might threaten the Republic's fragile institutions.

[30] Campbell 1958: 35ff.

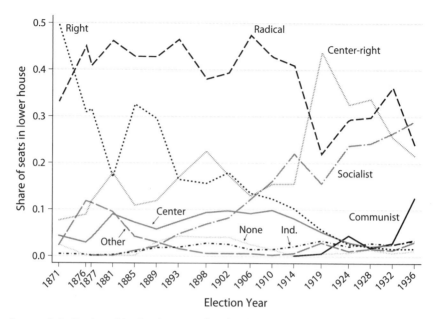

FIGURE 5.1. Partisanship in the French Chamber of Deputies during the Third Republic. For various party leanings, the chart lists the share of seats held during each legislature, whose start dates are represented on the x-axis. Source: Author's calculations using Graham 1984.

threat of monarchy and clericalism. Though the salience of these issues waned after the turn of the century, new foes, particularly socialism after the Russian Revolution and the rise of the right under the Bloc national in 1919 re-ignited anxiety among Radical politicians.

The heightened electoral competition that defined this era is of the sort that presents opportunities to entrepreneurial parties looking for ways to change the rules in their favor. As we have seen, with several transformations in the allocation of votes to seats (to proportional electoral rules and back, twice), adoption of the secret ballot, and adoption of reforms that enhanced parties' power, the legislature itself was not anti-reform. If a coalition of legislators believed it could capture the majority of women's votes and had the power to bring the change about, then women's enfranchisement could have become a political reality. The reason it did not happen may have been that the Radicals, though weak and searching for opportunities to change the rules, did not believe female voters would help them reach their goals.[31] In this political environment,

---

[31] As we have seen with the adoption, annulment, and re-adoption of electoral lists, they were not averse to all electoral changes.

centrist republican women who wanted to vote found themselves in a difficult situation.

SUFFRAGE MOBILIZATION UNTIL 1914

France is often hailed as the birthplace of feminism, but, like much of the politics in the country, its feminism was defined by extremes on both the right and the left that influenced the nature of mobilization on the issue of suffrage.[32] In 1836, just a few years before American women gathered in Seneca Falls, France's first feminist magazine, *La Gazette des femmes*, was founded, declaring women's right to be professionals, members of the civil service, and to exercise the vote.[33] The 1848 revolution saw a multiplication of feminist clubs and organizations that were quickly shut down as backlash mounted against the regime. But when the Third Republic began to stabilize, there was a surge of feminist activity, including the circulation of pamphlets, feminist periodicals, and the formation of suffrage organizations.

Whereas in the United States and the United Kingdom, the largest organizations that advocated for women's rights were explicitly non-partisan, in France women's rights organizations existed among the republican, moderate, conservative, catholic, and Socialist banners. Most of these groups had fewer than 200 members, but one, the Conseil national des femmes françaises (CNFF), claimed 21,000 members in 1901.[34] The leaders of the CNFF were primarily moderate republicans, but the organization did have a few Catholic and Socialist members. In general, the leaders of feminist organizations were nearly always from the middle classes and almost always from the urban areas of Paris and Lyon. Before the First World War, the suffragists were "Protestants, Jews, freethinkers, and atheists" holding positions as teachers, postal clerks, and students.[35]

From 1880 to 1914, French women's demand for the right to vote grew throughout the country. But, although feminist organizations existed in most places, the distribution was not necessarily even. Only five departments of the ninety-nine were completely devoid of feminist organizations, but more than half of the departments had fewer than two

[32] See, for example, Hause and Kenney 1984: 5–6; Offen 1994.
[33] Zeldin 1973: 347.
[34] Hause and Kenney 1984: 41–42.
[35] Ibid.: 43–44.

feminist organizations.[36] The Union française pour le suffrage des femmes (UFSF), a moderate suffrage organization that focused on procuring the female franchise in local elections, accounted for about half of the feminist organizations in the country as a whole. The UFSF was more prominent on the north and western coasts. It boasted 135 branches in total, with 21 branches in Paris alone. The Ligue française pour le droit des femmes (LFDF), a more radical organization with national aspirations (at least by 1900), had branches in seven departments in 1914. There was not a clear spatial distribution of the LFDF, except that several branches were located in the Somme and Pas-de-Calais (in the north, home to the industrial triangle).

Within each of these organizations, the most common means of eliciting suffrage support (whether the goal was local or national politics) entailed meetings among sympathizers and public outreach through specialized journals and the popular press. Other, more visible tactics, such as distributing handbills, aggressively lobbying politicians, or staging large demonstrations, were rarely employed. An attempt at marching on the Place Vendôme in 1904 was so unsuccessful at courting participants that no other large demonstration was organized for ten more years. But this reluctance to engage in public displays of suffrage activism began to change in 1914 after a bill favorable to suffrage, known as the *Buisson Report*, was briefly debated before being relegated to obscurity under a committee in the Chamber of Deputies.[37] General elections held that spring, on 26 April and 12 May 1914, brought the ouster of eighty-nine deputies who had voted to continue discussing the Buisson Report, leaving the Chamber deprived of many suffrage sympathizers. Around this time, suffragist organizations began to take more dramatic steps toward advocating for the vote.

As proof of women's desire for the vote, in May 1914 the magazine *Le Journal* organized a poll of women to see how many wanted the vote: the end result of the poll revealed 505,972 women in favor of voting rights against only 116 detractors.[38] With a population of around 40 million, the enthusiasm of 1.3 percent of people may seem modest, but suffrage organizers heralded this result as proof positive of the interest of French women in electoral politics. It emboldened cooperation among different segments of the suffrage movement for the first time, culminating in what

[36] The data come from Hause and Kenney 1984: map 5.
[37] The Buisson Report was part of the Chamber's debate on proportional representation.
[38] Hause and Kenney 1984: 188 and ch. 6.

is known as the "Condorcet" demonstration, in honor of the famous early espouser of women's equality. The demonstration brought together a federation of seventeen suffrage organizations to march on the Orangerie toward a statue of Condorcet on 5 July 1914. The demonstrations were estimated to have between two and ten thousand participants, with suffragists claiming the upper limit of support.

In what is perhaps just a cruel twist of historical fate, the Condorcet demonstration, which represented the first major act of cooperation among different branches of the women's movement, occurred just six days after Ferdinand and Isabella, the Archduke and Archduchess of Austro-Hungary, were assassinated in Sarajevo, in other words, just after the event that ignited the First World War. There is a sense that had it not been for France's entry into the war, and the political upheaval this engendered, the cooperative cross-organizational movement of suffragists, just beginning to cohere, might not have deteriorated. Instead, after the Armistice of November 1918, for reasons discussed later in this chapter, there would be no more moderate cooperation among the suffragists. Nevertheless, the end of the war brought a proliferation of new bills agitating for women's political inclusion to the parliamentary table.

WHY DID SUFFRAGE FAIL?

It was not for lack of opportunity that women's suffrage stalled in the Third Republic. From 1919 until 1935, more than forty bills related to women's suffrage rights, in one form or another, were introduced into the Chamber of Deputies. Many of these bills received majority support in the Chamber but stalled in the Senate. At least five such bills were debated in the Senate from after WWI until the abdication of parliamentary powers at Vichy, yet the Senate never gave way. (See table A.4 in appendix IV for a timeline of suffrage measures in France from 1919 to 1940.) Given all of these potential moments of reform, how can we make sense of this failure?

Several historians of the suffrage movement, including Paul Smith and Stephen Hause and Anne Kenney, have attributed the suffrage stalemate to the disincentives faced by the Radical Party. In line with the theoretical claims forwarded in this book, being both insecure in their position and worried that women would be under the thumbs of the priests, Radicals may have found reason to resist enfranchisement. Here I examine the evidence that incentives related to the clerical peril influenced Radical vote choice in three ways. First, I provide an overview of the debates on suffrage in the Chamber of Deputies, describing how Radical deputies often raised concerns about the impact of women's enfranchisement on the future of the Republic. Following that, I analyze roll-call votes in the Chamber and Senate, showing that Radical deputies' vote choices, in particular, were influenced by the salience of the religious cleavage, and that all parties were impacted by the overall level of political competition. Finally I turn to evidence on suffrage mobilization, looking at suffragists' response to the stalemate in 1919.

An Overview of Suffrage Debates

The pre-war Chamber of Deputies, elected in 1914 as the Republic's 11th legislature, voted in 1919 to extend votes to women. A bill originally introduced in the 10th legislature by Paul Dussaussoy (Pas-de-Calais) of the *Action libérale,* a Catholic republican party, was re-examined in October 1918 and sent to a committee, led by Louis Andrieux (Basses-Alpes) of the *Républicains de gauche,* beginning in January 1919. The bill, which would give women department-level suffrage for munici-pal, arrondissement, and general councils, was discussed in the Chamber of Deputies on 8, 15, and 20 May 1919. During the course of these discussions, two substitute proposals (*contre-projet*) were introduced in place of the bill. The first article of the substitute proposal, suggested by Jean Bon of the *Parti socialiste,* would give women suffrage on the same terms as men by decreeing that the electoral laws governing the entire elected assembly (meaning both the Chamber and Senate) are applicable to all French citizens without distinction of sex.[39]

The Chamber's debate on the original bill as well as the substitute proposal for full suffrage revolved around a few key themes, including women's role in public life, their "readiness" for political expression, and the nature of equality in the Third Republic. Some of the arguments raised can seem, today, to be quintessential examples of sexism in public discourse. Others, however, evince a much more strategic understanding of the effect of women's votes on the composition of the legislature and, hence, public life in France.

---

[39] See the *Journal officiel de la République française. Débats parlementaires.* Chambre (1880) (hereafter J.O.) 20 May 1919. The first article of the substitute bill, for full women's suffrage, reads "Les lois et dispositions régimentaires sur l'électorat et l'éligibilité à toutes assemblées élues sont applicables à tous les citoyens français sans distinction de sexe" (p. 2350). The article was voted on under the roll call (*scrutin*) N. 904 (pp. 2365–66). 441 voters, a 221 majority in favor of suffrage for all French citizens without distinction of sex.

Suffrage opponents in the Chamber argued that women would catalyze the death of the Republic, as their votes would be entirely under the sway of the priests.[40] A second set of opinions, issued by Augagneur of the *Parti républicain socialiste*, who eventually voted for the bill, and conservative republican Pierre-Étienne Flandin (Yonne) of the *Union républicaine radicale et socialiste*, who abstained from voting, contended that women's involvement should be limited to municipal and local suffrage because women were ignorant of politics and not yet mature enough for a full set of rights. (Of course, being indirectly elected, Senators were also quite concerned to keep women from the local franchise.)

Suffrage proponents, including the Socialist proposer Bon and the left-republican Andrieux, argued for the importance of voting for validating women's individualism, claiming that *"ceux qui ne votent pas ne comptent pas"*: those who do not vote do not count. Giving women votes would allow them to defend their lives as mothers or wives, and would develop their interests in political life. Women have unique virtues to bring to the public sphere and, in a democracy, should not be excluded. These leftist proponents gave little heed to their opponents' more dramatic claims about the peril of politics under votes for women. Bon, in particular, found the notion that France would be reorganized under a monarchy if votes were given to women absurd.

Toward the end of the 1919 debate, the discussion took on a more strategic tone. Would the Senate consider the expansion for full suffrage a move too far? Should the Chamber really pay heed to the Senate's conservative nature or was it the case that *"La Chambre des idées doit défendre de grandes et nobles idées"* (The Chamber of ideas should defend grand and noble ideas)? Would giving women the "experience" of the local vote allow the Chamber to, at a later date, gauge the "success" of women in engaging in public affairs? How, if the ballot is secret, will they be able to know the women's vote and know if it was a success? These concerns indicate that the consequences of women's suffrage were viewed, at least to some degree, through an electoral lens. French deputies were aware of the electoral impact that female voters might have on their own and the Senate's futures, and did not shy away from the obvious wish to know how women would vote before deciding whether to extend the franchise.

The opposition's concerns were not able, in the end, to overwhelm the roll-call vote. On 20 May 1919, the bill for full women's suffrage received

[40] Smith 1996; Zeldin 1973: 360.

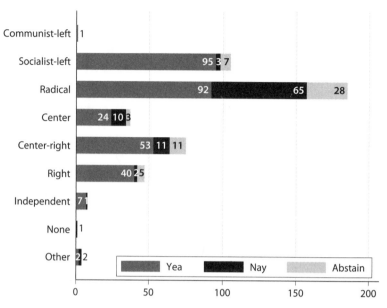

FIGURE 5.2. Support for Women's Suffrage in the Chamber of Deputies, 1919. The figure plots the number of deputies in each partisan grouping (out of 601 total), and, within parties, the number that supported, dissented, or abstained from the vote on a bill that would apply electoral rights regardless of sex. Source: roll-call votes coded from J.O., 20 May 1919; party tendencies calculated from Graham 1984.

97 votes against and 314 votes for. Nevertheless, from a strategic point of view the breakdown of these votes is telling: as figure 5.2 shows, nearly all opposition to the bill came from the Radicals—the centrist stronghold that maintained power through shifting coalitions during much of the period—while support came from both the right and the left. Only 1 percent of Socialists, 8 percent of the parties of the right, and 10 percent of conservative republicans voted against women's suffrage, yet nearly 21 percent of the Radicals and Radical Socialists voted against the measure. Radical members were also much more likely to abstain from voting, with 28 percent abstaining altogether. Although there were no speeches explicitly calling for party members to abstain from the roll-call vote, the high rate of abstention may reflect hesitation by members of the "party of universal suffrage" to so visibly contest a measure which would actually bring about universal suffrage.[41]

---

[41] The relationship between republicans and members of the Radical Party and universal suffrage was complex. The 1848 constitution granted universal suffrage and the people

Analysis of the 1919 Vote in the Chamber

Throughout the 1920s there were several roll-call votes taken in the lower chamber and many procedural votes in the Senate on the issue of votes for women.[42] Rather than analyzing all of these separate polls, I will focus on the first vote in each chamber after World War I ended. Two reasons underlie this choice. First, the 1919 vote in the Chamber produced visible divisions across the parties, but also produced heterogeneous results within parties. Later votes contained no such diversity: the rate of support grew to near unity on subsequent suffrage bills, leaving little room for empirical probing. To the degree that "cheap talk" was an issue, it would have been particularly acute after 1922 because the Senate's firm refusal to consider the Bon bill in 1922, and the debates and reports that accompanied that decision, firmly established the upper chamber's hostile position. Prior to those debates, it was at least possible that the Senate's vote may have gone in a different direction. In this sense, the 1919 bill in the Chamber presents the best opportunity to study "truthful" revelations of individual preferences for women's suffrage.

Secondly, while the Chamber's support for suffrage grew during the interwar period, the Senate's suffragism attenuated throughout the following decades. This was driven in part by the increasing presence of the Radical group in the upper chamber and, perhaps surprisingly, by the heightened conservativism of the youngest Radical representatives. In 1922, the group had 153 senators; in 1928, 189; and by 1938, the Radicals made up nearly two-thirds of the upper house. During the entire period, the average level of opposition by this group was between 72 and 84 percent.[43] The rising strength of the Radical group, and the group's persistent anti-suffrage stance give special resonance to the events in 1919 and 1922. As the Radical party's power waxed over the next twenty years, the window of opportunity for women's suffrage waned. For these reasons, the earlier votes are the most politically informative.

Expectations for Party Vote Choice

To guide the discussion of the roll-call votes, table 5.1 presents a modified version of the theoretical electoral logic presented in Chapter 2 that

---

promptly elected Louis-Napoléon Bonaparte president, ultimately bringing the Republic to its knees, and thereby giving life to the Second Empire. But when the 1871 constitution was being debated they did not restrict the male suffrage, in spite of the "ambivalence" that republicans had about the practice of universal suffrage. Offen 1994: 153–155; Bateman 2018.

[42] See table A.4 in appendix IV.

[43] Smith 1996: 151.

TABLE 5.1. Party Level Predictions. The boxes list which parties are expected to support suffrage when competition is low or high, and when the department was historically religious or secular.

	Political Competition	
	Low	High
Politically Religious	Right <	**Right**
Department	∨	∧
Secular Department	Left/Radicals <	**Left/Radicals**

summarizes my expectations of the divisions across parties on the issue of suffrage based on local-level characteristics. The horizontal axis represents the level of political competition, which can be thought of either as the level of competition in the department overall or competition in an individual legislator's district. The vertical axis represents the political religiosity of the department. The idea is that politicians will have beliefs about the future political loyalty of female voters depending on the entrenchment of the Church in a department's political life. Women in more politically religious departments will be expected to vote more conservatively—that is, with the Church and against the Republic—while women in less religious departments will be expected to be less conservative.

In light of the parliamentary discussion of women's enfranchisement, the first prediction is that the left parties will be the most supportive of suffrage, as it was often Socialists who proposed suffrage bills and who voiced the most enthusiasm in the Chamber of Deputies. We should also expect the parties of the right to be most favorable in more religious constituencies, and the Radical Party to be the least favorable. As in the book on the whole, I expect support for suffrage to be lowest in less competitive political environments, and that support falls when women are not considered allies of the party in question.

The Dataset Description

To explore the validity of this argument, I analyze support for suffrage by looking at how characteristics related to the religious cleavage, partisanship, and political competition correlate with average suffrage sentiment among members who served in the Chamber of Deputies from 1914 to 1919. In the 1914 election, 601 deputies were elected out of single-member districts *circonscriptions*. Ali Cirone has generously shared district level information on political competition in the 1914 election. To this I have added information on deputy-level party affiliation from Graham (1984), and information on the religious cleavage, measured at the departmental level, from Tackett (2014). (These indicators are described in more detail below.) This produces a deputy-level database that can be used to analyze suffrage support at the individual, party, or departmental level.

The key dependent variable is whether a given deputy voted "Yea" or "Nay" on the bill for women's suffrage in 1919. This roll-call vote was coded from *Journal officiel de la République française. Débats parlementaires:* 20 May 1919.

Measuring Political Competition

A key theoretical concept is political competition. For each deputy elected in 1914 we can measure various dimensions of political competition. Cirone (2017) codes all elections to the Chamber of Deputies based on whether they went to a second ballot, the effective number of parties in the final round of the election, the incumbency status of the legislator, whether legislators held multiple offices (*cumul des mandats*), and voter turnout as a share of registered voters. As in the analysis of the United States, I also calculate the ratio of votes won by the runner-up to the votes won by the winner in the final round, with higher values indicating a closer competition. Although these measures are initially recorded at the candidate (election) level, they can be aggregated to produce averages at the departmental level. I will focus specifically on the effective number of candidates, voter turnout, and the ratio of runner-up to winner, as with each of these a higher value indicates higher levels of political competition.

Measuring the Religious Cleavage

An implication of the argument is that Radical deputies from more politically religious departments would be less likely to vote for suffrage than Radicals from secular departments. The key independent variable of interest is thus the salience of the religious cleavage in the areas from which deputies are elected. I capture this using a variable called the *clerical peril*, which subtracts from one the share of priests in a given department that, during the French Revolution, swore fealty to the Civil Constitution of 1791.

In the wake of the first French Revolution, Radical members of National Assembly sought to vitiate the power of the Church through a series of reforms that included the abolition of tithes, direct election of the bishopric, the nationalization of church lands, and bringing the clergy into public employ.[44] The keystone of these reforms was a decree, issued in July 1790, that all members of the clergy (but particularly those with elevated positions in the hierarchy) take an oath of faith to the nation, the law, and the Civil Constitution. Priests who acquiesced to the state and took the oath are known as the "juring priests," those who refused, the refectory priests, were the "non-jurors" whose loyalty remained with the Vatican.[45]

Timothy Tackett, an historian and electoral geographer of the revolutionary period, argues that while the pattern of oath-taking does not correlate with earlier "maps" of politics, culture, or economics in France, future patterns of religious practice and the shape of political conflict thereafter conforms closely to the distribution of priests that took the oath in 1791. He writes:

> Substantially different regional reactions and trains of logic had come together in forming the oath geography [i.e., which priests committed to the constitution]. But, thereafter, the oath itself would rapidly set in motion a complex concatenation of action and reaction and would greatly intensify the polarization of clerical and anticlerical factions throughout the country. It served to unify, to "nationalize," the diverse forces of religious confrontation and thus contributed to the political realignment of French society.[46]

The ideological realignment that was set into motion by the conflict over the oath is reflected in voting patterns to the present day. Even political geographers such as William Brustein, who stress the social and material origins of contemporary partisanship, do not discount the important independent effect that the religious cleavage has had on political life in France.[47] Hence the share of priests who swore fealty to the civil constitution in 1791 may be a reasonable proxy for the depth of the religious cleavage across France's departments.

One question a reader might have concerns the utility of a measure of religiosity that dates to 1791 when data from the early twentieth century might be preferable. There are several reasons for this choice, both practical and theoretical. First, the French census did not specifically record respondents' religion, making an exact measure of religious belief

[44] Tackett 2014: 11–14.
[45] At the discretion of local political leaders, non-jurors could be forced out of the clergy. In a few departments, such as Rossillion, there are reports of the persecution of jurors.
[46] Tackett 2014: 299.
[47] Brustein 1988: 146ff. and table 18.

in the early 1900s impossible. But even if the census recorded information on religious belief, membership in the Catholic Church, or the frequency of church attendance around 1920, these measures are not good proxies for the religious cleavage because most people in France were Catholic around 1900 and still are to this day. Moreover, in the event that church attendance was a good indicator of anti-republicanism, the measure would likely suffer from bias due to simultaneity: if church attendance ebbed and flowed with the salience of religious issues in politics, we should expect higher levels of attendance in moments when the Church was trying to exert influence.

Substantively, understanding whether the clerical peril hindered suffrage does not require knowledge about Catholicism per se, but about the religious cleavage as driven by *political* Catholicism. In the words of Suzanne Berger, "The Catholics, politically defined, were a subset of religious Catholics who were made aware of the impact of politics on their lives principally through the impact of state decisions on the religious institutions to which they belonged and whose response to this impact was to line up on the side of the church."[48] Religious affiliation or even church attendance may not capture this political aspect of Catholicism in France. Indeed, there was substantial disagreement among Catholics as to the virtues of the republican form of government. Liberal Catholics were supportive of the Republic, while the integralists were committed to re-instating the church in all aspects of political life.[49]

Along with disbanding monarchy, weakening the strength of the powerful Church was a key tenant upon which the first three French republics were founded. In the era of the suffrage movement, which was also the beginning of mass politics in France, divisions over the church-state issue were foundational to the formation of political parties. As the heated vote in 1905 over public funding of Church schools demonstrated, the project was still incomplete at the dawn of the twentieth century.[50] But religious tensions became particularly heated after the First World War, when the conservative ruling coalition, the Bloc national, allowed the Vatican to re-establish an embassy in Paris.[51] Because the Catholic Church

[48] Berger 1974: 24.

[49] Berger 1987: 119, 122, 130.

[50] Until the 1905 vote, church-state conflicts had cooled a bit at the end of the nineteenth century. Pope Leo issued an encyclical statement stating that the Church was not linked to any particular form of government, and that Christians could accept republican governance (Sowerwine 2001: 66).

[51] Smith 1996: 126.

was a political actor in France, and church attendance could either represent an outlet for political expression and education or solely represent belief, which many republicans shared, a measure of church attendance in the 1900s is either uninformative about the religious cleavage or, worse, endogenous to the overall political milieu. On the other hand, given that priests' refusal of the civil oath was critical to the formation of political Catholicism, the share of oath-takers in a department may in fact be a good indicator of the religious cleavage in the Third Republic.

The map in figure 5.3 provides a glimpse of the clerical peril circa 1791. Generally, the center, southwest, and northeast (near the "industrial triangular") were the most secular and, arguendo, more republican, while the north, west, and south were the most religious.

CORRELATES OF SUFFRAGE SUPPORT IN FRANCE

What are the correlates of support for suffrage at the department level? The first question to tackle is whether there is a relationship between the clerical peril, partisanship, and support for suffrage. Second is whether this relationship is mediated by political competition.

Clerical Peril and Support for Suffrage

Figure 5.4 shows how the historical religious cleavage correlates with the position of the Radical Party (1914–1919) within a department. On average, there is about a 13-percentage-point gap in the Radical Party presence from more secular to more politically religious departments, suggesting that the Radical Party was not as prominent in places where the Church had a more important role in public life. Further, departments with a greater share of Radical members among its deputations to the Chamber were less supportive of suffrage overall. Geographically, support for suffrage was strongest in the center of France and in the southeast, while the Radical Party was strongest in the north and southwest. The southwest and northwest were also places where the religious cleavage was more dominant. The first question, then, is how the Radical MPs acted when they were located in the more historically religious departments.

Taking up this question, we can look at the raw data of the share of deputies that supported women's suffrage, by party, plotted against the entrenched religiosity of the department. Figure 5.5 divides departments into ten groups (deciles) based on the level of the clerical peril along the x-axis. The left side of the x-axis represents places that would have been more secular—where a greater share of priests sided with the Republic

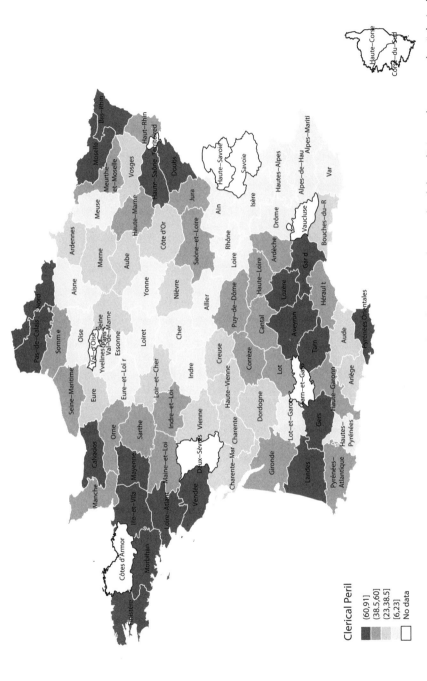

FIGURE 5.3. Map of the Religious Cleavage in France. The map plots the historical strength of the religious cleavage—the "clerical peril"—measured by 1 minus the share of priests that swore fealty to the 1791 Civil Constitution. Darker shades indicate more politically religious departments. Data come from Tackett 2014: appendix 2.

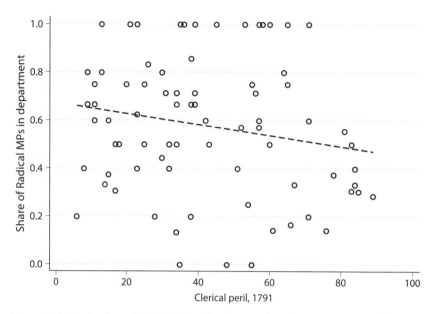

FIGURE 5.4. Radicals and Religiosity. The figure plots the percentage of deputies who were members of the Radical Party (1914–1919) in a given department based on the political religiosity of the department.

under the 1791 civil constitution—and the right side of the axis shows places where the religious threat to the Radical Party may have been greater. The overall vote choice of deputies is plotted by taking the average support for suffrage of parties on the far left and far right of the spectrum, and the average support of the Radical Party, within each decile bin of the clerical peril. The interspersed lines are from a local linear regression. Finally, the number of deputies in each decile of the clerical peril, by party, is listed in the figure.

Figure 5.5 shows a relatively constant correlation between support for suffrage and the political religiosity of the department for the parties of the left and right. In the most secular departments, nearly 100 percent of deputies from the left and right supported suffrage, while in the most historically religious department average support falls to around 85 percent. On the other hand, the Radical Party vote choice is much more sensitive to the historical religiosity of a department. In the most secular departments, about 75 percent of Radical deputies supported suffrage, while in the most religious departments, around 35 percent of deputies supported women's enfranchisement.

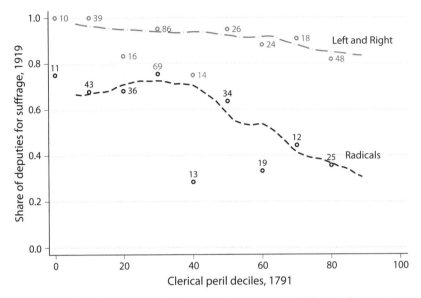

FIGURE 5.5. Clerical Peril, Partisanship, and Support for Suffrage. The x-axis represents 10-percentage-point groupings of the clerical peril, the y-axis depicts the overall share of deputy support for suffrage within parties. The numbers on the graph depict the number of deputies in that group.

The raw data suggest, therefore, that there is a correlation between the religiosity of a department and the Radical Party's support for suffrage. Historians have argued that fear of women's religiosity drove the Radical Party to resist women's enfranchisement. As we saw above, although the 1919 bill received majority support in the Chamber of Deputies, the key element of resistance came from within the Radical group. What the data in figure 5.5 indicate is that the resistance to women's suffrage in the Chamber tended to come from Radical members in politically Catholic districts.

Partisanship, Religiosity, and Suffrage Support

The theoretical argument made throughout the book is that politicians are motivated to support women's enfranchisement when they are subject to high levels of competition and when they believe women will be their political allies. We took one look at this issue above by seeing whether the Radical Party's support was related to the religious cleavage, and hence the threat to their own party's survival in certain areas of the country. I interpret the relationship in figure 5.5 as providing some evidence that Radical deputies in historically religious departments feared that women would not be allies. To complete the analysis, it is important to examine whether the parties that were likely to see women as allies were willing to support enfranchisement in general or only when political competition was high. My argument will be more compelling to the extent that I can show that competition conditions the relationship between religiosity and party support for suffrage.[52]

To analyze these relationships, in figure 5.6 I look at the individual deputy roll-call data within the Radical Party, departmental level information on religiosity, and information on the competitive landscape faced by that deputy in the 1914 election. The competition measures include the effective number of candidates in the final round of voting, the overall level of turnout, and the ratio of runner-up to winner. For each competition variable, I constructed three groups, "terciles," where observations that are in the bottom 33rd percentile of the distribution are coded as "Low competition," observations in the 34th to 66th percentiles are coded as "Medium competition," and observations above the 66th percentiles are coded as "High competition." Within these competition groups I examine the average proportion of Radical deputies that voted for suffrage in 1919 along the distribution of the clerical peril. Figure 5.6 presents correlations using both a linear fit of the relationship between suffrage support, religiosity, and competition, as well as with a "lowess" curve that estimates correlations for smaller subsets of the data. This allows us to see how overall levels of support for suffrage among Radical deputies varied based on political competition and the religious cleavage.

Runner-up to Winner. The ratio of runner-up to winner divides the share of votes won to the second largest party by the share of votes won by the winner. It provides an indication of how large a lead, on average, is held by the winners in each constituency. When this number is closer to one, the runner up is right on the winner's heels. This is an indication of high competition. When this approaches zero, the winner holds all the seats. This variable is left-skewed, meaning that there are more observations close to one than there are close to zero. The terciles

---

[52] The appendix lists average support for suffrage given various measures of competition and religiosity in table A.3.

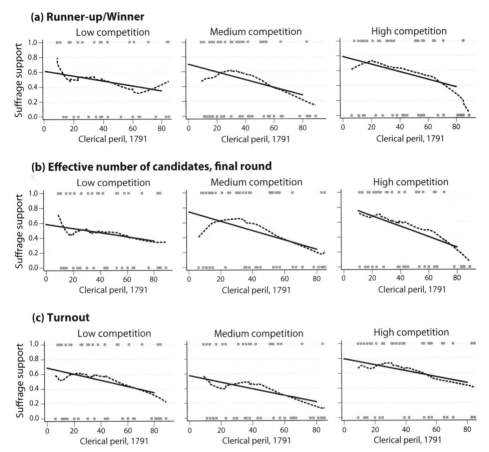

FIGURE 5.6. Raw Data Plots of Suffrage Support, the Religious Cleavage, and Competition. The figure depicts the proportion of Radical Party members that voted for women's suffrage (y-axis) given the historical religiosity of their departments (x-axis) and the level of competition. Decile bins of the clerical peril are formed with reference to all departments, hence the sample size can vary based on the number of Radical deputies across groupings of competition and religiosity. The scatterplot points show the relative sample size for each of the groupings. The solid line shows a linear fit of the bivariate correlation, while the dashed line is a lowess smoothed fit of the raw data.

cut the variable at values of 0.59 (winner has 63 percent of the votes), 0.85 (winner has 54 percent of the votes), and 0.99 (close to 50-50).

Figure 5.6, panel a, presents the relationship between the runner-up to the winner, the clerical peril, and Radical support for suffrage within parties. Across all levels of competition, highly religious departments received the lowest levels of support for suffrage from Radical deputies (between 30 and 40 percent voted yes in 1919). Notably, support for suffrage was higher in more secular departments. When competition was low (the winner won 63 percent of votes in their district), around 60 percent of MPs from secular districts supported suffrage. In the high-competition districts (the winner won only 50 percent of votes), around 80 percent of Radical deputies from secular districts supported suffrage. This gap suggests that Radical votes varied considerably with the religiosity and level of competition within districts.[53]

Effective Number of Candidates. The effective number of candidates tells us about how many people were, on average, vying for the same seat. We might suspect that places that are more ideologically homogenous will have fewer candidates and less competition, while more heterogeneous communities will have more competition and options in the electoral arena. In my data, the number of candidates ranges from one to four with the average around two, which is what we might expect in a single-member district system. The terciles are demarcated at 1.98, 2.02, and 2.97. Panel b of figure 5.6 shows the relationship between the effective number of candidates, the religious cleavage, and support for suffrage by Radical MPs. Overall, the findings mirror those from the ratio of runner-up to winner, although note that the slope of the bivariate correlation is much steeper in the high-competition case. When a deputy faced two or more competitors, he was much less likely to vote for suffrage in religious departments.[54]

Turnout. The final competition variable I analyze divides the number votes cast by the number of registered voters. High turnout is often a signal and a symptom of high competition. When everyone knows who will win (as is the case in less competitive districts), the marginal return to voting is low. But when there is uncertainty, every vote might count, which pushes turnout up. In the 1914 election, between 38 and 90 percent of registered voters actually cast votes, with the average falling around 77 percent. The terciles are demarcated at 75 percent turnout, 81 percent, and 88.4 percent. Panel c of figure 5.6 shows

[53] A similar exercise for the right and left shows that in these high-competition districts, we see much higher support of women's enfranchisement in the most religious departments for the right. Few left deputies are elected in these districts.

[54] A similar exercise for the right shows that they are more supportive of suffrage in competitive districts (measured by the effective number of candidates) that are more religious.

the relationship between the turnout, the religious cleavage, and support for suffrage among Radical MPs. The patterns of support are similar to the other measures of competition—Radical votes for suffrage fall in more religious departments. Here, though, it appears that Radical MPs were the most supportive of suffrage in the highest turnout environments.

Endogeneity Concerns

When social scientists analyze observational data and detect correlations between key variables of interest, one concern is whether an alternative explanation might actually account for the relationship depicted. In this study there are two potential issues. First is that the religious cleavage itself is driving political competition. Second is that competition alone explains the visible patterns. The utility of the clerical peril in 1791 as a proxy for the religious cleavage circa 1900 rests, in part, on the fact that future political outcomes can be traced to a defining moment more than one hundred years earlier. But to the extent that an important aspect of future politics is influenced by what happened in 1791, we might be concerned that all aspects of politics are linked to the past. That is, we might worry about the correlation between the religious cleavage and other indicators of competition. In this case, the two sides of the schematic in table 5.1 would be endogenous to one another either because the religious cleavage drives political competition or because some third factor drives both.

I hope to allay this concern by looking at the correlation between the clerical peril in 1791 and measures of political competition described above. These measures of high competition include the effective number of candidates in the final round of voting, the ratio of runner-up to winner, and turnout as a share of registered voters (where higher turnout implies a higher salience election).[55] There is virtually no correlation

---

[55] The online appendix (doi:10.7910/DVN/JZYGRB) contains scatterplots of the correlation between these measures of competition and religiosity. In addition, I also looked at other measures available from Cirone (2017). There was no correlation ($r = -0.6$) between the share of deputies that held multiple offices (*cumul des mandats*) and religiosity, and no correlation ($r = -0.11$) between the share of deputies who had been incumbents and the clerical peril. There was a positive correlation ($r = 0.35$) between the share of elections that went to a second round and suffrage support in more secular departments. I did not include this variable because the interpretation of the second ballot is complicated. On the one hand, this might in fact suggest a higher level of competition overall—with many dissimilar groups vying for political influence. On the other hand, a competitive first ballot might suggest low levels of coordination among ideologically similar groups. We might expect that a real threat

between competition and historical religiosity: on average, more secular departments and more religious departments fielded 1.9 candidates in elections to the Chamber of Deputies ($r = 0.18$); the ratio of runner-up to winner was 0.63 in historically secular departments and 0.64 in more religious departments ($r = 0.00$); and turnout was slightly lower in more secular departments (72 percent of eligible people voted) than in more religious departments (78 percent voted, $r = -0.21$). This suggests that the average level of competition was similar to competition in departments that were more historically religious, as in departments that were historically more secular. In addition, there also does not appear to be a simple correlation between competition and support for suffrage overall. The correlations range from 0.2 for the effective number of candidates in the final round and suffrage support to 0.08 for the ratio of votes for the runner-up over votes to the winner and support, suggesting that for Radical deputies, the relationship between competition and support was mediated by religiosity.[56] Finally, in results not shown, I looked at the social bases of leadership along the oath-taking spectrum. There is no correlation between the share of MPs elected in 1914 that were employed in the liberal professions and the share of priests who took the civil oath. But there is a slight negative correlation between property ownership of the deputies and oath-taking ($r = -0.18$) (though in most departments, the average ownership status was zero). Deputies from more secular departments were less likely to be landed and more likely to face a second ballot, at least in the 1914 election.

To summarize the findings, the descriptive analysis shows strong partisan dynamics in support for suffrage related to both the religious cleavage and political competition. As we have seen, in the 1919 bill voted on in the Chamber of Deputies, most MPs voted for suffrage, but there were high levels of dissent among Radical members. Radical members formed the majority of the Chamber at this time, but were found less commonly in the more historically religious departments: the most religious departments returned Radical members in 50 percent of their seats, while the most secular returned Radicals in about 63 percent of their seats. Overall, we see that the more religious a department, the less

---

from an ideological opponent group would minimize the overall number of parties as the threatened group sought to combine forces to overcome the challenger.

[56] Looking at the other measures of competition, there is a small correlation between the share of elections in a department that went to a second ballot and suffrage support ($r = 0.2$), and a very small negative correlation between the share of deputies that were incumbents and suffrage support ($r = -0.07$). Similarly for the dual mandates ($r = -0.07$).

likely the Radical members were to support suffrage. The second question I investigate in order to test chapter 2's theory of suffrage extension is whether the religious cleavage interacted with competition to influence Radical Party vote choice. The prediction, which is supported by the analysis, is that Radical MPs would have been less likely to support suffrage in competitive districts that were religious, because they stood to lose in such elections given the population of women within them. On the other hand, in more secular departments, Radicals would not face as great a threat, so Radicals should have been more likely to support franchise extension when competition was high. Finally, I investigated whether a third factor might be driving the relationship between religiosity, competition, and the Radical Party vote choice, but found no evidence that the religious cleavage itself influenced political competition, nor that competition alone is predictive of suffrage support. The relationship between competition and support for suffrage is therefore mediated by the historical religious cleavage. From this, I think it is possible to infer that legislators that think they will lose with women's suffrage will not support enfranchisement, but that when competition is high, legislators that have less to fear will be more inclined to support reform.

Blocking Suffrage in the Senate

Amidst considerable opposition by the Radical Party, the Chamber of Deputies nevertheless voted in favor of women's suffrage in 1919. Such luck was not to be had on the floor of the Senate. The Chamber's bill, which was sent for study under the Senate's Commission of Universal Suffrage (a standing committee), was never actually discussed. Instead, when the committee finally issued a report three years later—in 1922—a procedural vote on whether the bill's articles should be discussed failed. I highlight here the reasons for the negative procedural vote, pointing to issues from the debate that reveal the role that the religious cleavage played in fomenting the Radical senators' opposition.

Amongst the historians who study this period, it is generally agreed that the fate of the bill was sealed by the deliberate actions of Alexandre Bérard (Ain), a Radical senator who was the bill's *rapporteur*. As the reporter, Bérard would have been in charge of ushering the legislation through to discussion, but it was he who dragged his feet for nearly three years after the bill was sent up from the lower house, and he who marshaled the most persuasive arguments against its passage. The report, filed on 3 November 1922, has come to be known as "Bérard's

Fourteen Points."[57] These points, all of which recommended against granting women the vote, are worth reprinting in full:

Bérard's Fourteen Points:

1. The Chamber of Deputies surpassed its mandate in proposing such far-reaching legislation because it continued to sit past its scheduled termination in 1918 only to conduct the war effort.
2. Any legislation subversive of the established order must be thoroughly studied, and the country must be first consulted in an electoral campaign based on the issue.
3. French opinion does not approve of the change, not even in the large provincial cities; there is no trace of support in the small towns, much less in the villages.
4. The immense majority of French women, "so full of good sense," do not want to vote, do not want to leave home for the political arena: they know that their families would suffer as a result.
5. While women did give immense service to France during the war, they did so for love of the country, not in the expectation of a reward: it would be an insult to pay them for their patriotism.
6. Women have insufficient civic education for political rights; their uninformed participation would pose a grave threat to the Republic.
7. Some women do claim the vote, but they are only "an infinitesimal minority...a handful of incoherent feminists."
8. The assertion that women are needed in politics to secure major social reforms is contradicted by parliament's record of twenty years of attention to these matters: the Senate and the Chamber of Deputies do not need help in drafting legislation.
9. Feminists are beginning to threaten "an uproar in the streets, even violent revolution" like the Bolsheviks, and the Senate must not capitulate to their threats.
10. France has always guided other people toward liberty and is great enough to decide for herself, on reasoned argument and not on foreign examples, what legislation to adopt.
11. The "Catholic mentality" of the majority of French women, combined with the hostility of the Church toward the Republic and liberty, mean that women's suffrage would lead to clerical reaction.

---

[57] *Rapport n° 564, annexé au procès-verbal de la séance du Sénat du 3 octobre 1919.* Not available online from the J.O. but provided to the author by the National Archives.

12. Women's suffrage would be "a formidable leap into the unknown" that might produce the election of a new Bonaparte as universal suffrage did in 1848, and might thereby lead to a new Sedan.
13. Nature has given women "a different role than men... a primordial role" to attend to the "incomparable grandeur" of maternity and to the family, which is the basis of French society.
14. Women are different creatures than men, filled with sentiment and tears rather than hard political reason: their hands are not for political pugilism or holding ballots, but for kisses.

It bears emphasizing that many of these points are succinct reflections of nearly every argument made against women's suffrage throughout history and across the globe: The multitudes of citizens do not want the change; women themselves do not want the vote; women are not ready for the vote; women prefer their place in the home; women do not need to represent themselves; women will not beneficially aid politics; women should not barter for the vote; government should not capitulate to women's threats; government should not copy other countries; men and women have different places in society; women's dispositions make them better for lovemaking than policymaking. Yet there are also reasons, unique to France, that Bérard summons against the franchise.

In particular, points 2, 9, 11, and 12 hazard that female voters would threaten politics as they are; that suffrage would be subversive to the established order; that feminists are simultaneously "like the Bolsheviks," too militant to be incorporated into the Republic; and at the same time women fall prey to the "Catholic mentality," which would likely bring on a clerical reaction. Finally, even knowing these two things about women, it is probably true that giving women votes would lead to a great unknown, perhaps at the level of the 1848 extension of voting rights to all men. The irony of a Radical politician arguing against the 1848 expansion was not lost in the debate that followed on 22 November. The discussion, which was briefer than the debate in the Chamber, focused on two issues: whether the bill should be discussed at length, or whether in fact some other idea, like a "family vote" where all adults would have a vote plus one vote for each child given to the father, should be given the Senate's attention.

Senators from both the left and the right came forward for women's suffrage. Siméon Flaissières, a Socialist, argued that far from being an extreme force, women would emerge as a neutralizing force in politics.

Moreover, extending these rights would elevate the political status of women, which had heretofore been depressed because of their exclusion. Yet, he realized that there was an imbalance in the population that would lead women to be a majority of voters (especially due to France's deaths in the war, women were 60 percent of the adult population). To refute this concern, and to counter the claim that women were not ready for political inclusion, Flaissières recommended a voting age floor of 30 (the terms adopted in the UK in 1918). On the point of women being a scourge to the republic, Flaissières counted himself as a long-time supporter of this form of government, and argued that if he feared it would be shaken up by women's votes, he would become an opportunist, and vote against the measure.[58]

On the other side of the political spectrum, Gaudin de Villaine, a senator from the right who had also served for many years in the Chamber, explained that women should have the right to defend their own interests, and that, if we look at the example set by women in the United Kingdom, it is clear that they brought more conservatives to power.[59] Given the Catholic leanings of women in the country, de Villaine saw a conservative ally in female voters. Finally, François Albert (Deux-Sèvres), a member of the Parti républicain, radical et radical-socialiste, lobbied against discussion of the bill, claiming that since "nature does not jump," neither should the Senate on the issue of suffrage. Doubling the electorate, especially since male turnout had fallen in the previous election, was too risky to the Republic.

In all of these arguments we see the senators jostling with their myriad expectations about how women, as voters, would influence the electorate. Certainly there were some who argued, flat out, that women lacked the competence to exercise political choice. And certainly, too, there were some who believed in the principle of equality. Yet the very political nature of the arguments used in this discussion suggests that "fears for the Republic" was used as a rather thin guise to shroud "fears for my party" or even "fears for myself." This is evident in the roll-call on November 21, as the Radical senators were the only party that overwhelmingly voted against considering the measure further.[60] As Paul Smith writes, the idea

[58] "Si je sentais que le Gouvernement de la République fût exposé à être à ce point ébranlé par le vote des femmes, il est certain que je deviendrais, pour l'heure, opportuniste."

[59] "Voyez ce qui s'est passé en Angleterre; ce sont les femmes qui ont fait l'appoint des conservateurs et ont battu les travaillistes."

[60] In the Senate's procedural roll-call vote, 52 percent of the Senate voted "Nay" and so the bill was not discussed. forty-nine of seventy-four Radicals voted "Nay" with five

of the clerical peril "became an article of faith for leading Radical senators like Jean Jeanneney and the Sarraut brothers that to give women the vote would lead to events as catastrophic for the Third Republic as the declaration of manhood suffrage in 1848 had been for the Second."[61] Jean Pedersen may be right, then, in claiming that the way individual Radical legislators felt about women's suffrage stemmed from their views about democracy more generally.[62]

French Feminists' Response

After the bill passed the Chamber of Deputies in 1919, three long years passed before the Senate put the nail in the coffin. Thereafter, in spite of many successful bills presented in the Chamber, suffrage was nonstarter. The question, of course, is why? Certain macro-level arguments, such as the idea that differences in labor force participation of women in France versus the United States and the United Kingdom, cannot explain the variation across these cases. Women accounted for a higher share of the labor force in France than in Great Britain throughout the nineteenth century, and the fraction of employed women grew in France until the 1920s, while it stagnated in England after 1890.[63] On the other hand, France's later industrialization meant that more of its laborers (of both genders) were involved in agricultural activities and small-scale production than in England, leaving sectoral mix as a potential explanation. But France had experienced considerable urbanization by 1900 and was home to a large manufacturing sector not only in Paris, but also in areas like Lille, Roubaix, and Tourcoing—the "industrial triangle" located close to the Belgian border in the northeast of the country. Before the First World War there were two men to every woman on the factory floor, but after the war this rose to three. Moreover, France had double the number of married women at work as in England, and this shared work experience should have made it easier for French women to form a collective consciousness across class groups than elsewhere.[64]

A more compelling explanation for the failure of suffrage in the Third Republic can be found in how the suffrage organizations contrived to deal with the Senate's refusal to grant reform. Two key differences with the

---

abstentions. Source: roll call coded from *J.O. Senat 21 Nov 1922 scrutin n. 68*; party tendencies calculated from Graham 1984.

  [61] Smith 1996: 105.
  [62] Pedersen 2017.
  [63] Tilly and Scott 1987: figure 4-3, p. 68.
  [64] Zeldin 1973: 352.

French suffrage strategy set it apart from the UK and the US The first difference has to do with the French suffragists' reluctance to engage in spectacular actions like holding large rallies and marches. As Banaszak (1996b) and others have argued, direct action techniques like rallies were successful at courting more suffragists and raising the salience of the issue in the public sphere. The second, not wholly unrelated, reason for suffrage failure has to do with feminists' reluctance to expand the movement outside of the urban areas and across ideological divides, and the failure to form umbrella organizations as in the United States and Great Britain. Ultimately, the "feminization" of religion after 1870, which stemmed in part from the Catholic Church's involvement in female (more than male) education until 1906, created large social and cultural divisions between ordinary French women and bourgeois secular suffragists that may have precluded large-scale mobilization of the sort that emerged in the United States and the United Kingdom.[65]

French suffragists were arguably less demonstrative than their British or American counterparts. In part this might stem from French popular culture, in which memories of unflattering portrayals of women storming the Bastille, rioting for bread, or as participants in the Paris Commune were often summoned as cautionary tales against politically empowering a group of people that was inherently unpredictable.[66] If the suffragists were to push the boundaries of acceptable discourse and action, such as by pursuing militant actions, it might signal danger to the fragile republic and play into the hands of their adversaries. The concern not to appear too extreme was apparent before the Condorcet demonstration in 1914, where suffragist Caroline Rémy de Guebhard (known under her pen name Séverine), leader of the Union française pour le suffrage des femmes (UFSF) argued:

> One can claim one's rights without gnashing one's teeth; one can desire justice without preaching hate. Our feminism includes keeping our smiles, our senses of humour, and our good manners. ... We will arrive at our rights without reprehensible actions, with hands untouched by violence, with hearts not filled with resentment.[67]

[65] The feminization of religion in France, which was evidenced by higher levels of participation in religious orders and in attendance at church, has been discussed by several historians, including Smith (1996: 5), and McMillan (1991: 57). McMillan rejects the received scholarly view that French women were backwards and that the men were more modern, as well as the idea that French men were not religious in the nineteenth century. For our purposes the important point is whether enough politicians believed women to be hopelessly reactionary, rather than the validity of that claim.

[66] Duchen 2003.

[67] Quoted in Hause and Kenney 1984: 187.

Séverine's speech makes implicit reference to the strategies of women in other countries, signaling that mobilization in the French manner must take a decidedly different tone.

Yet, while French suffragists maintained a higher commitment to "femininity" in their movement, they allowed for less entrepreneurship within their organizations than the movements in the US or the UK and appeared to be less cooperative with women of different ideological positions. Although the larger organizations in the US and the UK—the National American Women's Suffrage Association in the US, and the National Union for Women's Suffrage Societies in the UK—attempted to organize power in a hierarchical manner, they also worked to establish good communication with branches and rely on the local knowledge and strategies of auxiliary branches. The statutes of the French UFSF, on the other hand, explicitly stated that auxiliary chapters could not undertake their own initiatives. "They could not approach their deputies or senators, could not appeal to their municipal council, and certainly could not organize a demonstration—all of these decisions were reserved to the Parisian Central Committee."[68] One possible interpretation of these stringent regulations is timidity: perhaps feminists were too concerned about perceptions of their behavior if they made more strident calls. This at least was a concern of militant suffragettes, such as Madeleine Pelletier.[69]

Another interpretation for the relative reluctance of French suffrage leaders to allow for diverse organizations and to stage large protest events relates to their expectations of French women as voters. Worrying too much about the other types of women that would enjoy the vote should reform pass, they were not always convinced that it was worth fighting for. This prejudice is on display in the letter of Emile Darnaud, a rural feminist, who wrote to a Parisian newspaper in 1914: "If you knew our villages! At the present time, to give the right to vote to women in France would be to give the priest in each village the ballots of all the women."[70]

The idea that votes for women would put extra ballots in the priests' pockets and could threaten the fate of the Republic was deeply held

---

[68] Hause and Kenney 1989: 217.

[69] Madeleine Pelletier has quite the biography: she emerged from the lower classes to become one of only a few female medical students and one of the first female psychiatrists in France. She campaigned for abortion rights and contraception, and was a vanguard of sexual liberation. She also was a socialist leader, becoming the first woman to represent a country delegation at the International. See Maignien and Sowerwine 1992 and Gordon 1990: 180.

[70] See footnote 1, this chapter.

and hard to shake. French suffragists "were deeply committed, both ideologically and personally, to a regime that appeared to be unstable. They could not assume the survival of liberal democracy, as English speaking suffragists did. ... They chose activities that did not threaten the bourgeois republic."[71] In part, this quiescence was a response to strong signals sent by the French government. Agents of the police force infiltrated all suffragist organizations, and large numbers of police were present at all suffragist demonstrations, suggesting a general willingness by the French government to intimidate suffragists that pushed boundaries.[72]

The evidence of a stalled movement is also apparent when we consider the expansion of suffrage activity over time. By 1914, feminist activity was well distributed over the countryside, and many of the departments had independently given women access to local voting rights. With the exception of Somme, Ardennes, and some of the coastal areas in the northwest and southeast, there is very little overlap between places where feminists were originally mobilized and places where deputies supported suffrage. This is further borne out if we consider how the Ligue française pour le droit des femmes (LFDF) grew after 1918. I examined religiosity and competition in places where the LFDF established branches after the war ended. Overall, the LFDF expanded into districts that were more religious on average (such as the Loire Atlantique and Nord), but which had a lower share of Radical members among its representatives to the Chamber of Deputies. Contrary to what Hause and Kenney suggest, I find that the LFDF established branches in places where Radical deputies were less supportive of suffrage on average, but the organization stayed away from the Radical stronghold in the southwest. Thus, while suffragists did not shy away from large departments with many anti-suffrage Radical MPs, the movement did not target the places with the greatest resistance.

At the same time that American Carrie Chapman Catt was devising a national strategy, known as the "winning plan," which helped push the Nineteenth Amendment past the finish line, in France, the movement was stalled. After 1919 the lack of a national strategy proved devastating. The loss in the Senate was both political—the Radicals, who were in a majority, voted overwhelmingly against it—as well as geographical—with the southwest showing no support for the bill. It does not appear that French suffrage organizations leveraged enough resources to push

---

[71] Hause and Kenney 1981: 806.
[72] Ibid.: 802.

the bill through when the opportunity arose: once the suffrage bill passed the lower house, they did not organize a strategy for passage in the Senate, even though the issue was drawn out for more than three years before debate. The three departments where French feminists had been very active, and the eleven where there was moderate feminist activity, brought 68 and 53 percent of the Senate votes, respectively. But where they did not organize there was little support for the suffrage bill, less than a third of the representatives, which meant, in the end, defeat.[73]

To be fair, the Balkanization of the suffragist strategy cannot only be blamed on Radical women, as the Catholic organizations, representing by far the largest share of French women in that era, were decidedly against suffrage until after the First World War. One reason French Catholic women may have resisted suffrage before WWI was Pope Benedict XV's stance against it. In some accounts the Pope is said to have changed his mind in 1919, the same year French Catholic women agreed to found an organization devoted solely to suffrage.[74] When Catholic organizations changed course after the war, advocating for women's inclusion, they feared a red-swing in government and maintained separate activities. The fear was heightened by the Russian Revolution, which began in the midst of the war. Avoidance of cooperation between the LFDF and Catholic organizations and the lack of a national strategy may reflect the suffragists' internalization of the larger divisions within French society— the monarchy versus the Republic. The priests versus progress.

CONCLUSION

Although the end of the First World War brought enhanced partisan competition—which might have provided a similar opportunity for voting rights reform in France as elsewhere—deep political cleavages worked against the suffrage movement throughout the remainder of the Third Republic. Even among French feminists, there was a sense that women's suffrage presented an existential threat to the French state. This revelation pitted the Radical Party against the country's more conservative forces, and, by extension, against female voters, whom the party believed to be overwhelmingly conservative. In the words of Pierre

[73] Hause and Kenny (1984), especially maps 11 and 12 and pp. 269–72.
[74] Hause and Kenney 1984: 216.

Marraud, a Radical senator from Lot-et-Garonne in the southwest (a region that overwhelmingly voted against suffrage),

> The woman of the Latin race does not feel, has not developed, in the same way as the woman of the Anglo-Saxon or Germanic races. Her position in the foyer is not the same. As a person, she is generally more absorbed in her Church, whose dogmatism she does not dispute. It is perfectly reasonable, then, that her legal status should be different.[75]

Women's exclusion was justified, in the minds of the foremost members of the party of "universal" suffrage, because of their unquestioning dogmatism, and because they continued to be educated by the Church in rural areas.

It may seem curious that clerical concerns would have been paramount nearly fifty years after the Republic was formed, but although issues related to the Church and the legitimacy of the Republic had receded during the first decades of the 1900s, they resurfaced in 1919 with the election of the center-right Bloc national. Under the leadership of Alexandre Millerand (Seine), a longtime deputy who had switched parties multiple times, and whom the Radical Party would later depose, Bloc members sought to re-establish diplomatic links with the Vatican by allowing for an Embassy of the Holy See to be installed in Paris. In 1921 the Senate agreed to this reform, stoking fear among many in the Radical anti-clerical camp that the government itself would be under threat if the power of the right grew.[76] Opposition to both policies overlapped in the Senate: of the 122 senators that detracted from women's suffrage, 107 also had resisted the embassy. This group comprised a full two-thirds of the anti-suffrage camp in 1922.[77] Radical anti-suffragism was therefore linked quite closely with Radical anti-clericalism. Party members feared not only for their party's future, but for the future of the regime itself, should women get the vote.

The leading histories of the suffrage movement take slightly different positions on why the suffrage movement was unable to overcome the Radical hurdles in the interwar period. Hause sees the problem as a failure of French feminism.[78] Leaders of Ligue française pour le droit des

---

[75] 1927. Quoted in Smith 1996: 124.
[76] Smith 1996: 159ff.
[77] Ibid.: 115.
[78] Hause and Kenney 1984: ch. 8.

femmes (LFDF), the major umbrella organization advocating for women's suffrage, selected an organization that was highly centralized, emphasizing activities in Paris to the neglect of the provinces. This strategy meant that the movement was too urban, too bourgeois, and too secular to integrate women in the countryside. Smith, on the other hand, notes that the movement did expand into many new territories throughout the twenties.[79] He documents the growth, in the interwar period, of the UFSF and the conservative and Catholic suffrage organizations the UNVF and the FNF, contesting the claim that feminism was weak after 1922. Instead,

> [women's suffrage] was not acceptable to important political players, and could only have occurred if one or a number of significant changes took place: either the Radicals changed their views on votes for women, or the Radicals diminished as a political power in the Republic, or an individual of equal power imposed women's suffrage by act of fiat.[80]

In Smith's view, electoral politics is the reason that suffrage reform failed in France.

The logic of women's suffrage suggests that both Hause's and Smith's accounts are correct. The party with the greatest disincentives to franchise reform held veto power in France's upper chamber, creating substantial barriers to women's enfranchisement throughout the period. Moreover, a fear of the "downstream" political effects of enfranchisement caused the mainstream suffrage movement to acquiesce to the Radical Party's opposition. The Radical suffrage organizations in Paris did not form ties with the Catholic suffragists, nor did they expand into the places where they faced the most resistance.

In the end, suffrage was imposed by fiat.[81] While still under German occupation, the French Committee of National Liberation, which met in Algiers in 1944, declared that women would have the right to vote in

---

[79] Smith 1996: 1960.

[80] Ibid.: 162.

[81] There were a few important moments in the interim period. Women actually experienced a retrenchment in labor force participation after the war (see Zeldin 1973: 352). But there were some very public advances for professional women. In 1936 Léon Blum (Aude), of the Parti socialiste, appointed three female undersecretaries to his cabinet. And, in February 1938, clause 215 of the Napoleonic Code, which required a woman to have her husband's authorization to enroll in school, open a bank account, or get a passport, was abolished.

the first elections of the Fourth Republic.[82] In initial discussions of how the constituent assembly would be constructed, many in Algiers felt that the old electoral registers, which included only men, should be used, and that the fate of women's votes should be decided by the plebiscite itself.[83] Several of the participants, however, declared in favor of women voting for the assembly and for women's rights to hold office themselves. These sentiments were ultimately carried.[84]

The existence of the measure is widely attributed to the advocacy of the conservative republican, and future president, Charles de Gaulle. But the reasons that the committee included the suffrage provision, and the degree to which de Gaulle himself is responsible, have been the subject of a small scholarly debate. On the one hand, scholars comment that de Gaulle came out in favor of women's suffrage as early as 1942, and, in the weeks before the constituent assembly was announced to the public, he gave a speech in which he called for the regime to be democratic in institutions and practice, and to have representation "élue par tous les hommes et toutes les femmes."[85] On the other hand, there were many visible moments in which de Gaulle made no mention of women's suffrage, such as in his inaugural speech to the committee in 1943. When he did mention the vote, "he did it without insistence, without grandiloquence, as if it were self-evident."[86]

[82] The women's provision was promulgated on 21 April and re-iterated by de Gaulle on 25 August when he returned to Paris.

[83] The issue was discussed on 27 December, 1943 and taken to a vote on 8 January 1944. On this date the committee gave unanimous approval to the principle of women's suffrage, but wanted to delay the decision for the constituent assembly, which at this point would be elected based on the male registers. In March the issue was again raised in discussions of who would elect the constituent assembly. Including women's votes was deemed problematic because it would effect the writing of new electoral lists (slowing up the date of the plenary election), and because of the statistical imbalance of women after many men had perished in the war. Decamont 1996: 110–11.

[84] On 22 March, Article 1 of the Ordonnance was debated. Originally only men would be electors of the constituent assembly. Robert Prigent vigorously combatted this provision, proposing an amendment justified by women's involvement in the war effort. The commission's president agreed, and the Prigent amendment was carried. Then on 24 March, women's eligibility to stand for local elections was discussed. Greneir forwarded an amendment in favor of women's passive suffrage, which was adopted 51 for and 6 against. Women voted for the first time in the plebiscite for an assembly to draft France's new constitution, held 29 April 1945. In all, 13 million women were enfranchised by the decree of 21 April 1944. Duchen 2003: 34–35.

[85] 18 March 1943. Quoted in Decamont 1996: 114.

[86] Author's translation, Du Roy and Du Roy 1994: 243.

Several scholars have suggested that the measure in Algeria was meant to bring France into the modern era and separate the new republic from the old; that looking around at all the other advanced powers, to be legitimate the new state must include votes for women.[87] Others have suggested that women's participation in wartime resistance earned them a seat at the table.[88] (Although, of course, this did not work as a rationale in the wake of the First World War.) Some, including de Gaulle and his son, Philippe, claim that he had always been on the side of suffrage, believing that women's sensibilities would help to moderate and stabilize society.[89] Others, including Theodore Zeldin and Joan Scott, point to the issue of partisanship, claiming that de Gaulle understood that female voters would help counterbalance the forces of fascism and socialism inside of France, and that women would provide electoral support for his party.[90] The political behavior of French women after the vote has been well studied. Although there was a gender gap in political participation between men and women of 7 to 12 points from 1940 to 1960, those women who did vote generally supported the right over the left. Zeldin reports that 85 percent of French women voted in the same way as their husbands, while unmarried women and widows had distinctive electoral preferences.[91] In the 1965 election, de Gaulle topped François Mitterrand by nearly 10 percentage points, almost exactly mirroring the gender gap in political support for de Gaulle.[92] Reading history backwards suggests that de Gaulle likely made the right call in heeding the logic of women's suffrage.

If political competition bolstered women's voting rights in the United States and the United Kingdom, it was not enough to secure the vote in France because the party with veto power in the Senate did not expect to win after reform. Secular French suffragists appear to have espoused views similar to those voiced by Radical politicians about the political preferences of the majority of women in the countryside, and may have halted the growth of their movement in response to political

[87] Bouglé-Moalic 2012: 310.
[88] Du Roy and Du Roy 1994: 256.
[89] Callon 2003: 27; de Gaulle and Tauriac 2003: 259, tome 2.
[90] Zeldin writes that de Gaulle found support for the vote among communists—who had many female supporters, and members of the Mouvement républicain populaire, France's new Christian Democratic Party, who wanted to win the votes of Catholic women. Zeldin 1973: 360. Scott 1998: 218–220. Although, as Duchen (2003: 34) points out, all parties tried to claim credit for the reform.
[91] Zeldin 1973: 360.
[92] Mossuz-Lavau 1994: 68.

concerns that stemmed from the religious cleavage. Not all suffrage movements remained as insular as that in France. As we saw, in the United Kingdom and in the West and North of the United States, the cleavages that divided women from one another were overcome to a large enough degree to allow suffragists to form broad coalitions and induce politicians to support reform. When political competition increased, and groups of politicians saw an advantage in courting female voters, women's suffrage became a political possibility.

6

Conclusion

The transition to democratic government is perhaps the most fundamental institutional innovation the world experienced in the past three hundred years. During this period, the once radical notion that a government is legitimate only if it acts with the consent of the governed has become commonplace, embodied in the constitutions of nations around the globe. Scholars have long recognized the novelty and importance of this shift, making the conditions under which countries undergo democratization a frequent topic for students of political economy and comparative politics. Despite this, the inclusion of women—a group that always constitutes about half the population in every country on earth and whose enfranchisement often marks the single largest extension of political rights within a nation's borders—has not yet made it into the canonical theories of democratization. This book points to several intriguing features of the politics of women's suffrage that need to be considered as we move toward a more holistic conception of democratization. It explored the conditions under which activists mobilize broadly, with encompassing goals that incorporate the needs of a wide variety of women, or narrowly, with relatively modest reform agendas that would affect only elite women. The theory suggests that broad-based movements are necessary for reform when a country has already moved toward a manhood franchise, but that these movements are difficult to build in societies riven by class, racial, ethnic, or religious cleavages. The scope of the movement influences the information politicians have about how women are likely to vote after the vote is extended, and politicians make their decisions on suffrage bills based on whether they think women can be mobilized for their group in future elections, and whether they need women's votes in order to win.

As anyone familiar with ideas about democratization will note, many of the same types of concerns and incentives that I suggest are important for women's political inclusion were also relevant for the inclusion of men. Why, then, have women been missing from mainstream theories of franchise reform, and what can the study of women's suffrage teach us about the process of democratization more generally? In this chapter I offer an account of the absence of women from theories of democratization, suggesting that three prominent features of this discourse exclude women almost by definition—the search for a "unified" theory of democratization, the primacy placed on "revolutionary" forms of mobilization for effecting political change, and the prominence of class politics in models of enfranchisement. Reliance on these concepts has meant not only that we have few competing ideas about how half of the world's population, in the majority of the world's countries, became voters, but also that we miss out on how democratization for men is fundamentally intertwined with democratization for women.

Traversing into speculative territory, I provide a brief sketch of how cross-national patterns of male and female enfranchisement might be understood together. Country-specific social cleavages, which systematically influenced the formation of electoral rules governing male participation, need to be theorized alongside patterns of gender inequality in order to make sense of the full trajectories of democratization within and across countries. But in order to form a theory of this nature, more work is needed to understand how overlapping inequalities within states promote or prevent the formation of social movements, including movements for democratic reforms like suffrage. In a world with overlapping inequalities, how can we make sense of the formation of a political consciousness? When will consciousness developed around a crosscutting cleavage— such as gender—dwarf other identities? Thinking through these questions will open up new ways of looking at social movements and episodes of democratization, and prompt new avenues for comparative investigation.

MISSING WOMEN IN THE STUDY OF DEMOCRACY

A rich scholarship on gender and politics considers how women have been on the front lines of regime transitions, and looks at how the process of transitions, and the nature of the state, influence women's ability to organize collectively and exert influence within states.[1] Yet the implications of this research have not been adequately incorporated into larger theories of democratic reform. Here, I suggest that there are three features of democratization scholarship—the search for a unified theory of democratization, the emphasis on revolutionary unrest as the catalyst for

[1] Alvarez 1990; Friedman 2000; Baldez 2002.

democratic reforms, and the reliance on class as the key locus of conflict—that have made women and studies about women invisible. Bringing women in, however, can lead to new theoretical insights about the nature of democratization.

The Search for a Unified Theory

Scholarship on democratization has vacillated between seeking theories that are highly detailed and contextually specific and those which are general and ostensibly timeless. Huntington, Juan Linz and Al Stepan, and Guillermo O'Donnell and Philippe Schmitter all fall into the former camp, offering historically grounded and highly contingent accounts of democratic transitions in specific countries or regions.[2] A recent explosion of theoretical research, sparked by the contributions of Acemoglu and Robinson, as well as Boix, but also visible in earlier texts by Dahl, Moore, Therborn, and Rueschemeyer et al., takes the latter approach, searching for a "unified" theory of democratization that has the power to explain both the transition to a democratic form of government and later improvements in the degree of democracy that a country achieves.[3] Along with accounting for transition and reform within countries, the essential feature of unified theories is that they are temporally unanchored—they should perform just as well in light of the revolutions in the late eighteenth century as they do for explaining the third, or even fourth, waves of democratization.

The ambition to form a unified theory of democratization merits recognition, but several problems arise when these unified theories are tested in actual cases. Depending on the exact time period in question, the specific measures of inequality and democratization, and which countries are included in the study, scholars come to very different conclusions about the link between inequality, revolutionary unrest, and democratization.[4]

---

[2] Huntington 1993; Linz and Stepan 1978; O'Donnell and Schmitter 1986. Huntington does not believe a unified theory of democratization is possible, while O'Donnell and Schmitter explicitly do not provide a theory of transitions from authoritarianism in Latin America in the third quarter of the twentieth century.

[3] Acemoglu and Robinson 2006: 15; Boix 2003: 2; Dahl 1971; Moore 1966; Therborn 1977; Rueschemeyer et al. 1992. Geddes (2007: 323) credits the single-theory approach with mixed results of large-N statistical studies. Przeworski et al. (1996), on the other hand, argue that transition and later consolidation need to be separated both analytically and theoretically.

[4] Wood (2000) contends that extreme inequality, coupled with class inequality can produce sustained insurgency from below, and drive elites to split and democracy to emerge in South Africa and El Salvador. In the cross-national literature, the big debate is whether inequality and democratization are related in an inverted-U shape (*pace* Acemoglu and

If Capoccia and Ziblatt are correct in their claim that democratization is not a single episode of transition but rather a "protracted and punctuated process," unified theories of democratization should place considerable weight on the conflicts that arise and political tactics that are used after an initial transition to democracy has transpired.[5] And yet the revolutions that led to regime change are often given primacy over the more mundane negotiations in countries that already forged a path to representative institutions. In this sense, it should come as no surprise that the unified theories have received mixed empirical support depending on the time periods analyzed and a country's institutional form: politics have very different flavors in authoritarian settings in comparison to democratic settings, and the same economic factors that may have mattered for democratization in the eighteenth and nineteenth centuries may not be mirrored in the twentieth.[6]

As Barbara Geddes highlights, structural features within a polity may also be different in earlier moments of democratization than those that happen later.[7] The configurations of power, the set of actors, and even the political conflicts may have changed across the regimes. In practice, though, unified theories allow the same groups, conflicts, and tactics that were important during a democratic transition to linger after the new government is established. When the initial conflict was between owners

---

Robinson 2006) or a U-shape (*pace* Boix 2003). Freeman and Quinn (2008) study changes in democracy scores over five-year intervals from 1955 to 2004 and between thirty-four and ninety-one countries (depending on the specification) and find mixed empirical support for implications of both theories. In line with Boix, Freeman and Quinn further suggest that asset mobility is correlated with positive changes in democracy scores, but only in autocracies (e.g., table 1, model 1.5; table 2, model 2.1.). Thus, while there is support for both unified theories, it is only in the context of autocratic regimes that are undergoing a transition, instead of episodes of democratic deepening. In one sense, these results vitiate an earlier study by Houle 2009, who studies 116 countries from 1960 to 2000, finding that inequality affects democratic consolidation but not transitions to democracy. Freeman and Quinn (2008: 58, 65, 75) argue that Houle's results are a function of his measure of inequality and on his omission of financial openness as a key dimension of the story. In another sense, though, the results are complementary: when tested in different contexts—using a set of countries that is either democratic or authoritarian, and temporal windows that are shorter or longer—neither of the leading empirical studies finds support for the unified theories across systems.

[5] Capoccia and Ziblatt 2010: 940.

[6] A recent book by Ansell and Samuels (2014) provides a nice example of a non-unified account. Whereas high landholding inequality reduces the probability that countries democratize, after a democratic transition, high levels of inequality increase the probability of further democratizing reforms.

[7] This gives additional theoretical reasons for separate models of the process. Geddes 2007: 331.

of different types of capital, between elites living in different geographic areas, or between classes struggling to overcome their subordination, these conflicts are presumed to persist once democracy is established.[8] This has resulted in unified theories wherein the politics of founding moments have been given more weight than subsequent configurations of power and interests.[9]

Studying women's enfranchisement makes this obvious. Before women gained the vote, most countries had already undergone a transition away from authoritarianism. The key decision-makers were no longer autocratic leaders but elected legislators with diminished coercive leeway. In these systems, electoral incentives inform both the decisions of legislators as well as the concerns of potential movement activists. What is more, since many of the early democracies initially included only a small segment of the male population, the groups that were left to contest their continued exclusion were undoubtedly more diverse than those that gained entry during an initial transition. Whether the excluded groups were ethnic or racial minorities, members of the poorer classes, or women, the barriers for collective action may have been more formidable than those faced by groups like the merchant classes. As the scholarship progresses, it seems fruitful to think again about how the nature of the struggle over democratization is shaped by the diversity of groups that are empowered during initial transitions and by the diversity of groups that remain excluded thereafter.

The Primacy of Revolutionary Unrest

A second way that the study of women's suffrage challenges theories of democratization relates to a favored mechanism of political change. Many scholars working in both the unified tradition and in the contextually bound accounts of democratization are drawn to the idea that "revolutionary mobilization" plays a key role in democratic reforms.[10] In much of the

[8] A recent formal paper by Xi (2014) takes the point that democratization occurs in stages, noting that across the world, countries extended franchise laws twice on average. Yet his stepwise model of franchise extension still only applies to male enfranchisement.

[9] Geddes (2007: 319) takes a similar line of argument even further, arguing that the process of transition itself needs to be disaggregated and subgroups need to be separately theorized. Some models may apply to transitions in Western Europe and the Americas, while others are better suited for the "third wave" cases.

[10] The model's intuitive appeal is hard to deny. We need only recall England's Glorious Revolution (1688), the French Revolution (1789) and American Revolution (1776), the Russian Revolution (1917) or the Chinese Revolution (1949) to agree that revolutionary unrest has existed and likely caused many momentous instances of regime change. This is

literature, revolutionary mobilization entails public displays of discontent against a regime that signal a willingness on the part of the citizens to use violence to achieve their ends. From the "Age of Revolutions" in the nineteenth century to the uprisings that brought the "Arab Spring," mass mobilization with the potential to foment a revolution has been a key factor in regime transition. And because many of the world's revolutions have led to major changes in the electoral franchise, scholars have been right to focus on the importance of revolutionary unrest as one key driver of democratization. What remains unclear, however, is the degree to which social unrest has undergirded franchise reforms *within* limited democracies, and, if it has, whether this unrest should be conceptualized as revolutionary.[11]

Although women were involved in agitating for suffrage reform in many more countries than has been acknowledged—in at least twenty-nine countries, independent women's movements challenged exclusionary voting rights—their movements were not revolutionary in the sense used by the quantitative litetature on male enfranchisement.[12] This is true even of the militant wings of the suffrage movement. The "suffragettes," as the militants were called, were sometimes violent and definitely challenged norms about women's behavior in the early twentieth century. They also selectively deployed violence in an attempt to gain inclusion in an established political system. But the purpose of these actions was to wrangle concessions rather than to force regime change.[13] In light of this, several scholars who have studied women's enfranchisement have determined that because women generally did not take up arms against the state, they were passive recipients of voting rights. Among social scientists, this idea is pervasive: in both formal models of women's enfranchisement and in empirical analyses of rights extensions to women, women are often depicted as passive recipients of rights.[14] One scholar

---

true even though the revolutionary mechanism was not present in nineteenth-century male franchise reform in the UK or the US. For example, Collier 1999; Haggard and Kaufmann 2012; Himmelfarb 1966; Keyssar 2000.

[11] Collier 1999. Note that this is true even in the case of Britain's second Reform Act, which Acemoglu and Robinson herald as a prime example of their theory.

[12] Chafetz et al. 1990: 308; Banaszak 1996b: 4.

[13] See footnote 32, chapter 2.

[14] Formal models include: Bertocchi 2010; Doepke and Tertilt 2009. Empirical papers: Bertocchi 2010; Braun and Kvasnicka 2013; Miller 2008. Doepke and Tertilt theorize that as societies' demands for human capital rose in the nineteenth century, men were voluntarily induced to support women's rights. While Braun and Kvasnicka posit that a lower fraction of women relative to men reduces the costs to men of enfranchising women, again taking

even goes as far as to claim that women's enfranchisement in the United States was exogenous to (meaning historically and therefore statistically independent of) women's mobilization for the vote.[15] While men conquered the right to vote by their own devices, the argument goes, women were merely granted these rights as pawns in a greater political game.[16]

Regardless of the tactics, a group mobilized for minor but substantive changes in the rules of the game, but that does not seek a new constitution, or a total re-ordering of society, is probably not revolutionary. Indeed, democracies generally allow for groups to form and hold meetings and to contest the rules in the public sphere. Often, groups agitating for more democracy are acting within the bounds of their society and are contesting injustice within a regime that they believe in fundamentally. This is not to say that suffragists had a fully inclusive vision of society—as we have seen, they often argued for inclusion within their society's very exclusive bounds—but rather that most people fighting for voting rights did not want a new regime.[17] To borrow a phrase from Rustow, these groups already knew "what political community they want to be a part of" and were guided by different motivations, and utilized different means to effect reform, than groups mobilized for regime change.[18]

By eliding the distinction between what movements want and the tactics they use, the democratization literature has incorrectly concluded that large-scale movements for reform must have revolutionary aims.[19] We see this play out in the quantitative literature on democratization, where there has been a tendency to conflate mobilization for reform with revolutionary unrest, and where the revolutionary mechanism wins support if any number of forms of collective action is correlated with reform.[20] Along with incorrectly attributing the causal factors of democratizing

---

women's agency off the table. Historically, though, men put up quite a fight against the expansion of rights to women. This included men in the labor movement, conservative men, and even liberals in many countries. Dubois 1991.

[15] Miller 2008.

[16] This idea finds its fullest explication in Przeworski 2009, 2010.

[17] In this sense, suffragists may be different from ethno- or religious-nationalist groups, the latter of which may prefer self-rule and employ more violent means as a result.

[18] Rustow 1970: 350.

[19] In this sense, the unified theories of democracy explain revolution—by which I mean a new beginning marked by regime change—instead of reform within the structure of a specific set of institutions.

[20] Several recent studies code strikes, protests, and waves of mobilization by men as instances of revolutionary unrest, regardless of whether the underlying aspiration of the mobilized was regime change. Przeworski 2009, 2010; Dasgupta and Ziblatt 2015; Xi 2014. See Nepstad (2011) for many examples of non-violent revolutions.

reforms, the conflation of mobilization with revolutionary aspirations has begun to mean, in a normative sense, that the only groups that can get credit for winning their own emancipation are those with revolutionary aims. This view is problematic on several levels, not the least because it discounts the ordinary democratic tactics and the important non-violent channels through which voting rights were obtained for women *and* for men.[21]

The Importance of Non-Class Politics

The final way in which incorporating women poses a challenge to most of the democratization literature relates to the specific cleavages that dominated political conflict over women's enfranchisement. Property rights or taxpaying status were used by many governments as a way to regulate male participation in the political sphere. These rules linked the right to participate to class-based characteristics, naturally elevating class distinctions in the politics of reform. Yet many countries had already abandoned income restrictions for male voters before the women's movement emerged. In Latin America and the United States, for example, literacy tests were common. Hence women were not always admitted to or excluded from the franchise strictly because of their class, and generally speaking class politics was not the most prominent feature of debates about women's enfranchisement.

To be sure, there is evidence that class concerns figured in some politicians' discussions of women's enfranchisement. For example, conservative politicians in New Zealand took an anti-suffrage stance because they feared that the women would champion liberal economic causes.[22] In a letter to a conservative MP, a fellow Kiwi conservative cautioned that extending the vote to women "will double the majority against us and make the country more communistic than it is already."[23] And right-wing dictators such as Manuel Odría in Bolivia hoped that women's conservativism would help stave off the communist threat. But, in general, other issues, such as social policy, religiosity, and affairs of state, were more of a concern.

---

[21] The democratization literature sees the "threat" of revolution as the basis of power, but in Nepstad's (2011) account, it is precisely the ability of non-violent resisters to maintain their non-violent tactics, regardless of the regime's oppression, that gives them the power to delegitimize the regime.

[22] Grimshaw 1972: quoted on p. 104.

[23] Letter from G. G. Stead, chairman of directors of *The Press*, to John Hall of the New Zealand Legislature. Quoted in Grimshaw 1972: 63.

More often, though, the actual political debates centered on how women's religiosity would influence social policy and on how women's natural pacifism might interfere with affairs of state. In contrast to the models described above, support for women's enfranchisement did not necessarily stem from the industrial parties or the industrial workers.[24] As the study of the United States shows, the agricultural states in the American West extended voting rights before the manufacturing states in the East.[25] This, in spite of the fact that the movement was largest in the industrial centers of New York and Massachusetts. Moreover, even within US states, voters from urban areas were more likely to vote against suffrage referenda than rural ones.[26] Over time the alliances could shift, such as in New York state, where the socialist party took suffrage on their platform in 1916, but these changes were not inherent to the interests of the economic sector. They emerged as a result of a concerted strategy pursued by the New York suffrage movement.[27]

In the world as a whole, too, support for women's enfranchisement was not driven solely by class-based preferences. In places where the Catholic Church was an important political actor, such as Chile in the early twentieth century, religious issues could drive conservative parties to be the primary proponents of reform within the national legislature.[28] In Europe, Christian Democratic parties that had worked to develop a Catholic political identity even among more secular Church members may also have supported the relatively early enfranchisement of women in Austria and Belgium.[29] As revealed in the chapter on France, it was often in response to fears of clerical control of government that parties

---

[24] This idea has a long history; from Marx, to Lipset (1960: ch VII), to Rueschemeyer et al. (1992), many scholars assume and argue that the working classes will be the instigators of democratic reforms.

[25] The states that enfranchised women before the Nineteenth Amendment had, on average, 3.9 cities with more than 25 thousand inhabitants in 1900. The states that did not had, on average, 4.5 cities at that size.

[26] McDonagh and Price 1985: 423.

[27] Lerner 1981.

[28] Valenzuela 1995. The first politician who defended suffrage in Chile was Abdón Cifuentes, a Catholic leader who made his views known in 1865. And, on 25 October 1917, several members of the Chilean *Conservadores*, the party associated with the Catholic Church, were the first to formally present a suffrage bill to parliament.

[29] Belgium's measure was limited until 1946. As Kalyvas (1996) shows, in several northern European countries the Catholic Church united with conservative parties in order to confront anti-Catholic liberalism. In these countries, Christian Democratic parties took on lives of their own but continued to use religious cleavages to maintain the salience of a Catholic political identity.

resisted women's voting rights.[30] In debates about women's enfranchisement, class-based political cleavages were therefore not always (nor even generally) the primary concern of political leaders. This fact vitiates an easy application of most models of franchise extension to the case of women's suffrage, but it also raises the question of whether class really was the primary cleavage during democratizing reforms for men.[31] To move forward, we may need to move back to the older work of scholars such as Lipset and Rokkan, which stresses the roles that political cleavages outside of class play in transformations of systems of governance.

Instead of Separate Analyses, Link Them

The challenges that women's enfranchisement raises for theories of democratization do not imply, however, that women's inclusion was completely different from men's. The context in which women's voting rights emerged—generally after an initial transition away from authoritarianism—is similar to that in which many other groups gained political inclusion. And cleavages other than class, and mechanisms other than revolutionary unrest, also describe many major episodes of male enfranchisement. Hence, in the final instance, the dynamics of women's struggle may not, as Rueschemeyer et al. suggest, require a whole separate analysis from the inclusion of other subordinate groups. Instead, I submit that the relationship between men's and women's incorporation needs to be understood as fundamentally intertwined. Based on a reading of suffrage politics in many countries and the research presented in the preceding chapters, I propose that cross-national differences in patterns of enfranchisement for men and for women can be linked as follows.

Politicians and suffragists operating in countries that had already granted manhood suffrage—without regard to property or literacy— would have had a difficult time justifying a piecemeal approach to women's enfranchisement. Hence where the male franchise was expansive, the only real option was universal suffrage. In this context, a narrow coalition for women's suffrage could not succeed for two reasons. First,

---

[30] Here I depart from the view of of Richard Evans (1977), an historian of Germany, who sees the late enfranchisement of women in Catholic countries like Greece, Spain, Italy, and France as stemming from traditional views of women's role in society. My contention is that parties with traditional views of women were happy to support women's political rights if it could help their own fortunes, while parties with more progressive views were happy to resist reform if they would suffer. The outcome depends on the nature of political competition and the strategies of the women's movement.

[31] Recent qualitative work by Haggard and Kaufmann 2012 suggests that most transitions to democracy were not fundamentally about redistribution.

the normative reason, that it was difficult to justify and write a suffrage law that enfranchised only elite women. Second, the strategic reason, that if only a small group of women demanded the vote, parties would not know very much about women's preferences as a whole, nor could they be assured of the ease of mobilizing the newly enfranchised women to vote. Parties would have to be shortsighted, or quite risk loving, to introduce that kind of uncertainty into coming elections. Thus, in countries where most men could vote, the women's suffrage coalition would have to be broad and secure the support of mass-based parties that were vulnerable to electoral threat in order for women to gain entry to the polls.

Conversely, in countries with a more limited male franchise, a key question was whether letting one group of women in would have a snowball effect requiring a more substantial electoral change. In British politics, this problem was often decried as the "thin end of the wedge." In places where elites were confident that they could continue to exclude large segments of women and men in the reform, women could gain entry on extremely limited bases. Kenya and South Africa may be examples where settler women were given voting rights without fear of having to extend voting rights to indigenous Africans.[32] In these places the women's suffrage coalition could remain narrow, and suffragists could seek support from vulnerable parties with centrist and conservative leanings.

But if pressure was already mounting for a more expansive male franchise, then elite women's suffrage might fail for fears that extending the vote to women would expose the "contradiction" of male exclusion. In this case, mass-based parties would begin to advocate for women's suffrage, hoping both to gain the resources and loyalty of the disfranchised women and also to increase pressure for universalist reform. In the event that mass male enfranchisement began to seem inevitable, conservative parties may have come around to the idea of women's enfranchisement, hoping, as they did so, that women's conservative votes would serve as a buffer for mass politics.[33] In this circumstance, centrist parties provided

---

[32] In Kenya, the right to vote and stand for office was given to European women in 1919, and to Asian men and women in 1923. In 1956, native Africans were given the vote subject to educational and property requirements. All restrictions were lifted in 1963 (Martin 2000: 209). In South Africa, in 1910 men could vote subject to property, education, and racial requirements. In 1930 whitehood franchise was granted. It was not until 1984 and 1994 that Africans and Indians were allowed to vote. Martin 2000: 351; Paxton and Hughes 2016: 53.

[33] Evans (1980) argues that German conservatives supported suffrage for this reason.

the last form of resistance, fearing, perhaps correctly, that they would be beaten by both sides.

Several examples, including the United Kingdom, might fit this argument: in Luxembourg, although there was no obvious suffrage activism, the conservative party seems to have supported women's suffrage in 1919 in collaboration with socialists (the liberal group dissenting) because the conservatives hoped to save the constitutional monarchy in the face of mounting pressures for a republic.[34] A similar pattern emerged in Belgium, where in 1919 conservatives capitulated to pressures for manhood suffrage, but only under the condition that war widows and mothers who lost their sons to war were given voting rights. Here, there is an interesting comparison to be made with Ziblatt, who stresses the importance of strong conservative parties for democratic stability. Notably, all the European countries that developed strong conservative parties early on were also early adopters of women's suffrage.[35]

The idea that women could provide a buffer to mass politics may also be relevant for electoral system changes such as the adoption of proportional representation. There is a big debate about whether conservative parties supported proportional representation and why, and whether party members faced different incentives at the local versus national levels.[36] These texts often consider the implications of different electoral system rules given the landscape of voting rights for men. But if it is true that contemporary observers in many countries perceived women to be a conservative political force, then women's suffrage and proportional representation may have been alternative strategies of dominance for conservative parties. Exploring this, and the relationship between patterns of enfranchisement for both genders, would be a fascinating subject for future work.

IMPLICATIONS FOR GENDER AND POLITICAL DEVELOPMENT

In addition to providing new theoretical perspectives on democratization, the politics of women's suffrage overlaps with and expands upon existing knowledge about advancing gender equality in the world at large. As

---

[34] Daley and Nolan 1994: 350.

[35] Martin 2000: 34; Ziblatt 2017.

[36] Boix 1999, 2010; Kreuzer 2010. Ahmed (2010) argues that the adoption of both proportional electoral rules and single-member districts were designed to contain the emergence of mass-based politics, but that the particular system chosen depended on conservative parties' strategies to contain socialism.

Denise Walsh has rightly noted, the critique voiced here and in other works about women's exclusion from "mainstream" comparative politics forgets that the concerns of feminism are larger than any subfield. What lessons can we learn about gender and political development?

First, as with women's suffrage, the efforts made by women's movements to mobilize across political cleavages have been just as important for producing other advances in equality. The near sea change in women's representation that has been ushered in by the adoption of electoral gender quotas in more than seventy countries provides a case in point.[37] Like suffrage, the reasons that quotas have been adopted are different for countries with different institutional contexts.[38] Within systems that have established electoral competition—limited democracies if you will— the pressure exerted by women's movements and electoral incentives have been key.[39] Divergent national choices on suffrage in countries that share some common features, such as in Bolivia, Argentina, Mexico, and Chile, boil down to whether women were able to organize across party lines and demand reform. In Bolivia, Argentina, and Mexico, these cross-cleavage collaborations proved essential for the adoption of electoral gender quotas, but in Chile, where women did not work to form a broad coalition, reform failed.[40]

Understanding the conditions under which women's movements have and can effectively mobilize across cleavages remains an important terrain for future scholarship. Some feminist political theorists have cautioned against theorizing women as a group because of their fundamental diversity, and critique a politics that tries to lump women from very different backgrounds together.[41] And as Laurel Weldon has argued, women from minority groups are often most effective when they organize outside of mainstream feminist organizations.[42] But if we agree with Iris Marion Young, feminist politics loses meaning if women cannot be conceptualized as a group, and so there are practical reasons to think of women as having certain shared experiences, even while acknowledging that

---

[37] Legally mandated quotas or reserved seats in parliaments have been adopted in more than seventy countries. In an additional thirty countries, more than sixty parties have adopted party-level gender quotas (Clayton and Zetterberg forthcoming).

[38] Krook 2010; Bush 2011.

[39] Weeks 2017 shows that interparty competition, spurred by a left threat, can drive conservative parties to support the adoption of quota laws. Party members that want to get control over candidate selection within their party (in order to push out local party monopolies) may also support gender quotas.

[40] Htun 2016.

[41] Most famously Judith Butler and Chandra Mohanty.

[42] Weldon 2011. Young 1994: 719.

laws, policies, and market conditions may affect women from different backgrounds differently. As Karen Beckwith has suggested, fragmentation "along cross-cutting cleavages makes identification of women's interests more challenging, but does not obviate women's shared interests."[43] If identity *groups* are bound by shared values, cultures, or traditions, identity *politics* are based in the creation of shared interests that can be transformed into demands for the representation of those interests in political institutions. The question then becomes how to create a sense of shared consciousness in spite of fundamental differences across women.

In moving toward a holistic account of transformations in gender equality, it helps to theorize the overarching structural features that influence feminist identification and mobilization across time and space. Conceptualizing the position of women within groups and then the relationship between groups might help us better anticipate whether and when women can organize collectively to effect major social and legal changes. We must also attend to the ways in which gender equality changes in nonlinear fashions. As Mala Htun writes, "Being excluded from power makes women conscious of belonging to a group; once they have power, this group identity tends to weaken and dissipate."[44] Reforms such as introducing property rights for women, or gender quotas, may make gender inequality retreat from the horizon and allow other injustices to rise to the fore. In other periods, falling inequality along other cleavages may facilitate, or at least make space for, feminist identification.

A second lesson stems from thinking about the way that different structures of political competition can set the stage for large policy changes. There is a large body of work on women's political activity during and after political transitions that links political openings—the realignment of party systems and regime change more generally—to advances in women's equality.[45] As we saw in the case chapters, moments when party politics were in flux, that were marked by higher levels of competition, were associated with women's enfranchisement. The evidence from the United States provides an additional layer of nuance to this idea by showing that competition, in combination with women's mobilization for suffrage, increased the statistical likelihood that women won the vote. But the fact that women's movements were most successful at securing voting rights during moments of heightened competition, or during realignments more generally, does not tell us very much about

---

[43] Beckwith 2014: 26. Weldon would agree (2011, ch 1).
[44] Htun (2004: 451).
[45] Friedman 2000; Alvarez 1990; Waylen 1994; Tripp 2015.

the landscape of gender equality thereafter. As Maxine Molyneux has argued about the agglomeration of states into the Soviet Union, initial attempts by the revolutionary regime to distinguish itself from the old regimes produced progressive gender laws that granted women equality within marriage and the right to control their fertility via abortion. When the period of transition ended, however, and the state attempted to gain control and expand its authority, it returned to older tropes about women in the family and ratcheted down its progressive gender legislation. This form of retrenchment in women's rights after what was seen by some as too hasty an expansion may be common after all major moments of reform, including suffrage.[46]

On a more pessimistic note, suffrage might be just another way in which laws are changed to grant women inclusion without allowing for substantive representation. And indeed, this would seem to be a big part of the conclusion drawn by scholars who have studied the aftermath of the Nineteenth Amendment in the United States.[47] But I want to warn against drawing too quick conclusions about the impact of women's suffrage for three reasons: first, to think about the impact of suffrage we cannot only consider what happened after the vote, but also need to understand all of the policy concessions that women were granted in lieu of the vote on the road to suffrage. The temporal gap between women's first request for voting rights and the eventual expansion was often long, and in the meantime many of the goals that suffragists initially desired, such as property rights, the right to divorce, the right to transact commercially, and so on, were granted along the way. These policy concessions should be traced and analyzed as part of the legacy of suffrage mobilization.

A second reason not to sound the death knell on the success of the suffrage movement is that the impact of women's mobilization may appear more significant on the subnational than at the national level.

---

[46] Molyneux 1985. See too Chafetz 1990. Stamiris (1986; 102) makes a similar point about how advances in Greek women's participation during the civil war in the 1940s, and their enhanced freedoms under German occupied zones, were wrested back in a counter-revolutionary period "by a dictatorship resting on the cult of the family."

[47] Harvey (1996) suggests that women were not able to transform themselves into a vote-producing machine and were sucked up into the larger party organizations. Corder and Wolbrecht (2016) show that for the most part, men and women tended to vote similarly (with women participating at much lower rates overall) in the first elections after the national amendment. Alpern and Baum (1985: 64) reject the idea that women were apathetic in the US (the post WWI period saw declining rates of voting overall), but, like Harvey, argue that the failure of women to vote as a bloc limited the policy concessions thereafter. But Anderson (1996) convincingly shows important qualitative differences in participatory norms after franchise reform.

If local competition and mobilization were important for politicians' individual incentives to support women's enfranchisement, we should expect women's empowerment to translate into local policy changes even if national-level policies prove more recalcitrant. Economists have studied the impact of suffrage on local school expenditures, educational attainment, and spending on child and maternal health, and they showed large and positive changes in these factors after suffrage in the United States.[48] We might think, therefore, that the political effects of suffrage should be theorized and evaluated at the local level.[49]

Finally, much more work needs to be done to understand, in a comparative context, the politics that undergird the fiscal effects of suffrage reform. Studying multiple countries before and after women's enfranchisement, political economists have found that suffrage mattered for the welfare state: women's suffrage increased social spending in Western Europe, in the OECD countries, and in Switzerland, and produced large and immediate changes in public health expenditures in the United States.[50] If the strategic elements that influenced the adoption of women's suffrage were also instructive for the policy changes that emerged thereafter, there should be a *political* link between enfranchisement of women and public spending. To investigate a political link between suffrage and social spending, three possible mechanisms could be considered in future work. First, female voters might have thrown their weight behind parties that had redistributive agendas. If early female voters cast their ballots disproportionately for progressive parties, then more generous welfare spending might have followed from the changing partisan landscape. Alternatively, parties of all ideologies might have perceived that women would prefer higher levels of social spending, and may have competitively matched each other's platforms in order to court women's votes.[51]

Finally, women's suffrage may have improved welfare state provision because women that cared about the social safety net won seats in national legislatures. Although legal discourse distinguishes between what is perhaps inaptly called "active" suffrage (the right to vote) and "passive" suffrage (the right to stand for office), and some countries actually conferred on women these rights at different times, most

---

[48] Miller 2008; Carruthers and Wanamaker 2015; Kuka et al. 2017.
[49] See Morgan-Collins 2017.
[50] Aidt and Dallal 2008; Bertocchi 2010; Abrams and Settle 1999; Miller 2008.
[51] This would be the prediction of the famous "median voter theorem" of Downs. It could be investigated by looking at parties' strategies of mobilization and through an analysis of party platform changes before and after enfranchisement.

countries reformed the laws allowing women to vote and stand for office at the same time.[52] Around the time of suffrage reform, many countries elected their first female representatives. In the US, Jeannette Rankin was elected to congress in 1916, four years before the Nineteenth Amendment was federally ratified.[53] In the UK, Viscountess Nancy Astor served in parliament from 1919 to 1945. In France, the first woman was elected prior to enfranchisement, in 1936.[54] The suffrage movement, which, it should be recalled, often grew out of demands for broader social reform along the lines of healthcare, sanitation, and educational reform, to name a few, produced leaders who might easily have transitioned into holding an elected office. To the extent that they shared the policy concerns of the broader movement, these women may have successfully advocated for social reform. Such was the case with British feminist Eleanor Rathbone, who became an independent MP from 1929 to 1946. She was a key player in the early formation of the British welfare state, and worked to ensure that newly established "family allowances" were allocated to wives instead of husbands.[55] The generations of women that gained leadership skills and political know-how through their involvement with the suffrage movement may have been instrumental for cementing the welfare reforms that followed the vote.[56]

Fundamentally, the extension of the right to vote to women was not, as some social scientists have suggested, merely or primarily a normative

[52] For example, Belgian women were given limited national voting rights in 1919, but also local voting rights and the right to stand for all elections in that year. Universal suffrage would wait until 1948. The Nepalese "interim" constitution of 1951 allowed women to vote under universal suffrage but not to stand for office (Daley and Nolan 1994: 351). The Netherlands allowed women to stand for office beginning in 1917 but not to vote until 1919.

[53] As for the argument about Western US "progressivity," Rankin appears to be the only woman ever to represent Montana in congress.

[54] The right to run for office does not appear to have been a primary goal of the suffrage movement, but typically only a few years passed after enfranchisement before a woman was elected to national office. Iceland extended the vote in 1915 and elected Ingibjörg H. Bjarnason in 1922. In Argentina the vote was won in 1947 and then four years passed before the first woman held national office. Lavrin (1994, 1995) is the key source on Latin American suffrage movements. Germany elected Marie Juchacz (SPD) and extended the vote in 1919. Belgium, with its limited suffrage rights in 1919, elected its first woman in 1921.

[55] See Pedersen (2004) and Holton (1996: 230).

[56] Carpenter and Moore (2014: table 5) provide some quantitative evidence for the oft-noted link between American women's activism in the abolitionist movement and women's later involvement in suffrage politics, the idea being that the skills and contacts gained in the earlier campaign translated into later political activism. In the context of the Norwegian independence movement, Skorge (2017) shows that women's political participation after independence was correlated with their ability to collect petition signatures in the pre-independence era.

issue. Though changing norms about women as citizens, and about citizenship more generally, are part of this history, these forces cannot account for the short-term reversals that propelled women to the polls. To be sure, in each country there were politicians that behaved as moral crusaders—who supported suffrage because of the justice of the cause, no matter the effects. Then there were some who were chauvinist stalwarts— who resisted suffrage though they knew deep down that it was "right." But a substantial group of people fell somewhere in the middle—they were neither moved by the norm nor set in their ways. Suffrage could not be wholly won, or wholly resisted, without the backing of this middle group. For them, the choice over whether to enfranchise women had to do with whether the ebb and flow of political competition, and the strategic choices made by organized women, led to an alignment of interests between suffragists and politicians.

Appendix

Measuring "Full" Suffrage

The dates of full suffrage used, for example, in figure 1.1 refer to the year in which legislation allowing for "active" suffrage for women passed the national legislature and became law. (Other studies may report the year of the first election in which women were eligible to vote.) The raw data and complete list of references used to code this variable are available with the book's replication files at doi:10.7910/DVN/JZYGRB.

Active suffrage pertains to the right to vote, which may be distinct from the right to "passive" suffrage, in other words, the right to stand for office. In some cases, women were granted passive suffrage before active. For example, Belgian women were granted passive suffrage but only local voting rights in 1919. Active voting rights were extended in 1945. In most cases both the right to vote and the right to stand for office were disbursed with the same piece of legislation.

I code a country as having extended franchise rights to women in the year of the first *major* extension that would have allowed women to vote. This would require more than half of all adult women to be eligible to vote. So, for example, Australia is coded as 1902 although aboriginal women were excluded because indigenous peoples constituted only 2 percent of the population in that decade; but South Africa is not counted until 1994, though white women were given the vote in 1930. Similarly Belize is counted as 1954, because the earlier extension in 1945 had age, racial, and property requirements which would have meant that only a small proportion of Belize's women could vote.

Importantly, my measure does not require that women and men face the same requirements. Thus women may be given voting rights but at a higher age floor than men, but so long as this enabled the majority of women to vote, it would count in my score.

I draw these dates from many sources, often using country case studies to find the exact day that legislation passed. Sources for individual country studies can be found in the book's online appendix. I also consulted with the following texts that list dates for several countries, including Collier 1999; Caramani 2004; Hammond 2004; Hannam et al. 2000; Przeworski and Sprague 1986; Ray 1918; Sivard 1985 (used by Paxton 2000). For the dates of female suffrage, my list is, I believe, the most comprehensive and the most accurate.

II RESEARCH ON THE UNITED KINGDOM

Data for this chapter were drawn from several sources. The raw data as well as replication files will be made available upon request. Electoral returns in the 1910–1914 by-elections have been hand-coded from McCalmont et al. (1971). General election returns from the January 1910 and December 1910 elections are available through Britain's Economic and Social Data Service in digital form (Field 2007). The Field (2007) data originate from Craig (1974), the most comprehensive source of parliamentary returns in British politics.

List of Archives Consulted

- CAB: National Archives, UK Cabinet Papers.
- CAC: Cumbria Archive Center, Carlisle, UK. The papers of Catherine Marshall and those related to the Election Fighting Fund.
- LHA: The Labour History Archive and Study Center (formerly the People's Library), Manchester, UK. The papers of Arthur Henderson and Henry Noel Brailsford, as well as the Labour Party's documentation of their alliance with the National Union.
- MLS: Manchester Archives and Local Studies, Manchester, UK. Microfilmed letters of Millicent Garrett Fawcett, much correspondence between her and Henry Noel Brailsford, and some documentation on the Election Fighting Fund.
- OBL: Oxford Bodleian Library, Oxford, UK. Microfilmed papers of Herbert Asquith. Typed minutes of deputations of suffragist organizations that he received as Prime Minister.
- PA: Parliamentary Archives, London, UK. Bound boxes of Lloyd George's correspondence while Chancellor or the Exchequer and Prime Minister.
- TWL: The Women's Library (formerly the Fawcett Library), London, UK. The papers of Millicent Garrett Fawcett, records of the National Union for Women's Suffrage Societies including election files and files and original minutes of the Election Fighting Fund. Note that as of 2014 the collection is housed at the London School of Economics and Political Science.

Text of the Conciliation Bills

From 1908 until 1911 there were two private member bills that would have given parliamentary franchise to women, and three bills that would have given local franchise to women. The text on the parliamentary franchise bills are below.

Women's Enfranchisement Act, 1908

A private member bill proposed by Henry York Stanger on 28 February 1908. Stanger was a Liberal, educated at Oxford. Elected in N. Kensington in 1906. Retired in 1910 (Stenton and Lees 1978, *Who's Who* II: 335). The bill passed a second reading. The text of the bill implied that the masculine words should include women with reference to the right to be registered as voters and voting (in other words, enfranchise women on the same terms as men). Among voters, the Liberals, Labour, and Nationalist groups supported this bill, which would have likely only added a few wealthy women to the registers. Within all party members, however, the Nationalist and the Unionist were overwhelmingly against the bill. In the chapter, this bill is described as being of type C.

Representation of the People Act, 1909

A private member bill proposed by Hon. Geoffrey William Algernon Howard, 19 March 1909. Howard was a Liberal, educated at Cambridge. Sat for Eskdale 1906–1910 until defeated. Sat for Wiltshire (Westbury division) 1911–1918 until defeated. Lost in N. Cumberland 1922. He was the private secretary to Herbert Asquith 1908–1910 (Stenton and Lees 1978, *Who's Who* III: 175). This bill would have allowed every person of a given age to vote, given three months residency. No voting shall be allowed in multiple constituencies. Any masculine words imply women. For this bill, which would have abolished plural voting and enfranchised women, only 24 percent of the MPs voted. The Liberals, Nationalist, and Labour supported in large percentages, though not a single Unionist voted for the bill. Yet among all members, only the Labour Party polled more than 50 percent support for a second reading. In the chapter, this bill is described as being of type D.

III RESEARCH ON THE UNITED STATES

A longer technical appendix for the research on the United States is available through Teele 2018.[1] This includes a discussion of the dependent variable of passage of full suffrage in US state legislatures using a database originally constructed by King et al. (2005), and the construction of a measure of political machine presence within cities and states from 1840 to 1920. This appendix also shows the lack of relationship between suffrage and the adoption of prohibition within US states.

IV RESEARCH ON FRANCE

Variable Definition and Sources

TABLE A.1. Summary Statistics for France.

Variable	Mean	SD	Min	Max
Dependent Variable:				
= 1 if deputy voted Yea on granting women equal suffrage in 1919	0.77	(0.42)	0	1
Independent Variables:				
Percent Oath Takers, 1791	57.21	(23.38)	9	94
Party: Left, Radical Center, Right				
Branches of the UFSF, 1914	1.55	(2.41)	0	21
Expansion of the LFDF	0.42	(0.77)	0	2
Number of Feminist Organizations, 1914	2.31	(1.74)	0	9
Total Feminist Activity 1904–1922	1.46	(0.91)	0	4
Provincial Papers Pro-Suffrage, 1911	0.41	(0.69)	0	2
District Magnitude	6.26	(6.56)	1	25
District Magnitude, logged	1.46	(0.82)	0	3.22
Number of Parties, 1919	2.72	(1.91)	0	7

[1] See doi:10.7910/DVN/EVYI2H.

TABLE A.2. Variables Used in French Roll-Call Analysis.

Variable	Description	Source
Dependent Variable:		
	= 1 if deputy voted Yea on granting women equal suffrage in 1919	See table A.4
Independent Variables:		
Percent Oath Takers, 1791	Share of priests in a department that swore fealty to the Civil Constitution of 1791. This is a proxy for the depth of cleavage. The higher the share of juring priests, the less salient is the religious cleavage. The data are at the department level, although for some departments there is district level data, and reflect the spring 1791 oath, supplemented by the summer figures when needed.	Tackett 2014: appendix III.
Party: Left, Radical Center, Right	Aggregated party leanings found in figure 5.1. Left represents the Communists and Socialists; Radicals are the Radicals and the Center (because of anti-clerical leanings); and Right includes Center-Right and Right.	Graham 1984.
Branches of the UFSF, 1914	Records the total number of branches of the UFSF, founded in 1909, at the department level.	Hause and Kenney 1984: map 4.
Expansion of the LFDF	Lists whether a department had a branch of the LFDF in 1914, or whether a branch was established 1918–1920.	Hause and Kenney 1984: map 8.
Number of Feminist Organizations, 1914	The number of feminist organizations in each department including branches of UFSF, LFDF, CNFF, smaller Parisian leagues, chapters of FFU, lodges of mixed masonry.	Hause and Kenney 1984: map 5.
Total Feminist Activity 1904–1922	Covers activity of all feminist organizations including branches of UFSF, LFDF, CNFF, smaller Parisian leagues, chapters of FFU, lodges of mixed masonry, and more. Lists whether activity level is "rare or non-existent"; "little"; "occasional"; "well-established"; "frequent."	Hause and Kenney 1984: maps 1–5 and 8.
Provincial Papers Pro-Suffrage, 1911	Tallies whether provincial newspapers are open to feminist contributions, listing either a zero, one, or two for two or more.	Hause and Kenney 1984: map 3.

TABLE A.2. Variables Used in French Roll-Call Analysis. *(Cont.)*

Variable	Description	Source
District Magnitude	Total MPs that represent a given department in the Chamber of Deputies.	Author's calculation 1984.
Number of Parties, 1919	The number of unique party tendencies of MPs, as reflected in figure 5.1 calculated at the department level.	Author's calculation from Graham 1984.

TABLE A.3. Competition, Religiosity, and Suffrage Support by Party. The average support for suffrage by deputies in areas defined by high or low competition (measured by the variable on the left-hand side) when in a secular or religious department is listed in the cells. The number of observations contributing to the calculation of each average is below.

		Low Competition		High Competition	
		Secular	Religious	Secular	Religious
Runner-up to Winner	Left	0.61	0.58	0.76	0.8
		3	6	6	5
	Center	0.54	0.48	0.78	0.82
		12	9	14	6
	Right	0.63	0.52	0.7	0.78
		2	13	4	10
Second Ballot	Left	0.2	0.2	0.74	0.77
		2	5	7	6
	Center	0.24	0.1	0.63	0.54
		10	6	16	9
	Right	0.27	0.18	0.54	0.53
		2	19	4	4
Dual Mandate	Left	0.36	0.43	0.86	0.96
		5	6	4	5
	Center	0.42	0.34	0.82	0.79
		15	8	11	7
	Right	0.38	0.38	0.77	0.78
		2	9	4	14

TABLE A.4. Timeline of Suffrage Bills in France.

Date	Description	Outcome
20 May 1919, CoD	Full suffrage bill. Contre-projet of MM Jean Bon and Lucien Dumont. Bill text: third column of page 2350, rephrased to vote on 2358: "Le lois et dispositions réglementaires sur l'électorat et l'éligibilité a toutes assemblées élues sont applicables a tous les citoyens français sans distinction de sexe."	Adopted: 441 voters; 221 majority. 314 Yea, 97 Nay. *Scrutin* N. 904, in J.O. chambre, p. 2365–66.
3 October 1919, Senate	Submission of a report by Alexandre Bérard (of the committee for universal suffrage) on M. Louis Martin's proposal to give women the vote.	Sent to Committee: Rapport n° 564, annexé au procès-verbal de la séance du Sénat du 3 octobre 1919.
November 1922, Senate	Discussion for two weeks on the Bérard report. Debates: 21 November 1922, J.O. Senat, p. 1370–79. Under Berard's recommendation, procedural vote taken over whether to advance the discussion: Bill text: "Passage a la discussion des articles."	Rejected: Senate not to consider bill's articles. 134 Yea, 156 Nay, 21 Nov 1922. *Scrutin* N° 68, in J.O. senat, p. 1386–87.
7 April 1925, CoD	Municipal and cantonal election bill. Supporters: Justin Godart, Joseph Barthelemy, Louis Martin. Bill text: (p. 2100, 2nd Column: Art. 1er.) "Le droit de vote et d'éligibilité est accordé aux femmes françaises pour les élections municipales et cantonales, dans les mêmes conditions que celles exigées des hommes." Debates (p. 2099–2110).	Adopted: 573 voters; 287 majority. 390 Yea, 183 Nay. *Scrutin* N° 248, in J.O. senat p. 2122–25.
June 1928	To initiate a discussion of women's suffrage law. M. Martin proposes 6 July 1928. Debate, J.O. senat, 19th June 1928 (p. 985).	Not Adopted: 224 voters; 142 majority. 116 Yea, 158 Nay. Roll call (p. 986) *Scrutin* N° 25:
March 1929	Initiate discussion of suffrage law.	Not Adopted: 174 Nay, 120 Yea.

TABLE A.4. Timeline of Suffrage Bills in France. (*Cont.*)

Date	Description	Outcome
June 1931	A resolution based on article 96 of French Constitution to proclaim electoral eligibility of women. Supporters: Marin. Bill text: (p. 2977, 3rd column). Debates: 11 June 1931 (p. 2976–77)	Not Adopted: 538 voters; 270 majority. 218 Yea, 320 Nay. *Scrutin* N° 590.
November 1933	Senate asked to discuss Martin's draft suffrage law. Debates J.O., 14th November 1933 (p. 1845–48)	Adopted: 275 voters; 138 majority. 166 Yea, 109 Nay. *Scrutin* N° 100, p. 1851–52.
1 March 1935, CoD	Full Suffrage Rights. Supporters: original bill by M. Fayssat for municipal rights, then a contre-projet substituted by M. Bracke. Bill Text (p. 794, 1st column) "Toutes les dispositions législatives fixant les conditions dans lesquelles sont assurés et s'exercent le droit de suffrage, ainsi que l'éligibilité qui en résulte, dans toutes les élections aux assemblées délibérantes sont et restent applicable aux deux sexes." Debates J.O. 1st March 1926 (p. 790–95)	Adopted: Roll call 531 voters; 266 majority. 426 Yea, 105 Nay. Scrutin N° 690, p. 809–10.
30 July 1936	Full suffrage. Supporters: M. Martin. Bill Text (p. 2223, 1st column) "Les lois et dispositions réglementaires sur l'électorat et l'éligibilité à toutes les assemblées élues sont applicables à tous les citoyens français, sans distinction de sexe." Debates J.O. 30 July 1936 (p. 2222, 2223).	Adopted: Unanimously. 495 voters; 248 majority. 495 Yea, 0 Nay. *Scrutin* N° 78.

References

Abrams, B.A., Settle, R.F., 1999. "Women's Suffrage and the Growth of the Welfare State." *Public Choice* 100: 289–300.

Acemoglu, D., Robinson, J. A., 2006. *Economic Origins of Dictatorship and Democracy*. Cambridge University Press.

Acemoglu, D., Robinson, J. A., 2000. "Why Did the West Extend the Franchise? Democracy, Inequality, and Growth in Historical Perspective." *Quarterly Journal of Economics* 115: 1167–1199. doi:10.1162/003355300555042

Adams, J., 2014. *Women and the Vote: A World History*. Oxford University Press.

Ahmed, A., 2010. "Reading History Forward: The Origins of Electoral Systems in European Democracies." *Comparative Political Studies* 43(8–9): 1059–1088.

Ahmed, A., 2013. *Democracy and the Politics of Electoral System Choice: Engineering Electoral Dominance*. Cambridge University Press.

Aidt, T. S., Dallal, B., 2008. "Female Voting Power: The Contribution of Women's Suffrage to the Growth of Social Spending in Western Europe (1869–1960)." *Public Choice* 134(3–4): 391–417.

Aidt, T. S., Jensen, P.S., 2011. "Workers of the World, Unite! Franchise Extensions and the Threat of Revolution in Europe, 1820–1938." SSRN.

Alexander, T. G., 1970. *"An Experiment in Progressive Legislation: The Granting of Woman Suffrage in Utah in 1870." Utah Historical Quarterly*.

Alpern, S., Baum, D., 1985. "Female Ballots: The Impact of the Nineteenth Amendment." *The Journal of Interdisciplinary History* 16(1): 43–67.

Alvarez, S. E., 1990. *Engendering Democracy in Brazil: Women's Movements in Transition Politics*. Princeton University Press.

Andersen, K., 1996. *After Suffrage: Women in Partisan and Electoral Politics before the New Deal*. University of Chicago Press.

Ansell, B. W., Samuels, D. J., 2014. *Inequality and Democratization: An Elite-Competition Approach*. Cambridge University Press.

Ansolabehere, S., Snyder, J. M., Jr., Steward, C., III, 2001. "The Effects of Party and Preferences on Congressional Roll-Call Voting." *Legislative Studies Quarterly* 26: 533–572. doi:10.2307/440269

Anthony, S. B., Brownell, S., Gage, M. J., Harper, I. H., Stanton, E. C., 1969 [1881]. *History of Woman Suffrage*. Volume I: 1848–1861. Arno Press.

Anthony, S. B., Brownell, S., Gage, M. J., Harper, I. H., Stanton, E. C., 1969 [1881]. *History of Woman Suffrage*. Volume VI. Arno Press.

Baldez, L., 2002. *Why Women Protest: Women's Movements in Chile*. Cambridge University Press.

Banaszak, L. A., 1998. "Use of the Initiative Process by Woman Suffrage Movements," in D. McAdam, A. N. Costain, and A. S. McFarland (eds.), *Social Movements and American Political Institutions*, 99–114.

Banaszak, L. A., 1996a. "When Waves Collide: Cycles of Protest and the Swiss and American Women's Movements." *Political Research Quarterly* 49: 837–860.

Banaszak, L. A., 1996b. *Why Movements Succeed or Fail: Opportunity, Culture, and the Struggle for Women's Suffrage*. Princeton University Press.

Bateman, D., 2018. *Disenfranchising Democracy: The Construction of the Electorate in the U.S.A., the U.K., and France*. Cambridge University Press.

Bawn, K., 1993. "The Logic of Institutional Preferences: German Electoral Law as a Social Choice Outcome." *American Journal of Political Science* 37: 965–989.

Beckwith, K., 2000. "Beyond Compare? Women's Movements in Comparative Perspective. *European Journal of Political Research* 37(4): 431–468.

Beckwith, K. 2003. "The Gendering Ways of States," in L. Banaszak, K. Beckwith, and D. Rucht (eds.), *Women's Movements Facing the Reconfigured State*. Cambridge University Press.

Beckwith, K., 2014. "Plotting the Path from One to the Other Women's Interests and Political Representation," in M. C. Escobar-Lemmon and M. M. Taylor-Robinson (eds.), *Representation: The Case of Women*. Oxford University Press.

Beeton, B., 1986. *Women Vote in the West: The Woman Suffrage Movement, 1869–1896*. Garland.

Behn, B., 2012. *Woodrow Wilson's Conversion Experience: The President and the Federal Woman Suffrage Amendment*. University of Massachusetts, Amherst.

Belchem, J., 2000. *A New History of the Isle of Man: The Modern Period 1830–1999*. Liverpool University Press.

Berger, S., 1974. *The French Political System*. Random House.

Berger, S., 1987. "Religious Transformation and the Future of Politics," in C. S. Maier (ed.), *Changing Boundaries of the Political: Essays on the Evolving Balance between the State and Society, Public and Private in Europe*. Cambridge University Press, 107–149.

Berman, D. R., 1987. "Male Support for Woman Suffrage: An Analysis of Voting Patterns in the Mountain West." *Social Science History* 11: 281–294.

Bermeo, N., 2003. "What the Democratization Literature Says—or Doesn't Say—About Postwar Democratization." *Global Governance*, 159–177.

Bertocchi, G., 2010. "The Enfranchisement of Women and the Welfare State." *European Economic Review* 55: 535–553.

Bidelman, P. K., 1976. "The Politics of French Feminism: Léon Richer and the Ligue Française pour le Droit des Femmes, 1882–1891." *Historical Reflections/Réflexions Historiques*, 93–120.

Blewett, N., 1965. "The Franchise in the UK, 1885–1918." *Past and Present* 32.

Boix, C., 2010. "Electoral Markets, Party Strategies, and Proportional Representation." *American Political Science Review* 104: 404–413.

Boix, C., 2003. *Democracy and Redistribution*. Cambridge University Press.

Boix, C., 1999. Setting the Rules of the Game: The Choice of Electoral Systems in Advanced Democracies. *American Political Science Review* 93: 609–624.

Boix, C., Miller, M., Sebastian R., 2013. "A Complete Data Set of Political Regimes, 1800–2007." *Comparative Political Studies* 46(12): 1523–1554.

Bouglé-Moalic, A.-S., 2012. *Le vote des Françaises: cent ans de débats, 1848–1944*. Presses universitaires de Rennes.

Braun, S., Kvasnicka, M., 2013. "Men, Women, and the Ballot: Gender Imbalances and Suffrage Extensions in the United States." *Explorations in Economic History* 50: 405–426.

Bridges, A., 1997. *Morning Glories*. Cambridge University Press.

Brustein, W., 1988. *The Social Origins of Political Regionalism: France, 1849–1981*. University of California Press.

Buenker, J. D., 1971. "The Urban Political Machine and Woman Suffrage: A Study in Political Adaptability." *Historian* 33: 264–278.

Burnham, W. D., 1986. *Partisan Division of American State Governments, 1834–1985*. Ann Arbor, MI: Inter-university Consortium for Political and Social Research [distributor], 1992-02-16. https://doi.org/10.3886/ICPSR00016.v1

Bush, S. S., 2011. "International Politics and the Spread of Quotas for Women in Legislatures." *International Organization* 65(01): 103–137.

Butler, M. A., Templeton, J., 2008 [1984]. "The Isle of Man and the First Votes for Women." *Women & Politics* 4: 33–47.

Butterfield, L. H., Friedlaender, M., Kline, M. J. (eds.), 2002. *The Book of Abigail and John: Selected Letters of the Adams Family, 1762–1784*. Boston: Northeastern University Press.

Callon J. E. (ed.), 2003. "Préface: Les débats de l'Assemblée consultative provisoire à Alger 3 novembre 1943–25 juillet 1944." *Journal officiel de la République française* (Paris, 1953).

Camhi, J. J., 1994. "Women against Women: American Antisuffragism, 1880–1920. In B. Arrighi (ed.), *Understanding Inequality: The Intersection of Race/Ethnicity, Class, and Gender*. Rowman Littlefield.

Campbell, P., 1958. *French Electoral Systems and Elections Since 1789*. London: Faber and Faber.

Capoccia, G., Ziblatt, D., 2010. "The Historical Turn in Democratization Studies: A New Research Agenda for Europe and Beyond." *Comparative Political Studies* 43: 931–968.

Caramani, D., 2004. *The Nationalization of Politics: The Formation of National Electorates and Party Systems in Western Europe*. Cambridge University Press.

Caraway, T. L., 2004. "Inclusion and Democratization: Class, Gender, Race, and the Extension of Suffrage." *Comparative Politics*, 443–460.

Carpenter, D., Moore, C. D., 2014. "When Canvassers Became Activists: Anti-slavery Petitioning and the Political Mobilization of American Women." *American Political Science Review* 108(3): 479–498.

Carruthers, C. K, Wanamaker, M. H., 2015. "Municipal Housekeeping the Impact of Women's Suffrage on Public Education." *Journal of Human Resources* 50(4): 837–872.

Catt, C. C., Shuler, N. R., 1923. *Woman Suffrage and Politics: The Inner Story of the Suffrage Movement*. Charles Scribner's Sons.

Chafetz, J. S., Dworkin, A. G., Swanson, S., 1990. "Social Change and Social Activism: First-Wave Women's Movements around the World." *Women and Social Protest*, 302–320.

Chowdhury, N., Nelson, B. J., Carver, K. A., Johnson, N. J., O'Loughlin, P., 1994. "Redefining Politics: Patterns of Women's Political Engagement from a Global Perspective," in B. J. Nelson and N. Chowdhury (eds.), *Women and Politics Worldwide*. Yale University Press, 3–24.

Cirone, A., 2017. *Essays on Historical Political Economy: The Case of the French Third Republic*. PhD diss, Columbia University.

Clark, L. (1984). "Schooling the Daughters of Marianne." *Textbooks and the Socialization of Girls in Modern French Primary Schools*, Albany, NY: State University of New York Press.

Clayton, A., Zetterberg, P., forthcoming. "Quota Shocks: Electoral Gender Quotas and Government Spending Priorities Worldwide." *The Journal of Politics*.

Collier, R. B., 1999. *Paths toward Democracy: The Working Class and Elites in Western Europe and South America*. Cambridge University Press.

Colomer, J. (ed.). 2002. *The Handbook of Electoral System Choice*. Springer.

Cook, B. A., 2002. *Belgium: A History*. Vol. 50. Peter Lang Inc, New York.

Congressional Globe, 39th Congress, 2nd Session, 11 December 1867.

Connelly, K., 2013. *Sylvia Pankhurst: Suffragette, Socialist and Scourge of Empire*. London: Pluto Press.

Conover, P. J., 1988. "The Role of Social Groups in Political Thinking." *British Journal of Political Science*, 51–76.

Corder, J. K., Wolbrecht, C., 2016. *Counting Women's Ballots*. Cambridge University Press.

Cox, G. W., 2009 [1987]. "Swing Voters, Core Voters, and Distributive Politics," in I. Shapiro, S. C. Stokes, E. J. Wood, and A. S. Kirshner (eds.), *Political Representation*. Cambridge University Press.

Cox, G. W., 2005. *The Efficient Secret: The Cabinet and the Development of Political Parties in Victorian England*. Cambridge University Press.

Craig, F. W. S., 1987. *Chronology of British Parliamentary By-Elections, 1833–1987*. Chichester, UK: Parliamentary Research Services.

Craig, F. W. S., 1972. *Boundaries of Parliamentary Constituencies 1885–1972*. Chichester, UK: Political Reference Publications.

Craig, F. W. S. (ed.), 1974. *British Parliamentary Election Results 1885–1918*. SN: 5673 from ESTDS database. London: Macmillan.

Crasnow, S., 2015. "The Measure of Democracy: Coding in Political Science," in L. Huber (ed.), *Standardization in Measurement: Philosophical, Historical and Sociological Issues*. Routledge.

Crook, M., Crook, T., 2007. "The Advent of the Secret Ballot in Britain and France, 1789–1914: From Public Assembly to Private Compartment." *History* 92: 449–471.

Dahl, R. A., 1971. *Polyarchy: Participation and Opposition*. Yale University Press.

Daley, C. Nolan, M. (eds.), 1994. *Suffrage and Beyond: International Feminist Perspectives*. NYU Press.

Dangerfield, G., 2011 [1935]. *The Strange Death of Liberal England, 1910–1914*. Transaction Publishers.

Darsigny, M. 1990. *L'épopée du suffrage féminin au Québec, 1920–1940*. Université du Québec à Montréal.

Dasgupta, A., Ziblatt, D., 2015. "How Did Britain Democratize? Views From the Sovereign Bond Market." *The Journal of Economic History* 75(1): 1–29.

David, P. T., 1972. "How Can an Index of Party Competition Best be Derived?" *The Journal of Politics* 34(2): 632–638.

Davis, A. Y., 2011 [1981]. *Women, Race, & Class*. Vintage.

Decamont, F., 1996. "La préparation des ordonnances a Alger: Le vote des Femmes, in Fondation nationale des Sciences politiques Association française des constitutionnalistes" (ed.), Le rétablissement de la légalité républicaine (1944): actes du colloque 6, 7, 8 octobre 1994 organisé par. *Editions Complexe*, Bruxelles, 101–117.

de Gaulle, P., Tauriac, M. (2003). *De Gaulle mon père*. Paris: Plon.

Doepke, M., Tertilt, M., 2009. "Women's Liberation: What's in It for Men?" *Quarterly Journal of Economics* 124: 1541–1591.

Dubin, M. J., 2007. *Party Affiliations in the State Legislatures: A Year by Year Summary, 1796–2006*. McFarland.

DuBois, E. C., 1998. *Woman Suffrage and Women's Rights*. NYU Press.

DuBois, E. C., 1991. "Woman Suffrage and the Left: An International Socialist-Feminist Perspective." *New Left Review* 186: 20–45.

DuBois, E. C., 1987. "Working Women, Class Relations, and Suffrage Militance: Harriot Stanton Blatch and the New York Woman Suffrage Movement, 1894–1909." *The Journal of American History* 74: 34–58.

Dumas, A., 2016. "Le droit de vote des femmes à l'Assemblée législative du Québec (1922–1940)." *Bulletin d'histoire politique* 24(3): 137–157.

Dupont, A., 1972. "Louis-Alexandre Taschereau et la législation sociale au Québec, 1920–1936." *Revue d'histoire de l'Amérique française* 26(3): 397–426.

Duchen, C., 2003. *Women's Rights and Women's Lives in France 1944–1968*. Routledge.

Dunning, T., 2012. *Natural Experiments in the Social Sciences: A Design-Based Approach*. Cambridge University Press.

Du Roy, A., Du Roy, N., 1994. *Citoyennes!: Il y a cinquante ans, le vote des femmes*. Paris: Flammarion.

Edwards, L., 2004. "Chinese Women's Campaigns for Suffrage: Nationalism Confucianism and Political Agency," in L. Edwards and M. Roces (eds.), *Women's Suffrage in Asia: Gender, Nationalism and Democracy*. London: RoutledgeCurzon, 127–151.

Edwards, L., Roces, M., 2004. "Introduction: Orienting the Gobal Women's Suffrage Movement," in *Women's Suffrage in Asia: Gender, Nationalism and Democracy*. London: RoutledgeCurzon.

Engels, F., 2010 [1884]. *The Origin of the Family, Private Property and the State*. Penguin UK.

Englander, S., 1992. *Class Conflict and Coalition in the California Woman Suffrage Movement, 1907–1912: The San Francisco Wage Earners' Suffrage League*. Edwin Mellen Press.

Evans, R. J., 1980. "German Social Democracy and Women's Suffrage 1891–1918." *Journal of Contemporary History* 15: 533–557.

Evans, R. J., 1977. *The Feminists: Women's Emancipation Movements in Europe, America, and Australasia, 1840–1920*. New York: Croom Helm.

Federici, S., 2004. *Caliban and the Witch*. Autonomedia.

Ferree, M. M., Mueller, C. M., 2004. Feminism and the Women's Movement: A Global Perspective, in *The Blackwell Companion to Social Movements*, 576–607.

Field, W., 2007. *British Electoral Data, 1885–1949* [computer file]. SN: 5673. Colchester, Essex: UK Data Archive [distributor]. doi:http://dx.doi.org/10.5255/UKDA-SN-5673-1

Flexner, E., 1995 [1959]. *Century of Struggle: The Woman's Rights Movement in the United States*. Belknap Press.

Folbre, N., 1982. "Exploitation Comes Home: A Critique of the Marxian Theory of Family Labor," *Cambridge Journal of Economics* 6(4): 317–329.

Ford, L., 1991. *Iron-Jawed Angels: The Suffrage Militancy of the National Woman's Party, 1912–1920*. Lanham, NY: University Press of America.

Foster, R. F., 2014. *Vivid Faces: The Revolutionary Generation in Ireland, 1890–1923*. Penguin UK.

Free, L. E., 2015. *Suffrage Reconstructed: Gender, Race, and Voting Rights in the Civil War Era*. Cornell University Press.

Freeman, J. R., Quinn, D. P., 2008. "The Economic Origins of Democracy Reconsidered." *American Political Science Review* 1: 1–23.

Friedman, E. J., 2000. *Unfinished Transitions: Women and the Gendered Development of Democracy in Venezuela, 1936–1996*. Penn State Press.

García-Jimeno, C., 2012. "The Political Economy of Moral Conflict: An Empirical Study of Learning and Law Enforcement under Prohibition." Mimeo.

Geddes, B., 2007. What Causes Democratization? in C. Boix and S. Stokes (eds.), *Oxford Handbook of Comparative Politics*. Oxford University Press, 317–339.

Genest, J.-G. 1996. *Godbout*. Les éditions du Septentrion.

Gilman, C. P. 1911. *Suffrage Songs and Verses*. New York: The Charlton Company.

Gimpel, J., 1993. "Reform-Resistant and Reform-Adopting Machines: The Electoral Foundations of Urban Politics, 1910–1930." *Political Research Quarterly* 46: 371–382.

Goffman, E., 1977. "The Arrangement Between the Sexes." *Theory and Society* 4: 301–331.

Goldin, C., 1994. "Understanding the Gender Gap: An Economic History of American Women." *Equal Employment Opportunity: Labor Market Discrimination and Public Policy*. Hawthorne, NY: Walter de Gruyter.

Goldin, C., Sokoloff, K. L., 1982. "Women, Children, and Industrialization in the Early Republic: Evidence from the Manufacturing Censuses." *Journal of Economic History*, 741–774.

Gordon, F., 1990. *The Integral Feminist: Madeleine Pelletier, 1874–1939: Feminism, Socialism and Medicine*. Polity.

Graham, J. Q. J., 1984. "French Legislators, 1871–1940: Biographical Data." Inter-university Consortium for Political and Social Research, 1984.

Green, E. C., 1997. *Southern Strategies: Southern Women and the Woman Suffrage Question*. University of North Carolina Press.

Grimes, A., 1967. *The Puritan Ethic and Woman Suffrage*. Oxford University Press.

Grimshaw, P., 2004. "Settler Anxieties, Indigenous Peoples and Women's Suffrage in the Colonies of Australia, New Zealand and Hawai'i, 1888 to 1902," in L. Edwards and M. Roces (eds.), *Women's Suffrage in Asia: Gender, Nationalism and Democracy*. London: RoutledgeCurzon, 220–239.

Grimshaw, P., 1972. *Women's Suffrage in New Zealand*. Auckland University Press.

Gunter, R. 2017. *More Than Black and White: Woman Suffrage and Voting Rights in Texas, 1918–1923*. PhD diss., Texas A&M University.

Gustafson, M., 2001. *Women and the Republican Party, 1854–1924*. University of Illinois Press.

Haggard, S., Kaufman, R. R., 2012. "Inequality and Regime Change: Democratic Transitions and the Stability of Democratic Rule." *American Political Science Review* 106: 495–516. doi:10.1017/S0003055412000287

Hainmueller, J., Mummolo, J., Xu, Y., 2017. "How Much Should We Trust Estimates from Multiplicative Interaction Models? Simple Tools to Improve Empirical Practice." SSRN, doi:http://dx.doi.org/10.2139/ssrn.2739221.

Hammond, G., 2004. *Women Can Vote Now: Feminism and the Women's Suffrage Movement in Argentina, 1900–1955*. University of Texas at Austin.

Hancock, A.-M., 2016. *Intersectionality: An Intellectual History*. Oxford University Press. Hannam, J., Auchterlonie, M., Holden, K., 2000. *International Encyclopedia of Women's Suffrage*. Abc-Clio Inc.

Hansard Online (ed.), 1910. HC Deb 12 July 1910.

Hansard Online (ed.), 1912. HC Deb 28 March 1912.

Hansard Online (ed.), 1913. HC Deb 06 May 1913.

Harmer, H. J. P., 1999. *The Longman Companion to the Labour Party, 1900–1998*. London: Longman.

Hartmann, H., 1976. "Capitalism, Patriarchy, and Job Segregation by Sex." *Signs* 1.

Harvey, A. L., 1996. "The Political Consequences of Suffrage Exclusion: Organizations, Institutions, and the Electoral Mobilization of Women." *Social Science History* 20: 97–132.

Harvey, A., Mukherjee, B., 2006. "Electoral Institutions and the Evolution of Partisan Conventions, 1880–1940." *American Politics Research* 34: 368–398.

Hause, S. C., Kenney, A. R., 1984. *Women's Suffrage and Social Politics in the French Third Republic*. Princeton University Press.

Hause, S. C., Kenney, A. R., 1981. "The Limits of Suffragist Behavior: Legalism and Militancy in France, 1876–1922." *The American Historical Review*, 781–806.

Himmelfarb, G., 1966. "The Politics of Democracy: The English Reform Act of 1867." *Journal of British Studies* 6: 97–138.

Hirshfield, C., 1990. "Fractured Faith: Liberal Party Women and the Suffrage Issue in Britain, 1892–1914." *Gender & History* 2: 173–197.

Hobsbawm, E., 2010 [1989]. *The Age of Empires*. New York: Vintage Books.

Hoff, J., 1991. *Law, Gender, and Injustice: A Legal History of US Women*. NYU Press.

Holton, S. S., 1996. *Suffrage Days: Stories from the Women's Suffrage Movement*. Routledge.

Holton, S. S., 1986. *Feminism and Democracy: Women's Suffrage and Reform Politics in Britain, 1900–1918*. Cambridge University Press.

Houle, C., 2009. "Inequality and Democracy: Why Inequality Harms Consolidation but Does Not Affect Democratization." *World Politics* 61: 589–622.

Htun, M. 2003. *Sex and the State: Abortion, Divorce, and the Family under Latin American Dictatorships and Democracies*. Cambridge University Press.

Htun, M., 2004. "Is Gender Like Ethnicity? The Political Representation of Identity Groups." *Perspectives on Politics*, 439–458.

Htun, M., 2016. *Inclusion without Representation in Latin America: Gender Quotas and Ethnic Reservations*. Cambridge University Press.

Huntington, S. P., 1993. *The Third Wave: Democratization in the Late Twentieth Century*. University of Oklahoma Press.

Jayawardena, K., 1986. *Feminism and Nationalism in the Third World*. Zed Books.

Jones, A., 1972. *The Politics of Reform 1884*.

Jones, D. J. J., 1972. *The Asquith Cabinet and Women's Suffrage: 1908–1914*. PhD diss., Memorial University of Newfoundland.

Kalyvas, S. N., 1996. *The Rise of Christian Democracy in Europe*. Cornell University Press.

Katz, J. N., Sala, B. R., 1996. "Careerism, Committee Assignments, and the Electoral Connection." *American Political Science Review* 90: 21–33.

Kelly, V., 1996. "Irish Suffragettes at the Time of the Home Rule Crisis." *History Ireland*, 33–38.

Kent, S. K., 1987. *Sex and Suffrage in Britain, 1860–1914*. Princeton University Press.

Keyssar, A., 2000. *The Right to Vote*. Basic Books.

Khan, B. Z., 1996. "Married Women's Property Laws and Female Commercial Activity: Evidence from United States Patent Records, 1790–1895." *Journal of Economic History* 56: 356–88.

King, B. G., Cornwall, M., Dahlin, E. C., 2005. "Winning Woman Suffrage One Step at a Time: Social Movements and the Logic of the Legislative Process." *Social Forces* 83: 1211–1234.

Kleppner, P., 1983. "Voters and Parties in the Western States, 1876–1900." *The Western Historical Quarterly* 14: 49–68.

Kraditor, A. S., 1981. *The Ideas of the Woman Suffrage Movement, 1890–1920*. Norton.

Kreuzer, M., 2010. "Historical Knowledge and Quantitative Analysis: The Case of the Origins of Proportional Representation." *American Political Science Review* 104: 369–392.

Krook, M. L., 2010. *Quotas for Women in Politics: Gender and Candidate Selection Reform Worldwide*. Oxford University Press.

Krook, M., Mackay, F. (eds.), 2010. *Gender, Politics and Institutions: Towards a Feminist Institutionalism*. Palgrave MacMillan.

Kuka, E., Kose, E., Shenhav, N., 2017. "Women's Enfranchisement and Children's Education: The Long-Run Impact of the U.S. Suffrage Movement." Paper presented at *American Political Science Association conference*.

Larson, T., 1970. "Woman Suffrage in Western America." *Utah Historical Quarterly* 38: 7–19.

Lavrin, A., 1995. *Women, Feminism, and Social Change in Argentina, Chile, and Uruguay, 1890–1940*. University of Nebraska Press.

Lavrin, A., 1994. "Suffrage in South America: Arguing a Difficult Cause." C. Daley and M. Nolan (eds.), *Suffrage and Beyond: International Feminist Perspectives*, NYU Press.

Lee, W., Roemer, J. E., 2006. "Racism and Redistribution in the United States: A Solution to the Problem of American Exceptionalism." *Journal of Public Economics* 90(6–7): 1027–1052.

Lerner, E., 1981. *Immigrant and Working Class Involvement in the New York City Woman Suffrage Movement, 1905–1917: A Study in Progressive Era Politics.* PhD diss., University of California, Berkeley.

Liddington, J., Norris, J., 1978. *One Hand Tied Behind Us: The Rise of the Women's Suffrage Movement.* London: Virago.

Lieberman, E. S., 2005. "Nested Analysis as a Mixed-Method Strategy for Comparative Research." *American Political Science Review* 99: 435–452.

Linz, J., Stepan, A. (eds.), 1978. *The Breakdown of Democratic Regimes.* Baltimore: Johns Hopkins University Press.

Lipset, S. M., 1960. *Political Man: The Social Basis of Modern Politics.* New York: Doubleday.

Lipset, S. M., Rokkan, S., 1967. *Party Systems and Voter Alignments: Cross-National Perspectives.* Free Press.

Lizzeri, A., Persico, N., 2004. "Why Did the Elites Extend the Suffrage? Democracy and the Scope of Government, with an Application to Britain's Age of Reform?" *Quarterly Journal of Economics* 119: 707–765.

Llavador, H., Oxoby, R. J., 2005. "Partisan Competition, Growth, and the Franchise." *Quarterly Journal of Economics* 120(3): 1155–1189.

Loos, T., 2004. "The Politics of Women's Suffrage in Thailand," in L. Edwards, M. Roces (eds.), *Women's Suffrage in Asia: Gender, Nationalism and Democracy.* London: RoutledgeCurzon, 170–194.

Lunardini, C. A., 1986. *From Equal Suffrage to Equal Rights: Alice Paul and the National Woman's Party, 1910–1928.* NYU Press.

Macías, A., 1982. *Against All Odds: The Feminist Movement in Mexico to 1940.* Westport, CT: Greenwood Press.

Mackie, T. T. and Rose, R., 1991. *The International Almanac of Electoral History.* London: Macmillan, 3rd edition.

Mahoney, J., Goertz, G., 2004. The Possibility Principle: Choosing Negative Cases in Comparative Research. *American Political Science Review*, 98(4): 653–669.

Marino, K. M., 2018. *Feminism for the Americas: The Making of International Human Rights Movement.* Chapel Hill: UNC Press.

Maignien, C., Sowerwine, C., 1992. *Madeleine Pelletier, une féministe dans l'arène politique.* Editions de l'Atelier.

Manow, P., Palier, B., 2009. "A Conservative Welfare State Regime without Christian Democracy? The French Etat-Providence, 1880–1960," in K. Van Kersbergen and P. Manow (eds.), *Religion, Class Coalitions and Welfare State Regimes*, 146–175.

Marilley, S. M., 1996. *Woman Suffrage and the Origins of Liberal Feminism in the United States, 1820–1920.* Harvard University Press.

Markoff, J., 2003. "Margins, Centers, and Democracy: The Paradigmatic History of Women's Suffrage." *Signs* 29: 85–116.

Marshall, S. E., 1997. *Splintered Sisterhood: Gender and Class in the Campaign Against Woman Suffrage.* University of Wisconsin Press.

Martin, M., 2000. *The Almanac of Women and Minorities in World Politics.* Westview Press.

Mayhall, L. E. N., 2000. "The South African War and the Origins of Suffrage Militancy in Britain, 1899–1902," in I. C. Fletcher, L. E. N. Mayhall, and P. Levine (eds.), *Women's Suffrage in the British Empire: Citizenship, Nation, and Race*. Psychology Press.

Mayhew, D., 1986. *Placing Parties in American Politics: Organization, Electoral Settings, and Government Activity in the Twentieth Century*. Princeton University Press.

McAdam, D., Tarrow, S., Tilly, C., 1996. "To Map Contentious Politics." *Mobilization: An International Quarterly* 1: 17–34.

McCalmont, F. H., Vincent, J. R., Stenton, M., 1971. *McCalmont's Parliamentary Poll Book: British Election Results 1832–1918*. Brighton, UK: Harvester Press.

McCammon, H. J., Campbell, K. E., Granberg, E. M., Mowery, C., 2001. "How Movements Win: Gendered Opportunity Structures and US Women's Suffrage Movements, 1866 to 1919." *American Sociological Review* 49(70): 49–70.

McCammon, H. J., Campbell, K. E., 2001. "Winning the Vote in the West: The Political Successes of the Women's Suffrage Movements, 1866–1919." *Gender and Society* 15: 55–82.

McCammon, H. J., 2003. "Out of the Parlors and into the Streets': The Changing Tactical Repertoire of the US Women' Suffrage Movements." *Social Forces*, 81(3): 787–818.

McConnaughy, C., 2013. *The Woman Suffrage Movement in America: A Reassessment*. Cambridge University Press.

McDonagh, E., 2002. "Political Citizenship and Democratization: The Gender Paradox." *American Political Science Review* 96: 535–552.

McDonagh, E. L., 1989. "Issues and Constituencies in the Progressive Era: House Roll Call Voting on the Nineteenth Amendment, 1913–1919." *The Journal of Politics* 51: 119–136.

McDonagh, E. L., Price, H. D., 1985. "Woman Suffrage in the Progressive Era: Patterns of Opposition and Support in Referenda Voting, 1910–1918." *American Political Science Review* 79: 415–435.

McKibbin, R., 1974. *The Evolution of the Labour Party, 1910–1924*. Oxford, UK: Clarendon Press.

McLean, I., 2001. *Rational Choice and British Politics: An Analysis of Rhetoric and Manipulation from Peel to Blair*. Oxford University Press.

McMillan, J. F., 1991. "Religion and Gender in Modern France: Some Reflections." *Religion, Society and Politics in France since 1189*, 55–66.

Mead, R. J., 2004. *How the Vote Was Won: Woman Suffrage in the Western United States, 1868–1914*. NYU Press.

Mies, M., 1980. *Patriarchy and Accumulation on a World Scale: Women in the International Division of Labour*. Zed Books.

Miller, G., 2008. "Women's Suffrage, Political Responsiveness, and Child Survival in American History." *Quarterly Journal of Economics*, 1287–1327.

Mill, J. S., 1989. *The Subjection of Women*. MIT Press.

Mitchell, B. R., 2007a. *International Historical Statistics: Africa and Asia*. London: Macmillan.

Mitchell, B. R., 2007b. *International Historical Statistics: Europe, 1750–2005*, 6th edition. Palgrave Macmillan.

Mitchell, B. R., 2003. *International Historical Statistics: The Americas, 1750–2000*, 5th edition. Palgrave Macmillan.

Molony, B., 2004. "Citizenship and Suffrage in Interwar Japan," in L. Edwards and M. Roces (eds.), *Women's Suffrage in Asia: Gender, Nationalism and Democracy*. London: RoutledgeCurzon, 127–151.

Molyneux, M., 1985. "Family Reform in Socialist States: The Hidden Agenda." *Feminist Review* 21: 47–64.

Montes-de-Oca-O'Reilly, A., 2005. *Towards the Recognition of Women's Political Rights in Mexico: The Suffragists' Voices (1884–1953)*. PhD diss., University of Texas at Dallas.

Moore, B. J., 1966. *Social Origins of Dictatorship and Democracy: Lord and Peasant in the Making of the Modern World*. Cambridge, UK: Beacon Press.

Mossuz-Lavau, J., 1994. "Les électrices françaises de 1945 à 1993." *Vingtieme siecle. Revue d'histoire*, 67–75.

Morgan-Collins, M., 2017. "The Electoral Impact of Newly Enfranchised Groups: The Case of Women's Suffrage in the United States." Paper presented at the *American Political Science Association* conference, 2016.

Morgan, D., 1972. *Suffragists and Democrats*. Michigan State University Press.

Morgan, K. O., 1975. *Keir Hardie: Radical and Socialist*. Weidenfeld and Nicolson.

Morgan, K. J., 2006. *Working Mothers and the Welfare State: Religion and the Politics of Work-Family Policies in Western Europe and the United States*. Stanford University Press.

Moschos, D. M., Katsky, D. L., 1965. Unicameralism and Bicameralism: History and Tradition. *Boston University Law Review* 45: 250.

Nepstad, S. E., 2011. *Nonviolent Revolutions: Civil Resistance in the Late 20th Century*. Oxford University Press.

Neuman, J., 2017. *Gilded Suffragists: The New York Socialites Who Fought for Women's Right to Vote*. NYU Press.

Nohlen, D., 2005. *Elections in the Americas: A Data Handbook: Volume 2 South America*. Vol. 2. Oxford University Press on Demand.

Nohlen, D., Grotz, F., Hartmann, C. (eds.), 2001. *Elections in Asia and the Pacific: A Data Handbook: Volume I: Middle East, Central Asia, and South Asia*. OUP Oxford.

Nohlen, D., Krennerich, M., Thibaut, B., 1999. *Elections in Africa: A Data Handbook*. Oxford University Press.

Novotny, P., 2007. *This Georgia Rising: Education, Civil Rights, and the Politics of Change in Georgia in the 1940s*. Mercer University Press.

O'Donnell, G. A., Schmitter, P. C., 1986. *Transitions from Authoritarian Rule: Tentative Conclusions about Uncertain Democracies*. Johns Hopkins University Press.

Offen, K. M., 2000. *European Feminisms, 1700–1950: A Political History*. Stanford University Press.

Offen, K., 1994. "Women, Citizenship and Suffrage with a French Twist, 1789–1993." *Suffrage and Beyond: International Feminist Perspectives*, 151–170.

Olson, M., 1971. *The Logic of Collective Action: Public Goods and the Theory of Groups*. Harvard University Press.

Ostrogorski, M., 1891. "Woman Suffrage in Local Self-Government." *Political Science Quarterly* 6: 677–710.

Pankhurst, E., 1914. *My Own Story*. Hearst's International Library Company.

Pankhurst, E., 1913. "Freedom or Death" speech. Hartford, CT.

Paxton, P., 2000. "Women's Suffrage in the Measurement of Democracy: Problems of Operationalization." *Studies in Comparative International Development* 35: 92–111.

Paxton, P., Hughes, M. M., 2016. *Women, Politics, and Power: A Global Perspective*. CQ Press.

Pedersen, J. E., 2014. "'Speaking Together Openly, Honestly and Profoundly': Men and Women as Public Intellectuals in Early-Twentieth-Century France." *Gender & History* 26(1): 36–51.

Pedersen, J., 2017. "Suffrage and the French Exception," paper presented at the American Historical Association annual conference, Chicago, IL.

Pedersen, S., 2004. *Eleanor Rathbone and the Politics of Conscience*. Yale University Press.

Pincus, S., 2007. "Rethinking Revolutions: A Neo-Tocquevillian Perspective," in C. Boix and S. C. Stokes (eds.), *The Oxford Handbook of Comparative Politics*. Oxford Handbooks Online.

Postel, C., 2007. *The Populist Vision*. Oxford University Press.

Przeworski, A., 2010. *Democracy and the Limits of Self Government*. Cambridge University Press.

Przeworski, A., 2009. "Conquered or Granted? A History of Suffrage Extensions." *British Journal of Political Science* 39: 291–321. doi:10.1017/S0007123408000434

Przeworski, A., 1999. "A Minimalist Conception of Democracy: A Defense," in I. Shapiro, C. Hacker-Cordón (eds.), *Democracy's Value*. Cambridge University Press, ch. 2.

Przeworski, A., Alvarez, M., Cheibub, J. A., Limongi, F., 1996. "What Makes Democracies Endure?" *Journal of Democracy* 7(1): 39–55.

Przeworski, A., Sprague, J., 1986. *Paper Stones: A History of Electoral Socialism*. University of Chicago Press.

Pugh, M., 2000. *The March of the Women: A Revisionist Analysis of the Campaign for Women's Suffrage, 1866–1914*. Oxford University Press.

Pugh, M., 2001. *The Pankhursts: The History of One Radical Family*. London, UK: Vintage Books.

Pugh, M., 1985. "Labour and Women's Suffrage," in K. D. Brown (ed.), *The First Labour Party, 1906–1914*. London: Croom Helm.

Pugh, M. D., 1974. "Politicians and the Woman's Vote 1914–1918." *History* 59: 358–374.

Rallings, C., Thrasher, M., Craig, F. W. S., 2000. *British Electoral Facts, 1832–1999*. Aldershot, UK: Ashgate.

Ramirez, F. O., Soysal, Y., Shanahan, S., 1997. "The Changing Logic of Political Citizenship: Cross-National Acquisition of Women's Suffrage Rights, 1890 to 1990." *American Sociological Review* 62: 735–745.

Ray, P. O., 1918. "Woman Suffrage in Foreign Countries." *The American Political Science Review* 12: 469–474.

Roberts, D., 1994. *Killing the Black Body: Race, Reproduction, and the Meaning of Liberty*. Vintage.

Rolf, D., 1979. "Origins of Mr. Speaker's Conference During the First World War." *History* 64: 36–46.

Rucht, D., 2003. "Interactions between Social Movements and States in Comparative Perspective." in L. A. Banaszak, K. Beckwith, and D. Rucht (eds.), *Women's Movements Facing the Reconfigured State.* Cambridge University Press, 242–274.

Rosanvallon, P., 1992. *Le sacre du citoyen: Histoire du suffrage universel en France* Paris: Editions Gallimard.

Rosenstone, S. J., Behr, R. L., Lazarus, E. H., 1996. *Third Parties in America: Citizen Response to Major Party Failure.* Princeton University Press.

Rubenstein, D., 1991. *A Different World for Women: The Life of Millicent Garrett Fawcett.* Ohio University Press.

Rueschemeyer, D., Stephens, E. H., Stephens, J. D., 1992. *Capitalist Development and Democracy.* Oxford, UK: Polity Press.

Rustow, D. A., 1970. "Transitions to Democracy: Toward a Dynamic Model." *Comparative Politics* 2: 337–363.

Sanday, P., 1981. *Female Power and Male Dominance: On the Origins of Sexual Inequality.* New York: Cambridge University Press.

Salmon, P., 2009. "The House of Commons," 1801–1911, in C. Jones (ed.), *A Short History of Parliament.* Woodbridge, UK: Boydell Press.

Sarkees, M. R., Wayman, F., 2010. *Resort to War: 1816–2007.* Washington, DC: CQ Press.

Schattschneider, E., 1960. *The Semisovereign People.* New York: Holt, Rinehart and Winston.

Schattschneider, E., 1942. *Party Government.* New York: Farrar and Rinehar.

Schedler, A., 2002. "The Menu of Manipulation." *Journal of Democracy* 13: 36–50. doi:10.1353/jod.2002.0031

Scheve, K., Stasavage, D., 2011. "Democracy, War, and Wealth: Lessons from Two Centuries of Inheritance Taxation." *American Political Science Review* 1: 1–22.

Schumpeter, J. A., 1950 [1942]. *Capitalism, Socialism and Democracy,* 3rd edition. Harper and Row.

Schuyler, L. G., 2008. *The Weight of Their Votes: Southern Women and Political Leverage in the 1920s.* Chapel Hill: University of North Carolina Press.

Scott, J. W., 1998. *La citoyenneté paradoxale: Les féministes françaises et les droits de l'homme.* Paris: Albin Michel.

Searle, G. R., 1992. *The Liberal Party: Triumph and Disintegration, 1886–1929.* Houndmills, UK: Macmillan.

Sechrist, R. P., 2012. *Prohibition Movement in the United States, 1801–1920.* ICPSR08343-v2. Ann Arbor, MI: Inter-university Consortium for Political and Social Research [distributor], 10–26.

Shefter, M., 1994. *Political Parties and the State: The American Historical Experience.* Cambridge University Press.

Shortridge, R. M., 1978. "Voting for Minor Parties in the Antebellum Midwest." *The Indiana Magazine of History,* 117–134.

Sivard, R. L., 1985. *Women... A World Survey.* Washington, D.C.: World Priorities.

Skocpol, T., 1992. *Protecting Soldiers and Mothers.* Belknap Press of Harvard University Press.

Skorge, O., 2017. "Petitioning and the Mass Mobilization of Women." Paper presented at the American Political Science Association Conference.

Smith, D. A., Fridkin, D., 2008. Delegating Direct Democracy: Interparty Legislative Competition and the Adoption of the Initiative in the American States. *American Political Science Review* 102: 333–350.

Smith, P., 1996. *Feminism and the Third Republic: Women's Political and Civil Rights in France, 1918–1945*. Clarendon Press.

Sowerwine, C., 2001. *France since 1870*. Palgrave.

Stamiris, E., 1986. "The Women's Movement in Greece." *New Left Review* 158: 98–112.

"Statistics of Cities Having a Population of over 25,000: 1903 and 1904." US Bureau of the Census. Washington, DC: Government Printing Office, 1905.

Stokes, S. C., 2001. *Mandates and Democracy: Neoliberalism by Surprise in Latin America*. Cambridge University Press.

Strom, S. H., 1975. "Leadership and Tactics in the American Woman Suffrage Movement: A New Perspective from Massachusetts." *The Journal of American History* 62, 296–315.

Stuart, G. H., 1920. "Electoral Reform in France and the Elections of 1919." *American Political Science Review* 14: 117–123.

Tackett, T., 2014 [1986]. *Religion, Revolution, and Regional Culture in Eighteenth-Century France: The Ecclesiastical Oath of 1791*. Princeton University Press.

Tanner, D., 1983. "The Parliamentary Electoral System, the Fourth Reform Act and the Rise of Labour in England and Wales." *Historical Research* 56: 205–219.

Teele, D., 2014. "Ordinary Democratization: The Electoral Strategy that Won British Women the Vote," *Politics & Society* 42(4): 537–561.

Teele, D., 2018. "How the West Was Won: Competition, Mobilization, and Women's Enfranchisement in the United States," *Journal of Politics*.

Terborg-Penn, R., 1998. *African American Women in the Struggle for the Vote, 1850–1920*. Indiana University Press.

Therborn, G., 1977. "The Rule of Capital and the Rise of Democracy." *New Left Review* 103: 3–41.

Tilly, L., Scott, J. W., 1987. *Women, Work, and Family*. Psychology Press.

Tingsten, H., 1937. *Political Behavior: Studies in Election Statistics*. London: PS King.

Towns, A. E., 2010a. *Women and States: Norms and Hierarchies in International Society*. Cambridge University Press.

Towns, A., 2010b. "The Inter-American Commission of Women and Women's Suffrage, 1920–1945." *Journal of Latin American Studies* 42(4): 779–807.

Tripp, A. M., 2015. *Women and Power in Post-Conflict Africa*. New York: Cambridge University Press.

Trounstine, J., 2009. *Political Monopolies in American Cities: The Rise and Fall of Bosses and Reformers*. University of Chicago Press.

Turner, E. R., 1913. "The Women's Suffrage Movement in England." *American Political Science Review* 7(4), 588–609.

Valenzuela, E. M., 1995. "Catolicismo, anticlericalismo y la extensión del sufragio a la mujer en Chile." *Estudios Públicos* 58: 137–197.

Vellacott, J., 1993. *From Liberal to Labour with Women's Suffrage: The Story of Catherine Marshall*. Montreal: McGill-Queens University Press.

Vetter, L. P., 2017. *The Political Thought of America's Founding Feminists*. NYU Press.

Ward, M., 1982. "'Suffrage First, Above All Else!' An Account of the Irish Suffrage Movement." *Feminist Review*, 21–36.

Washington, E. L., 2008. "Female Socialization: How Daughters Affect Their Legislator Fathers Voting on Women's Issues." *American Economic Review* 98: 311–332.

Waylen, G., 1994 "Women and Democratization: Conceptualizing Gender Relations in Transition Politics," *World Politics* 46.3: 327–354.

Weeks, A. C., 2017. "Why Are Gender Quota Laws Adopted by Men? The Role of Inter- and Intra-Party Competition." *Comparative Political Studies*.

Weldon, S. L. 2011. *When Protest Makes Policy*. Ann Arbor: University of Michigan Press.

Wheeler, M. S., 1995, "Introduction: A Short History of the Woman Suffrage Movement in America," in *One Woman, One Vote: Rediscovering the Woman Suffrage Movement*, M. S. Wheeler (ed.). Troutdale: NewSage Press.

Wingerden, S. A., 1999. *The Women's Suffrage Movement in Britain, 1866–1928*. London: Macmillan.

WCTU (ed.), 1884. Minutes of the National Woman's Christian Temperance Union. Chicago, IL. Woman's Temperance Publication Association.

Wood, E. J., 2000. *Forging Democracy from Below: Insurgent Transitions in South Africa and El Salvador*. New York: Cambridge University Press.

Xi, T., 2014. "Reform or Revolution? Theory and Evidence on the Role of the Middle Class in the Rise of Universal Male Suffrage." *Journal of Theoretical Politics* 26: 283–311.

Young, I. M., 1994. "Gender as Seriality: Thinking about Women as a Social Collective." *Signs* 19: 713–738.

Zeldin, T., 1973. *France, 1848–1945*. Oxford, UK: Clarendon Press.

Ziblatt, D. 2017. *Conservative Parties and the Birth of Democracy in Modern Europe, 1848–1950*. New York, NY: Cambridge University Press.

Index

Acemoglu, Daron, 16, 30n34, 107n59, 179, 182n11
Ahmed, Amel, 188n36
amendment: as a decoy in the UK, 60, 75n61; ease of procedure, 31, 34n41; procedure in France, 124; at US federal level, 23n19, 84n2, 94 (*see also* Nineteenth Amendment); in US states, 87n11, 113, 125
American Women's Suffrage Association (AWSA) (US), 95
Anthony, Susan B., 23n19, 93–95, 98, 108, 126, 127n126
anti-suffragists, 36n47, 39, 41–42, 55, 63, 68, 77, 84, 87n2, 92, 96, 107, 184. *See also* liquor lobby
Argentina, 15, 189, 193n54
Asquith, Herbert, 50, 51n4, 55–64, 76–80, 196
Auclert, Hubertine, 28n32, 133n2
Australia, 1n2, 28, 195
Austria, 8, 11, 24, 185
authoritarianism, 181, 186. *See also* regime transitions

Banaszak, Lee Ann, 9n15, 12n24, 88n12, 102, 113, 123n97, 168
Bateman, David, 52n6, 148n41
Beckwith, Karen, 190
Belgium, 8, 8n14, 185n29, 188, 193n54
Bérard, Alexandre, 135, 163–65, 201; and Fourteen Points, 164–65
Berger, Suzanne, 134, 153
Blatch, Harriet Stanton, 106
Boix, Carles, 3n4, 16n3, 23n1, 32, 179, 179n4, 188
by-election: definition of, 64, 67n48; importance of to UK suffrage (*see* Election Fighting Fund (EFF))

Canada, 4n7, 4n9, 25. *See also* Québec
capitalism: industrialization and economic

development, 4n3, 17–20, 53, 139n1, 141, 154, 167, 185
Catholicism, 8, 11, 134, 185. *See also* cleavages, political
Catt, Carrie Chapman, 83, 87n10, 91, 106, 125, 170
Cecil, Lord Robert, 78–79
Chile, 4n7, 29, 44, 185, 189
Christian Democratic Parties, 175n90, 185
citizenship, 11n21; and suffrage rights, 18n10
class, social: and own suffrage, 35n43, 185n24; and UK Political Parties, 57–58, 66; upper class, 7, 23, 27, 39, 41–42, 64n2, 92, 99, 177, 187; and women's suffrage, 42, 64n36, 89–92, 106–7; working class in France, 141
cleavages, political, 6–8, 30–31, 38–39, 42, 177–78, 184, 189–90; and cross-cleavage mobilization, 145, 169, 176, 181; and gender quotas, 189
competition, political, 6–13, 27, 30–44; measures of, 68, 114, 151; and warfare, 25; and women's movements, 6, 44, 190
consciousness, feminist, 40, 95, 97, 167, 178, 189–90
Conseil national des femmes françaises (CNFF) (France), 143
Conservative Party (UK). *See* Tories (UK)
conservatives: and France, 134, 140, 146, 153, 166, 188; and support for suffrage, 10, 37n50, 187–88
culture, political, 87, 121–22, 168, 190. *See also* frontier states

Dahl, Robert, 5n10, 179
Delaware, 85–86, 87n11, 113
democracy: definition of, 5, 5n10; democratization, 178–88; limited, 7, 15, 29, 31, 43, 182, 189; measures of, 16, 16n3; quality of, 33n39; theories of,